INFAMOUS BODIES

INFAMOUS

BODIES

SAMANTHA PINTO

Early Black Women's Celebrity and the Afterlives of Rights

Duke University Press *Durham and London* 2020

© 2020 DUKE UNIVERSITY PRESS All rights reserved
Printed and bound by CPI Group (UK) Ltd, Croydon, CR0 4YY
Designed by Courtney Leigh Richardson
Typeset in Avenir and Adobe Caslon Pro

Library of Congress Cataloging-in-Publication Data

Names: Pinto, Samantha, author.
Title: Infamous bodies : early Black women's celebrity and the afterlives of rights /
Samantha Pinto.
Description: Durham : Duke University Press, 2020. | Includes bibliographical
references and index.
Identifiers: LCCN 2019054804 (print) | LCCN 2019054805 (ebook) | ISBN 9781478007838
(hardcover) | ISBN 9781478008323 (paperback) | ISBN 9781478009283 (ebook)
Subjects: LCSH: Wheatley, Phillis, 1753–1784. | Hemings, Sally. | Baartman, Sarah. |
Seacole, Mary, 1805–1881. | Bonetta, Sarah Forbes, 1843?–1880. | Women, Black,
in popular culture. | African American women in popular culture. |
Women, Black—Legal status, laws, etc. | African American women—Legal status,
laws, etc. | African American feminists. | Womanism. | Fame—Social aspects.
Classification: LCC HQ1163 .P56 2020 (print) | LCC HQ1163 (ebook) |
DDC 305.48/896073—dc23
LC record available at https://lccn.loc.gov/2019054804
LC ebook record available at https://lccn.loc.gov/2019054805

Cover art: *Too Many Blackamoors #2*, 2015. © Heather Agyepong. Commissioned by Autograph
ABP. Courtesy the artist.

Contents

First, I need to acknowledge with gratitude earlier versions and scraps of this manuscript that appeared in *Ariel* (on Mary Seacole) and in *Palimpsest* (on Sally Hemings).

Second, the mass gratitude: To audiences at Brown, Wisconsin, Georgetown, Princeton, UT AADS, and UT English, you made this book stronger. To the NEH, UT AADS, The Harry Ransom Center, Georgetown Internal Grants, and my long-time departmental homes at Georgetown, English and African American Studies, as well as African Studies and Women's and Gender Studies, thank you for time and money that supported this book. Thanks especially go to my fellow founding African American Studies scholars and staff at Georgetown, who helped make a department happen while always celebrating research achievements.

Third: I could never thank everyone who has kept me afloat these past few years. I could write epic paragraphs about all below for their numerous positive interventions into my writing life.

To Courtney Berger at Duke for talking to me as wisely and as transparently now as she did when I was a whippersnapper many years ago, to Sandra for her unflagging support, to my two amazing anonymous readers who made this book so much better (though all flaws are my own), to the press board for believing in my ability to pull this book through to the end, to everyone at Duke University Press who is making sure this thing gets printed and looks beautiful, and to my notes editor Joanne Muzak, my proofer Mishana Garschi, and my research assistants Mary Galli and Jewel Pereyra: thank you.

My Georgetown colleagues are family now, despite my departure: Thank you to Pam Fox (truly, she, Mark, and Ana will always be family), Ricardo Ortiz (my number one supporter from before day one and fellow UCLA alum), Nicole Rizzuto, Jennifer Fink, Dana Luciano, Christine So, Patrick O'Malley, Lindsey Kaplan, Soyica Colbert, Robert Patterson, Rosemary Ndubuizu, and Sherally Munshi. Thanks also to Marcus Board, Cóilín Parsons, Nathan Hensley, Leslie Hinkson, Gwen Mikell, John Tutino, Brian Hochman, Mimi Yiu, Carolyn Forche, Mark McMorris, Joy Young, David Gewanter, Sarah McNamer, Lena Orlin, Donna Even-Kesef, Jessica Marr, Jill Crenshaw, Karen Lautman, Scott

Taylor, Lori Merish, Kate Chandler, Kathryn Temple, Al Miner, Meredith McKittrick, Linda Blair, Sheila Foster, Ashley Cohen, Shiva Subbaraman, and so many others who made my daily life wonderful.

I am forever in delightful debt to Heather Houser, JK Barret, Neville Hoad, and Gretchen Murphy. My thanks also go to Jennifer Wilks, Sue Heinzelman, Judy Coffin, Cherise Smith, Julia Lee, Frank Guridy, Deborah Paredez, Kali Gross, Meta Jones, Helena Woodard, Philippa Levine, Stephanie Lang, Eric Tang, Ted Gordon, Willy Forbath, Bobby Chesney, Dan Rodriguez, Larry Sager, Jane Cohen, Liz Cullingford, and Ward Farnsworth. Bill Powers did so much for my family—may he rest in peace. Always, always I appreciate the incomparable Jenny Sharpe, the immensely generous Yogita Goyal, the enormously kind Liz DeLoughrey, the formational mentorship of Richard Yarborough, the creative exuberance of Harryette Mullen, and the beyond intellectually and otherwise generous Helen Deutsch. Brent Edwards and Eva Cherniavsky are giving beyond measure, in addition to their brilliance. The continuing support of Eve Dunbar, Sangeeta Ray, Angela Naimou, Alex Hernandez, Lindsey Green-Simms, Juliet Hooker, Sarah Cervenak, Libby Anker, Wendy Belcher, Britt Rusert, Amber Musser, Sara Matthiesen, Ali Moore, Crystal Parikh, Melanie Ho, Joyce Lee, Shane Vogel, Lisa Hills, Robert McRuer, Keidra Morris, and Kathleen Washburn, have made my life so much better. Everything I write or think is in and with the memory of the beautiful and brilliant Sam See.

All praise goes to my sanity crew, all of whom I could go on for pages about as remarkably hilarious, endlessly supportive humans: Tshepo Masango Chery, Aida Levy-Hussen, Marcia Chatelain, Emily Owens, Heather Houser (again), Gayle Wald, Lahra Smith, Holly Dugan, Emily Russell, Jennifer Chang, La'Tonya Rease Miles, Paige Harden, Leema Berland, Ally Hamilton, Amy Foshko, Jennifer Stamberger Evans, Cecily Parks, Leslie Oster, and Louise Bernard. You all buoy me. Thank you. I wouldn't have gotten out of my bed from grad school onward without Denise Cruz being my intellectual and cookie-sharing rock, from way back and in every circumstance. And I would not get through my days or my work without the constant, hilarious, and whip-smart support of Jennifer Nash, who reads my trash and somehow finds gold, including every single word of this manuscript multiple times. All of these women are everything you want friends and colleagues to be, and they are brilliant and funny and honest and wonderful.

Sometimes it felt like I was writing this book against the will of my children, Finn and Tegan (and my dogs, Leroy and Chester [who I hope is somewhere with salty pork products in abundance]), but nothing made me appreciate the process of writing more than its contrast with the needs of dependent beings. I love them all, and they prove that love is really a strange beast. They are delightfully silly and fully themselves. I'm thankful for their care providers and teachers, especially Rachel Lambert and Lacey London. Thank you also to the Pintos, the Beales, the Magdalinskis, and the Hannons for being my families. And thank you to the friends with whom we spend our weekends for putting up with me and giving us sustainable parenting company on the regular.

Everything in my life is possible because of Sean Williams. In the course of writing this book, we had made our two-body problem a four-body problem, and I frequently gave up on the logistics of life. He kept and keeps every single thing and being going, including me, all while cracking jokes and writing his own smart stuff and teaching torts and looking like he's still in his twenties. I love him more than anything, and if I'm exhausted and it looks hard, he's exhausted and he makes it look easy.

INTRODUCTION

INFAMOUS BODIES, CORRECTIVE HISTORIES

In law, rights are islands of empowerment. To be unenlightened is to be disempowered, and the line between rights and no-rights is most often the line between dominators and oppressed. Rights contain images of power, and manipulating those images, either visually or linguistically, is central in the making and maintenance of rights. In principle, therefore, the more dizzyingly diverse the images that are propagated, the more empowered we will be as a society.—PATRICIA J. WILLIAMS, *The Alchemy of Race and Rights*, 1991

We have many estimable women of our variety, but not many famous ones. The word famous is applied to a person who is "celebrated in fame or public report, renowned, much talked of . . . used in either a good or bad sense, chiefly the former." It is not well to claim too much for ourselves before the public. Such extravagance invites contempt rather than approval. I have thus far seen no book of importance written by a negro woman and I know of no one among us who can appropriately be called famous. This is in no way a disparagement. . . . We start too near a former condition [slavery] to have any famous work in science, art, or literature expected of us. It is not well to ship the paddle wheels before we have steam to move them. . . . I do not find it consistent to enlarge the list of famous negro women. Many of the names you have are those of admirable persons, cultivated, refined, and ladylike. But it does not follow that they are famous. Let us be true and use language truthfully.—FREDERICK DOUGLASS, in response to a request for names of "Noted Negro Women," 1892

For a brief moment in early 2016, months before her career-defining visual album *Lemonade* dropped, entertainer and icon Beyoncé Knowles Carter was tied to a rumored film project on Sarah Baartman, the early nineteenth-century African performer known in Europe as the Venus Hottentot. Baartman, performing in Europe from 1810 until her death in France in 1815, is perhaps the most infamous of bodies when thinking through the global tragedy and travesty that defines the relationship between Enlightenment modernity and black womanhood. The gossip of the rumored casting spread quickly and was just as quickly critiqued by both South African groups and popular think-piece websites such as *Feministing*, media blog *Blavity*, and hip hop magazine *Complex*. Ultimately, the link between Beyoncé and the biopic was disavowed by the popular icon's camp with a public statement in *Billboard* (Platon 2016) asserting that while "Beyoncé is in no way tied to this project . . . this is an important story that should be told."

This double-pronged statement of distance and recognition engages the minefield of black feminist thought and its relationship to cultural representation. Baartman's legacy has been one of infamy—one that locates the tragedy of antiblackness in her performing body and its fate. Debates about Baartman center on the politics of representing exploited black women's bodies and the attendant risk of repeating the injuries such exploitation caused and continues to manifest in the contemporary moment. Some also look to Baartman's past to find liberatory, resistant, and reparative possibilities in her performative resilience and its reiterations, and others advocate for Saidiya V. Hartman's (2008) caution about reproducing the violence of the archive of enslavement and colonialism by narrating black suffering for white audiences, which she outlines in "Venus in Two Acts."[1] Hartman nonetheless reinvests in the power of representation as she outlines the work of "critical fabulation," a process that attempts "both to tell an impossible story and to amplify the impossibility of its telling" (11). The early 2016 public reception of the possibility of Beyoncé reproducing Baartman, and then her camp's simultaneous disavowal of the project and recognition of the significance of Baartman's story inhabit the difficult desires—inclusive of failure and impossibility—that constitute black women's history and its cultural afterlives.

Beyoncé herself has also been a lightning rod and litmus test for black feminist politics, tightly controlling her message, image, and brand even as her status as a "racial icon" has catapulted her to unheard of levels of public recognition as well as critical attention from black feminist public luminaries such as bell hooks, Melissa Harris-Perry, and Angela Y. Davis. Pre-*Lemonade* Beyoncé, who is often seen as apolitical in her hyperfeminine performance, gives way to a recognizably politicized Beyoncé in much of this attention. If, as Nicole R. Fleetwood (2015a) compellingly argues, the "racial icon" is unique in its simultaneous evocation of veneration and denigration, Baartman seems to inhabit too much of the latter for even the post-*Lemonade*, politically venerated Beyoncé—the one with a Black Panther Party–inspired, black nationalist aesthetic in her 2016 Super Bowl performance of "Formation"—to rehabilitate for her considerable fan base. Beyoncé's balancing act of recognizing the significance of Baartman's infamous story while simultaneously refusing the intimacy of representing her body on screen suggests that Baartman's iconography still exceeds the boundaries of a black political imaginary of historical recovery or clear critique. Instead, Baartman is rendered *almost* unrepresentable by Beyoncé's camp precisely because of the very "problem" of black women's representation that she embodies and provokes over two hundred years after her death.

Infamous Bodies takes seriously the genealogy of black women celebrities who undergird Beyoncé's and Baartman's formations along with the political worlds and work of black women's cultural representation. As Frederick Douglass's 1892 letter quoted in the epigraph attests, the well-known author and abolitionist refused the category of famous to black women, including Phillis Wheatley, Sally Hemings, Sarah Baartman, Mary Seacole, and Sarah Forbes Bonetta, all of whom he likely had encountered in print (let alone fellow black women writers, speakers, and activists with whom he shared print and stage). Douglass lays bare the anxiety around black fame and its tenuous yet significant place in Western political economies—that it might be feminized and sexualized in object and subject if its political and cultural meaning were to become more capacious to include the infamous, sexualized, feminized labor in which black women's representational economies traffic in the public sphere. Following Hartman, *Infamous Bodies* eschews both the "heroic" and the "tragic" as adequate frames to ask how figures such as Baartman are both erased in political histories and "come to stand for too much" (Crais and Scully 2009, 6), in Baartman's biographers' words, not just in their own historical times but also in contemporary cultural negotiations of race, rights, and social justice. *Infamous Bodies* examines the political and cultural trajectories of famous black women of the late eighteenth and early nineteenth centuries whose legacies stretch into the twenty-first century.

This book studies cultural representations of Baartman, African poet Phillis Wheatley, enslaved subject of scandal Sally Hemings, Victorian-era Jamaican nurse Mary Seacole, and royally adopted African "princess" Sarah Forbes Bonetta. Their complicated biographies push the term celebrity beyond noting exceptional black women who make it into the archive—beyond correcting Douglass's exclusions. Instead, celebrity becomes a particular genre of black political history, one that foregrounds culture, femininity, and media consumption as not merely reflective of, ancillary to, or compensation for black exclusion from formal politics, but as the grounds of the political itself. *Infamous Bodies* reimagines these celebrity genealogies both as they critically intersect with the formation of human rights discourse around individual civil rights and entitlements, and as they represent a variety of black women's experiences as embodied political subjects of modernity who engage with pleasure, risk, violence, desire, ambition, and vulnerability. *Infamous Bodies* considers how they have been disciplined into the poles of heroic ascent into the affirmative recognition of rights or descent into tragic lack of agency as well as how they have exceeded these boundaries. Reading early black women's celebrity promises not repair of historical injuries but a method of interpretation that assumes the vulnerabilities of black women's embodiment as the starting point and future of progressive political projects—with "bodies" signifying both the material body *and* its representational insistence and repetition. Critical itineraries around social justice, then, are here premised on vulnerable embodiment not as a tragic problem to be solved, but as the premise of living and as the object of institutional care rather than cure.

Black women celebrities are also at the cultural, critical, conceptual, and representational center of debates about rights, humanity, and freedom. Within this frame, I explore how key concepts in the formation of rights as they are commonly known, forged in the late eighteenth and early nineteenth centuries— such as freedom, consent, contract, citizenship, and sovereignty—have been shaped by these cultural figures and contemporary transnational understandings of the politics of race, gender, sexuality, and rights. These "understandings" have frequently taken the form of heated debates about the value of rights— especially for Left critique that sees a tainted origin as an endpoint unto itself. *Infamous Bodies* takes these critiques of rights discourse as its starting point. In the spirit of Patricia J. Williams's own capacious desire for more and different rights as a black feminist political goal, this book looks elsewhere for a proliferation of genealogies of the political that center on black women's embodied experience and reception.[2] These histories include the shadow of rights discourse in varying and important ways, as well as point to and construct other modes of concatenating political meaning.

Baartman's reception and representation and the discussion of Beyoncé's embattled "right" to play her then participate in but also disrupt some of the major economies of what this book fashions as the corrective histories of early black women celebrities that continue to undergird black political thought. *Corrective histories* are the multiple reanimations of these infamous lives and texts that are meant to figure more contemporary political and social investments in struggles for black freedom and that start from a premise of either skepticism at the white feminized sphere of celebrity or revel in its public and resistant possibilities as they read "beyond" the mere surface of celebrity culture. This book traces the routes of these infamous bodies, these black women celebrities who maintain uncomfortable relationships to existing political discourses of race, rights, and representation. It does so through its analysis of a wide-ranging archive that includes newspaper accounts, legal proceedings, paintings, political cartoons, photographs, letters, poetry, contemporary visual art, novels, films, television scripts, plays, documentaries, children's books, monuments, memorials, speeches, autobiographies, biographies, histories, literary criticism, political theory, and other rich scripts that make up the enormous category of what we might call the culture of celebrity. Some of these act as corrective histories, even as they can also act as critical fabulations that maintain a deep skepticism about rights discourse and liberal humanism as pathways to liberation. Some may still find themselves in the grip of the conceptual limits of Enlightenment modernity, frames that assume, however complexly, that diagnosing failure or resistance is the endpoint of black cultural representation and politics. Here, instead, I investigate the critical attachments and desires that append to these histories and figures—generously and hopefully generatively—to map alternative routes through the genealogy of black women's representation and, in Gayatri Chakravorty Spivak's (1999) terms, "re-presentation" and its relationship to political thought beyond the corrective model.

Like Jennifer C. Nash's (2019b) work on moving away from a "defensive" affect of black feminist intellectual practice as exclusive property, moving away from the corrective can be both exposing and exciting for the future of the field. Celebrity repetition conjures up the Morrisonian "re-memory" of not just the material trauma done to black women's bodies in the past but also the critical trauma enacted through their simultaneous elision and exploitation in academic discourse. This project then converges on the feminist scholarly sites of critical fabulation, representation, and re-memory—alongside Diana Taylor's (2003) concepts of the archive and the scenario as the delicate delineation of that which is recovered through history versus that which is reperformed within a familiar structure, genre, or scene with the open possibility of difference—to animate discussions about the reception and reproduction of early black women celebrities in multiple forms and forums across modern history.

These celebrity lives dovetailed with the era often identified as the age of Enlightenment, which, following Avery Gordon's (2008) designation "New World modernity," I refer to as Enlightenment modernity—the historical point that simultaneously solidified the discourses of the "Rights of Man" and the enslavement of African peoples. Baartman both crystallizes and disrupts the rights-based poles of freedom and unfreedom, resistance and submission, as well as agency and exploitation that are formed during this historical period. Baartman is an enduring racial icon, and her corrective histories also intersect with the contemporary currency of both mainstream rights-based political understandings of personhood and antiracist movements that challenge the rhetoric of human rights as able to engineer black freedom.[3] Both discourses engage with the complicated work of "the making and maintenance of rights" that Williams describes in the epigraph, in that they expose rights as a set of fictions, performances, and constructions that are far from organic or "self-evident," in Thomas Jefferson's own infamous words. This book enters into these heated debates with eyes toward stretching visions of black political futures into alternative interpretive economies that imagine politics beyond rights (including rights critique) in black feminist thought. "Re-membering" these figures for this book thus represents not just a rehearsal of past traumas, but the recognition of holding the injury at the same time that one builds from and upon it, as in *Beloved*'s (Morrison [1987] 2004) own construction of the infamous afterlives of enslavement; this means materially holding both temporalities at once, rather than seeking trauma's impossible resolution. In the insightful words of one of this manuscript's anonymous reviewers, then, this book takes up representation not as a black feminist search for truth but as a black feminist analytics of "truth effects."

In tracing the work that Baartman and her fellow early black women celebrities do to undergird the imagined possibilities for living and representing black feminist lives across two centuries, *Infamous Bodies* seeks to find alternate sequences of meaning and strategies of interpretation that include but do not center on the stories critics already tell and know about the aims and possible outcomes of black political and social life (and death). These configurations hinge on the figures of decidedly difficult subjects—black women who are "famous" enough to have currency in the repeating scene of black iconography within the modern era, but who are also "infamous," or defined by their lack in comparison to the kinds of rights-bearing, rights-demanding, resistant, or agentic subjects that one might more obviously seek in creating antiracist political theories. In Michel Foucault's (1967, 161) formulation of "infamous men," he argues for an infamy defined by a metric of lost-to-history but for their "encounter with power" that marks them in the archive. I repeat that frame with a difference here, arguing that the "record" of encounter includes not just bureaucratic biopolitical and legal archives but the afterimages—Joseph Roach's (2007) term for the ways and forms that celebrity presence lingers, materially and otherwise—of early black women's celebrity in the public sphere. Hence, this project focuses on famous black women—akin to Fleetwood's (2015a) "racial icons," Kimberly Juanita Brown's (2015) "repeating bod[ies]," Uri

McMillan's (2015) "embodied avatars," and Daphne A. Brooks's (2006) "bodies in dissent"—whose public infamy renders them difficult subjects for racial heroism.

Douglass excludes these figures from "appropriate" black political vision, even as doing so "masks the import of the very centrality (of black women and their bodies) organizing transatlantic slavery and its resonant imprint" (K. J. Brown 2015, 8). Expanding Brown's "resonant echoes of slavery's memory" (8) to include other types of colonialist, labor, and performance histories, I focus here not on making these celebrity figures more appropriately known or seen—"famous," in Douglass's view of the term—but to question the available modes of hailing black women subjects into known-ness, into visibility, in the very moments that make them politically viable. McMillan's and Brooks's critical formulations, which always keep their eyes on this political impossibility rendered in their subjects' performances in the late nineteenth and early twentieth centuries, ground my own move away from redressive terms of analysis for black performance and authorship.

Because each figure in this book also troubles the line between free and enslaved, they have become contested, thick subjects that black studies and black feminist studies have returned to again and again in an effort to "work the contradiction," as Angela Y. Davis (2016, 125) refers to the methodology of feminist practice. *Infamous Bodies* thinks through the stakes of the debates surrounding these figures in their own time and beyond, and the way those corrective histories—both in disciplinary terms of reading in a "corrective" mode that aims "to remedy misreadings" (Nash 2017, 119) and in a broader sense, of the "stories [that] matter," Clare Hemmings's (2011) description of the narratives feminist studies has of itself as a field—have animated critical attachments around the sign and scene of "black women" and "black feminism." In doing so, I locate routes of black feminism that challenge the very terrain recognized as the political, or of what and how to understand the desired trajectories and outcomes of calls for social justice around race, gender, and sexuality. In other words, I question the ground that reads pre-*Lemonade* Beyoncé as lacking the political gravitas to pull off the balancing act of representing the story of Baartman but post-*Lemonade* Beyoncé as somehow better able and equipped in her recognizable political formations to redress the unredressable, to remake the tragedy of black abjection into an afterlife of political triumph.

These counterintuitive choices, traced here as the central figures of black political subjectivity, also expose possibility in the legal definition of "infamous" as a description "[of a person] deprived of all or some citizens' rights as a consequence of conviction for a serious crime" (*OED* 2017). The ontological "crime" of being black, and of being a black woman, has arguably defined the extremes of deprivation experienced in Enlightenment modernity, as well as desires for a revolutionary politics based on positive rights and freedoms. *Infamous Bodies* traces the ways these celebrity figures have been disciplined into laboring for the corrective histories of particular political visions—and also imagines, with artists, thinkers, and the figures themselves, a politics premised on the body, and embodied experiences of women of color.[4] It takes into account infamy not only as a criminal category, but a sexual one that appends particularly to feminine and feminized bodies and acts in the public sphere, marking a constant duality of "access" as risk and reward.

In what follows in this introduction, I expand on why celebrity is a vibrant and necessary terrain where the political is made through rather than against feminine embodiment. I then trace how, in particular, black feminist scholars—historians, cultural critics, and theorists—have worked through and on agency as a critical and problematic terrain in which to imagine the quotidian construction of black women's political subjectivity. I pay particular attention to both the obvious and subtle ways that race, rights, and humanity have been inextricably yoked together and critiqued in the work of political theorists before me in black, African, African-diaspora, postcolonial, feminist, queer, and critical ethnic studies. Next, I explore how vulnerability as a political theory might be a generative hermeneutic frame to consider the particular labor of black women, and their reception, in the public sphere. Finally, with particular attention to recent critiques in feminist and African American literary and historiographic study that call attention to the place of critical desires in constructing histories, traditions, and political legacies (not to mention objects of study), I briefly describe my archive as I move through the work of each chapter in imagining the lives and afterlives of five key black women celebrities of the era. This introduction maps out black feminist thought as the powerful and undercited base for a reconception of the political writ large, describing a politics from where the vulnerable figures of my study stand, as they were and as they are repeated, remembered, and reread.

Black Celebrity, Black Effect, and Black Study

In 2018's "Black Effect," The Carters (the artistic collective moniker for Jay-Z and Beyoncé on their joint album *Everything Is Love*) list their "Black Effect(s)"— the commodities, qualities, and features that evince their still-black cultural bonafides and that, in the song's formulation, invite criticism from but also have the potential to silence their haters. Namechecking the Jay-Z–owned streaming service Tidal, forewarning forthcoming documentaries on Trayvon

Martin (in the wake of the acclaimed Jay-Z–produced Kalief Browder documentary), and claiming "I'm like Malcolm X," Jay-Z rhymes until the three-minute mark, when Beyoncé takes over:

I'm good any way I go, any way I go (go)
I pull up like the Freedom Riders, hop out on Rodeo
Stunt with your curls, your lips, Sarah Baartman hips
Gotta hop into my jeans, like I hop into my whip.

Beyoncé's range here includes civil rights and conspicuous luxury consumption as well as a callback to the Baartman controversy: a reclaiming of fictional phenotypic racial categorization by "owning" Baartman's embodied legacy as Beyoncé's own, the locus of her and Baartman's fame and their infamy as well as their performative livelihoods.

The corrective histories of "nonheroic" black women such as Baartman, those one might characterize as infamous rather than famous, include and engender a deep suspicion of the feminized public sphere of celebrity as the domain of the political, much as do earlier dismissals of Beyoncé's political heft pre-*Lemonade*, skeptical of her lack of overt engagement with recognizable race politics due to her focus on the pop culture domains of love, wealth, personal loss, fashion, and beauty. I suggest infamy as a frame, then, because it also includes the disapproving public attention of fame, as well as a legal valence in its history as describing a state of rightlessness (Paik 2016), a deprivation of rights as legal "consequence" (OED 2017). But in Foucault's designation of infamy as visibility only due to an encounter with power, embodied black womanhood during this period stands as a public conviction turned question, a stripping of what one might think of as basic human rights if one was to think of "rights" as even existing before the categories of "black" and "woman." In choosing to focus on the formation and circulation of celebrity figures, I consciously engage the vulnerabilities, pleasures, and risks of representation, including objectification.[5] Celebrity bodies and attachments to academic objects of study can elicit similar commitments, surprises, and desires from their audiences, where "political desire is always excessive—excessive to the conditions, imaginations, and objects that are used to represent it" (Wiegman 2012, 26).

The infamous bodies of Wheatley, Hemings, Baartman, Seacole, and Bonetta inspire and occupy these terrains of political desire—always confounding, thwarting, and interrupting the idea "that if only we find the right discourse, object of study, or analytic tool, our critical practice will be adequate to the political commitment that inspires it" (Wiegman 2012, 2–3). As black women in the public sphere, these five figures exert varying levels of recognized "authority" over their representational spheres in their own moments and beyond, challenging their transhistorical audiences' interpretive devotions by insisting on a "fame" that does not rely on the kind of precision of accomplishment Douglass implores when thinking about black women's contributions to the race in the opening epigraph. Instead, these five figures largely move us away from the illusory control of self-authorship and self-representation as the central or only way to understand black feminist cultural resistance, and hence away from visions of (un)agency and its attendant genres of heroism and tragedy as the model of black political subjectivity. These figures are, to call on Ann duCille (1994), one route to both engaging and disrupting black women as "hot" political/intellectual/academic objects of attention that pushes up against the understandable impulse to authentication and ownership that duCille ambivalently unpacks.

Like the work of Brooks and McMillan, I retain the possibility of alternative readings of seemingly overly scripted performances of black women's embodiment, but I focus on methodologies that consider *critical* dissent and distance more than a focus on the political intent and capacities of black women cultural producers. Brooks's (2006) conceptualization of the "viability" of black women's bodies and performances, in particular, informs the work of this book, as a way to reconsider the intimacy that "star images" (Richard Dyer's [(1986) 2013] term for the constellation of texts of and around the celebrity) create between celebrity and audience—one that renders agency as an impossibly *unpure* question rather than as a definitive critical location (Brody 1998). Brooks, McMillan, Jennifer DeVere Brody, and other scholars of black celebrity and embodiment, along with scholars of black erotics, form the critical and creative space for the archive of *Infamous Bodies*, one which spans particularly wide historical, geographic, and generic terrains to create a genealogy of modern political subjectivity that hinges on the work of black women's embodiment in the cultural sphere.[6]

The celebrity as a figure—as a decidedly modern creation of the same formational time period of rights themselves—begins to get at this unique space of intimacy and inquiry. If Dyer's ([1986] 2013) conception of the "star image" and "star text"—and his later trenchant reading of whiteness in filmic celebrity—rests on the height of the Hollywood star system that so many theorists of the modern find themselves grappling with, one might also join other celebrity studies theorists and historians in thinking through the canny strategies of "extraordinary ordinariness" cultivated in the eighteenth and early nineteenth centuries, including Monica L. Miller's (2009) work on the formation of the black dandy and Francesca T. Royster's (2003) work on Cleopatra.[7] Joseph Roach (2007, 13) links modern celebrity's appearance to the "deep eighteenth century," arguing that the period "is the one that isn't over yet. It stays alive among us as a repertoire of long-running performances. In fact some of them we can't get rid of, hard as we might try: chattel slavery and colonialism, for example, still exist as themselves here and there and as their consequences everywhere. The deep eighteenth century is thus not merely a period of time, but a kind of time, imagined by its narrators as progress, but experienced by its subjects as uneven developments and periodic returns." Leo Braudy (1997, 595) refers to this period as the "democratization of fame," where, "since the eighteenth century, the imagery of fame has been more connected with social mobility than with inherited position, and with social transcendence as an assurance of social survival." Sharon Marcus (2019) dates celebrity to the nineteenth century, and she retains Roach's focus on the technologies of celebrity while also scrambling definitions of agency and authorship through her feminist concept of "drama"—making audiences, fans, consumers, media producers, and stars all performers on a stage of narrative creation and social meaning-making.

Braudy and Roach locate the discourses of Enlightenment and fame/celebrity as intertwined, "predicated on the Industrial Revolution's promise of increasing progress and the Enlightenment's promise of ever expanding individual will," and "inseparable from the ideal of personal freedom. As the world grows more complex, fame promises a liberation from powerless anonymity" (Braudy 1997, 297). Following Brody's (1998) foundational work on how the centrality of blackness was used to create an anxious illusion of white purity in Victorian English culture, I point to the ways that black women's constant embodied cultural presence in this earlier era undergirds the very core of political discourse of the time. Following Sharon Marcus (2019) out of the historical real time of celebrity development, this project insists on the significance of cultural production and reception—the optics and narratives of race, their "making and maintenance" (P. Williams 1991) work—as a mode that labors alongside law and civic participation in the public sphere to make the "drama" that constitutes and reconstitutes the afterlives of rights.

This "drama" displaces a primary critique that locates celebrity culture squarely within the realm of Marxist theory. *Infamous Bodies* critically and curiously explores what capitalism's seeming products—celebrity and commodity culture—afforded through and opened up for black women's embodiment. This approach refuses to consider the formal realms of law and politics proper as exempt from commodification, but more importantly, it takes seriously the social economy that provided women the most access as producers, objects of attention, and as audience/consumers.[8] The feminized public sphere, that of celebrity culture, is another site of Foucault's (1967) production of infamy, the "encounter with power," the scene/scenario that makes black women legible in the archive, or gives us access to their archive. How, this book asks, can public performances of black femininity be taken seriously, not in the way they approximate the formal sphere of politics as it is already known but in how they articulate a different form of "politics"—the political as a category of analysis that asks how a certain genre or milieu imagines, organizes, and governs social relations, rather than as a strict designation and disciplining of a singular formal realm. This includes and exceeds the feminist credo of "the personal is political," as *Infamous Bodies* refuses to make what was excluded from the formal realm of the political recognizable only in its relationship to the conceptual terrain already "known" to be politics. Instead, I argue that celebrity itself marks an important terrain to remake ideas and ideals of what constitutes the political, particularly in black studies.

My analysis then builds off of the work of black feminist emplotments of "the modern" that have shifted the terrain of political and aesthetic interpretation toward black women's celebrity. Jayna Brown (2008), Shane Vogel (2009), and Anne Anlin Cheng (2011), for instance, position black women performers and cultural producers at the center of modern aesthetic practice: for Brown, black women's embodied subjectivity defines "the modern woman" in the early twentieth century; for Vogel, it is in their "spectacular" publicity that black women's sexuality transforms the political subject; for Cheng, the convergences between the display of black skin and modernist aesthetics produce a new sense of "surface" meaning—surface as meaning—in the same era. Cheng provocatively marks her focus on surface as a conceptual repositioning fundamentally linked to the struggle over the political: "It is the crisis of visuality—rather than the allocation of visibility, which informs so much of current liberal discourse—that constitutes one of the most profound challenges for American democratic recognition today" (171). Celebrity can materially embody a history of racial formation that shows not just the well-known hegemonies but also the seams and breaks of such narratives—the idiosyncratic iterations of meaning that public circulation threatens and promises. In the orbit of celebrity comes the intersection of race, sexuality, gender, and nation in the relics of fame: the art objects left behind, the performances that both conform to and conflict with dominant narratives of identity, the globalized market for racialized celebrity in the contemporary moment of late capital, and the rush to memorialization as reparation. These images and after-images shape modernity and can reshape our political imaginations within it.

Celebrity presents a different frame than heroism for what we know and why we know it about black women in the public sphere of Enlightenment modernity—taking seriously what gets recorded in the modern age of media, whether that be portraiture prints in circulating manuscripts for a rising literate audience or early photographic practice in the Victorian era. In looking to figures who are not race heroes, or "race women" (Carby 1987)—difficult celebrities who, in Celeste-Marie Bernier's (2012, 26) words, disrupt "the politics and poetics of otherwise excessively sensationalized, grossly oversimplified, and willfully misunderstood acts and arts of Black male and female heroism"—I move away from icons and archives of those who have traditionally been thought of as representing "race as a form of charismatic self-display" (Stephens 2014, vii). Instead, I view my subjects and their "excessively sensationalized" afterlives as staging the radical uncertainties of what Fred Moten (2003) calls the "thingness" of blackness in the antiblack world, in a manner that refuses many of the existing terms of memorialization even as they drag its affective terrain.[9] The infamous bodies taken up in this book are both material and spectral, repeated and distributed in both quotidian and exceptional cultural flows. Celebrity and its cultures matter through and beyond their original iterations, and point to innovative futures in theorizing race if decoupled with the search for self-authorship and agency as the ultimate ends of political imagination. By emphasizing iconic figures like Baartman, this book takes black aesthetics seriously—like Beyoncé's claiming of "Sarah Baartman hips" as a political "Black Effect" that stands uneasily aside and within legacies of traditional protest narratives and uplift narratives. It is to the particular problems of public intimacy for considering black women's political meaning within and beyond agency, inside and outside of the academy, that I now turn.

Black Feminist Visions of Agency, Rights, and Humanity

At the center of the corrective histories traced in this book are the longstanding debates around, claims of, calls for, and challenges to "agency" in black feminist thought. Agency often marks the grounds for and limits of discourse around political action and inaction in feminist discourse, and as such, it functions much like rights discourse in the above critiques, with a focus on vulnerable actors. Wheatley, Hemings, Baartman, Seacole, and Bonetta constitute and represent the tension point of the agency/submission crisis in black feminist studies. They have all represented, at different stages, the hopes, dreams, and failures of black political freedom and politics in the time of modernity—utopic and dystopic, heroic and tragic, resistant and complicit. As flashpoints and flesh, these figures operate in ways that confound ideas and ideals around human will, choice, and volitional action that are organized around the masculine subject. Rights discourse also occupies this constructed terrain where one is either oppressor or oppressed, as legal scholar Patricia Williams (1991) has mapped and which she herself pushed back upon, refusing to abandon rights to this permanent dichotomy. Historians of enslavement in the Americas have been grappling with this political bind of rightlessness for the advancement of rights for many years—how to represent enslaved peoples as "human" while also making visible the obliterating violence and terror of the chattel slavery system.[10] Theories like that of Orlando Patterson's (1982) "social death" have been used to imagine the absence of agency for enslaved peoples in the white public sphere or in political understandings of will. And while Patterson himself is clear to mark social death as a designation that does not exclude the vibrant lives and socialities of enslaved peoples among themselves, his terminology has lived on in efforts to both dig into the capacious injury of enslavement and to develop a richer portrait of enslaved lives that centers on already recognizable political resistance.

Black feminist historiography has, of course, resided in this both/and space at its very inception and core, especially in the study of black women's lives under enslavement. In their work on enslavement and black women's sexuality, Deborah Gray White (1999), Jennifer L. Morgan (2004), Stephanie M. H. Camp (2004), and Brenda Stevenson (2013) have laid out an early map of the common intersection of black women's simultaneous lack of rights and, in Harriet A. Jacobs's infamous characterization, their carving out of "something akin to freedom" within enslavement (Jacobs [1861] 1988, 60). In a post–black nationalist period, these scholars resisted the strains of enslaved heroism and masculine resistance that Toussaint L'Ouverture, Nat Turner, Douglass, and other icons offered of armed rebellion, physical fight, or at least flight from enslavement. In doing so, black feminist historiography also had to negotiate a representational terrain that involved both the politically recognizable promise of coding quotidian expressions of human feeling as "resistance" and redress, as well as the equally recognizable narratives of tragic and totalizing injury.[11] This work, which must somehow balance the demands of critiquing both white devaluation of black women's lives and black political paradigms of resistance that are built on models of masculine individualism, has, along with woman of color feminist theory, remade and continued to push an analytical model that imagines black women's subjectivity as the paradigmatic political subject. Historians and cultural critics of black women's sexuality and sexual labor have created an underresourced theoretical/conceptual space for political theory that this book seeks to recenter beyond agentic models.[12]

Agency as a concept is linked to the currency and language of political power, born of fantasies of ideal rights and their deserving subjects that came of age during Enlightenment, an era defined through science, invention, and massive-scale, systemic brutality predicated on an invented emphasis on biological difference—namely, race and gender—which endured postemancipation. Scholars such as Paul Gilroy, Saidiya Hartman, Lisa Lowe, and Edlie Wong have exposed how liberal humanism and its statist forms were constructed through chattel slavery, colonialism, imperialism, postemancipation, and the fictions of "free labor" as a means to dangle access to full citizenship rights for some at the expense of others, and to sustain capitalism through the very language of individual rights, liberty, and personal responsibility—even through the vehicle of the law itself. These scholars, as well as Roderick A. Ferguson, Lisa Cacho, Angela Naimou, and others working in ethnic and queer studies have brought attention to what Ferguson (2003, viii) calls the "liberal capital of equality" that Enlightenment modernity inaugurated and that continues in the contemporary neoliberal moment. This critical ethnic studies scholarship labors alongside four other bodies of scholarly inquiry that frame the question of this period and its "echoes" (in the formulation of Joan Wallach Scott [2011] and as expanded by Lisa Ze Winters [2016]) in contemporary political debates over rights: postcolonial studies' deep investigation of modernity as a political, geographic, historical, and cultural designation; human rights histories and critiques of the universality of rights and uneven development; African studies' interpretations of rights through a rubric of responsibility and duty, not individual entitlements; and renewed interest in investigating and excavating the category of "the human" in black studies.[13]

These lines of thought around agency and rights are deeply gendered. For instance, to think of romance or tragedy as the genre of modernity, following David Scott (2004), takes on a wholly different political valence when centered on the political and social labor of black women. Rather than rely on narratives that circumscribe certain experiences of sexual and gender violence as irrecoverable and unredemptive in an effort to rescue, condemn, or abandon agency or rights, these renegotiations of the human in relationship to black subjectivity can emphasize the deep and varied attachments these terms have to culture itself—to the making of social life, meaning, and knowledge and to culture's possibilities to stage, disrupt, and remake personhood through imaginative, embodied practice.[14] It is here, alongside the work of Fleetwood (2015a) and Salamishah Tillet (2012) on black iconography's shaping of the dominant public and the civic imagination, that I locate the celebrity figures of this text as those who emerge at the crux of generative debates around the definitions and meaning of political agency, and who shaped, challenged, and continue to shape and challenge the institutional sites that uphold and contest them. Black feminist theories on and around agency offer the opportunity to expand on Regis Fox's conception of the "liberal problematic" (2017) and Crystal Parikh's "embodied vulnerability" (2018) as the basis for a different conception of politics that includes but does not limit itself to narratives of will, agency, or injury. Like the radical statement by the Combahee River Collective (1978)—wherein they vow to "organize around our own needs"—this project maps how certain black women's bodies, like Baartman's, have been appended to rights discourse and how that places black women as political subjects in a constant creative and interpretive state of injury and repair. How might conversations about needs and risks act as generative of a different conception of black political subjectivity?

Intimacy and Vulnerability

Early black women celebrity figures and figurations pose the modern world as one constituted and characterized not by the ideal of the liberal subject but by a radical state of public vulnerability. In *Private Bodies, Public Texts*, Karla FC Holloway (2011, xx) argues that "human legibility is determined by a stratified recognition of personhood. Public discourse proceeds from the version of eligibility that certain bodies produce," where "private individuation is rarely an opportunity" (7) for marginalized raced and gendered bodies. She continues by asserting that "the experiences of women and black Americans are particularly vulnerable to public unveiling" (9), easily exposed, read, known, and seen by and to the public even as they are not recognized with full public personhood. To remain unrecognizable in the purview of rights and yet inevitably public in the sphere of culture/the social—here marks the impasse of black women's celebrity bodies, a feminized twist on Hartman's thesis in *Scenes of Subjection* around black personhood and criminality.

Patricia Williams (1991, 24) counters the will to either champion or suspect black women's visibility, understating: "I continue to ponder the equation of privacy with intimacy and of publicity with dispossession." Stepping back from the immediate calculus of commodification as bad and interiority, or a retreat from public exposure, as a good, Williams's "equation," when thought of with Roach's (2007, 36) formulation of female eighteenth-century celebrity, foregrounds the difficult "public intimacy" fostered by celebrity—and its "simultaneous appearance of strength and vulnerability in the same performance, even in the same gesture." In this frame, one that questions the very terms of private and public spheres as feminist historians have done for decades (Hine 1989b; Kerber 1988), the figures in this book offer us an opportunity to imagine rights formation through a black feminist politics that decenters recovery and repair from the assumed "damage" of public vulnerability. Taking seriously Janell Hobson's (2017a) argument that "celebrity feminism . . . invites us to view public women beyond arguments about victimization and agency," *Infamous Bodies* explores vulnerable critical attachment to feminist critique and to its objects of study that are as visceral and affectively bound as fandom, including the "haunts" of respectability and suspicious reading. This study then offers a hermeneutic of vulnerability that imagines intimacy as an embodied "sensation" (Musser 2014) across what theater and performance scholar Soyica Diggs Colbert (2017, 7) terms a "temporal multiplicity" of black celebrity.[15] If the figures in this book have been stuck between the racist publics and antiracist counterpublics that claim them, I route them through their infamy, rather than either recovering or disavowing it, as a way to critically and generatively read vulnerable attachments to them.

This book, then, follows Christina Sharpe's (2016, 134) invocation of what she calls "wake work," citing poet Dionne Brand: "here there is disaster and possibility . . . and while 'we are constituted through and by continued vulnerability to this overwhelming force, we are not only known to ourselves and to each other by that force.'" When Sharpe references "continued vulnerability," she suggests that critical territory as part of what is already known to and as black subjectivity in modernity. Narratives around each of these five figures expose vulnerabilities in the political futures of social justice. Following contemporary black feminist critics such as Fleetwood (2010), Aida Levy-Hussen (2016), and Nash (2014b)—who critically take up and critique the desire within African American visual, cultural, and literary studies to read representation as the site of injury but also the site of cure, repair, and healing—I do not claim that critics *should* feel differently but rather recognize these critical desires as productive of particular trajectories of interpretation—and suggest opening up to other political desires and questions. Here, I engage Williams's speculative "proliferation" of rights and Claudia Tate's (1998) theory of "desirous plenitude," "a critical strategy for analyzing a unique form of desire—the implicit wishes, unstated longings, and vague hungers inscribed in" (178) African American art

and literature, as ways to upend foreclosed readings of vulnerable black feminine embodiment, even as Tate and Williams do not offer utopic methods that
solve the "problem" of black feminist embodiment. Tate locates a hermeneutic
focused on "the plenitude of a writer's fantasmatic pleasure [that] also exceeds
reason, prohibition, and indeed possibility" (188). Here, I take on affects that
include and exceed pleasure and the "radical fantasy of surplus delight," (188)
exceeding the agentic author/performer to consider the critic, the spectator,
and the audience in constructing the subjects of "black political longing," in
Aliyyah Abdur-Rahman's (2012) terms. I expand on Tate's practice of reading,
then, in form, genre, geography, era, and feeling, but I retain her insistence that
"the fantasy of personal plenitude complicates expressions of the elusive goal
of freedom in black texts" as my central jumping off point for reconsidering
interpretive practices around early black women's celebrity (189).

Beyoncé's Baartman controversy unearths and performs the contradictory,
competing, and seemingly compulsory desires surrounding black women's political subjectivity and how bound critical attachments are to the sphere of
cultural representation. Even the noncasting has cultural reverberations—the
think pieces, the rethink pieces in light of Beyoncé's more recognizable political formations in *Lemonade*, the mock-up trailers of a potential Beyoncé-as-
Baartman film, the citing of Baartman's body as one of Beyoncé's comfortable
inhabitations of her blackness in "Black Effect," and even Morgan Parker's
2016 poem "Hottentot Venus" in the *Paris Review*, later reprinted in her 2017
collection *There Are More Beautiful Things Than Beyoncé*. In Parker's poem (which
she explicitly states in a 2016 *Paris Review* interview that she wrote in the
wake of the Beyoncé-as-Baartman controversy), she fiercely opens:

> I wish my pussy could live
> in a different shape and get
> some goddamn respect.
> Should I thank you?

If Elizabeth Alexander's (1990) Baartman poem offers a first-person meditation on black interiority, Parker's Baartman confronts the externality of black
women's sexuality as a mode of cultural production, of authorship, and of paid
labor. Her Baartman narrates the vulnerability not just of her own body, but
how black women's cultural labor so frequently is deployed to shore up the
vulnerability of white audiences:

> No one worries about me
> because I am getting paid.

I am here to show you
who you are, to cradle
your large skulls
and remind you
you are perfect.

Parker invests in Baartman as what José Muñoz (2007) calls a "Vulnerability Artist," a performer who leaves herself open to the affects of others, though she does not promise repair.

Infamous Bodies holds this focus on mutual but radically uneven experiences, effects, and aesthetics of vulnerability but, like Parker, moves away from a focus on the possibility of mutual reparations; instead, I focus on the critical desires to read for repair and resistance. Resituating infamous women like Baartman in relationship to the formation of law and rights allows for a skeptical view of scholarly itineraries and opens up flexibility in methods of interpretation—the questions critics feel we can ask while still maintaining deep, ethical commitments to our subjects of study and to the complex world they have helped to create. This book resists reading black feminist theory as a "normalizing agenc[y]" that "fantasize(s) the subject's liberation into autonomy and coherent self-production [while also] imagin[ing] the possibility of doing so as the singular goal of interpretive practice as a whole" (Wiegman 2012, 33, 23–24). Like Wiegman, and in the vein of Nash's black feminist method of "letting go" (2019a), I imagine ways to read that render critical practice vulnerable, not to destroy it but to embrace a state of risk that refuses critique as (only) a mode of shoring up, of certainty.

White patriarchal supremacy has conflated rights with the absence of risk, deploying a strategic refusal to bear harm to the self even as it burdens risk on others (the examples, just when one thinks of stand-your-ground laws or hate speech, are staggeringly present). Such an overdetermining structure creates a political situation where to let up any pressure on the constant narrative of black suffering, risk, and injury feels like one is giving up on a political future, save for minor pauses for black excellence or triumphs over overwhelming antiblackness. Recent popular terminology such as "toxic masculinity" and "white fragility" can help here to think about the psychic nature of risk and the way narratives and capacities for vulnerability absorb cultural formations of rights-as-entitlements and ties to agency. With these structures and structures of feeling of white patriarchy in mind, I turn toward vulnerability in the feminist imagination.

The language of vulnerability referenced by Christina Sharpe (2016), by Kimberly Juanita Brown (2015, 8) in her work on vulnerability as both openness to violence and "open to reading" (which is echoed in Julietta Singh's concept of "vulnerable reading" [2018]), by Crystal Parikh's (2017) investment in embodied vulnerability as a means to articulate human rights otherwise, and by Darius Bost, La Marr Jurelle Bruce, and Brandon J. Manning (2019) as remaining "radically available" both to injury and to feeling across various temporal frames and moods, is an evocative affective vocabulary that has its own cultural, political, social, and legal history. Vulnerability evokes injury, threat, precarity, and paternalism as well as concomitant displays of the force of the security state and rhetorics of personal entitlement and responsibility. Alexandra S. Moore (2015), however, has asked the field of literary human rights study to decouple securitization from vulnerability, seeing the former as a particular appeal to the normalization of the liberal humanist subject that some feminist articulations of human rights traffic in (as deconstructed in the work of Wendy Hesford and Rachel Lewis [2016]), and the latter as a mode of relationality (Moore 2015). Judith Butler (2016, 25) has also turned to vulnerability as a mode of understanding and imagining possible nonviolent resistance, or nonmilitaristic and inclusive ways to politically reveal and collate that move from the presupposition that "loss and vulnerability seem to follow from our being socially constituted bodies, attached to others, at risk of losing those attachments, exposed to others, at risk of violence by that exposure."[16] Elizabeth Anker (2012) and Parikh follow up on this with particular investments in the "embodied vulnerability" (Parikh 2017, 36) of the subjects of human rights—for Anker, a concern with the materiality of bodies without an attachment to their coherence and absolute repair; for Parikh, a deep engagement with the unruly desires that constitute human subjects and literary imaginings of other, more just worlds, each taking seriously the unevenly distributed but "shared bodily exposure to the world" (36) as the *subject of* rights, as well as a *desire for* rights (rather than a constant will to the nonnormative). For critic Candace Jenkins (2007), this positionality is particular for what she terms "black intimate subjects"—defined by she calls a foundational "doubled vulnerability" to bodily exposure that, following Du Bois, is inherent in the experience of being a black human seeking relation and finding scrutiny in the social world.

Following Jenkins, I remain skeptical of some of the more utopic aspects of vulnerability as political and reading practice,[17] tracing from her careful work on the particularity of black vulnerability a new way into legal theorist Martha Albertson Fineman's vulnerability theory—one reworked through a tradition and trajectory of black feminist approaches to political subjectivity—most saliently Christina Sharpe's claiming of black women's subjectivity as "internal" to "all US American post-slavery subjects" (2010, 182, 187). Fineman's theory in many ways builds on the famous capabilities theory of Martha C. Nussbaum (2003) and Amartya Sen (2004), but instead of focusing on people's ascension to well-being, vulnerability theory assumes a state of risk and need: "If vulnerability is understood to be an inherent and inevitable aspect of what it means to be human, and also as the source of social institutions and relationships, it must necessarily be the foundation for any social or political theory. The universal political and legal subject we construct should reflect the reality that we all live and die within a fragile materiality that renders us constantly susceptible to both internal and external forces beyond our control. The social contract that binds society together should be fashioned around the concept of the *vulnerable subject*, a construct that would displace the autonomous and independent liberal subject that currently serves to define the core responsibilities of policy and law" (Fineman 2014, 307).

Within this vulnerability there is not a flattened common injury, but specific variances of experience that demand the studied strengthening of the institutions—what Fineman calls "the responsive state" (2010b)—that create and support what Fineman deems "resilience." In her terms, "Resilience is a product of social relationships and institutions. Human beings are not born resilient. Resilience is produced over time through social structures and societal conditions that individuals may be unable to control. Resilience is found in the material, cultural, social, and existential resources that allow individuals to respond to their vulnerability (and dependencies)" (Fineman 2010a, 362–63). Or as she reframes it in a different context, "recognition of vulnerability does NOT reflect or assert the absence or impossibility of agency—rather, it recognizes that agency [in the form of resilience] is causally produced over the life course and is limited and constrained by the sources and relationships available to any specific individual. Vulnerability theory asserts that agency or autonomy—like the concept of resilience . . . should always be understood as particular, partial and contextual" (2015a). The language Fineman uses is a call for a recognition of structurally and temporally unequal assumptions of risk and a call for responsible care in the face of such structural inequity (2014, 613). Even as I write this, though, I bristle at the suggestion that we might organize a politics around a capitulation to the world that is, rather than as we might wish to see it in heroic terms—where we would all have access to autonomy, dignity, sovereignty, and individual consent without harming or risking the lives of others.

Vulnerability takes seriously, politically, the desires and attachments to the very systems that fail us—what Lauren Berlant (2011) terms "cruel optimism"—and how that intersects with the ways public culture already collectively imagines the compromised lives, deaths, and afterlives of the five figures in this book. Under impossible circumstances that categorically refuse rights, agency, autonomy, dignity, and self-determination, one might pause in championing these categories, however tempered by utopic definition, as political goals. Vulnerability is a politics that speaks from, to, and with the materiality of something like Hortense J. Spillers's (1987) "flesh," which imagines what is left after the obliteration of what we think we know to be human and exposes the fictions of rights and their mythic tenets of personhood. If "the condition of black life is one of mourning," as Claudia Rankine (2015) has hauntingly headlined, and the key practitioners of this living and mourning are black women, then perhaps it is time that, following Anker (2012), we, as critics, refuse the fantasies of both dignity and "bodily integrity" that have never been the province of the marginalized and the vulnerable—particularly black women. This sentiment also infuses Holloway's (2011) reading of black bodies as public texts[18] that leave us, as scholars and as political subjects, critically vulnerable (Campt 2017; C. Sharpe 2010, 2016). Vulnerability as a reading practice, then, is not a race to the bottom, so to speak, but a call to consider the "bottom" as constitutive of political subjectivity, rather than its margins or lack (Stockton 2006). Such a reading practice aims to retain the specificity of black women's experience but to refrain from treating vulnerability as exceptional or unusual trauma, even as it is historically specific and unevenly distributed.

Infamous Bodies imagines ways—with and through expressive cultures—of vulnerably inhabiting the political that might exist with, from, and beyond the site of known critique. I push against the assumed use of history as rescue, as corrective, as a critical mission of human rights and social justice. In doing so, this book attempts to build a case that positions violence, trauma, desire, pleasure, risk, and vulnerability as inextricably linked to, and unevenly distributed by, human embodiment. This book assumes the presence of these tense partners in sociality as the collective base of *being* a political subject, rather than as categories either one inhabits or to which one aspires. It imagines, in other words, black women's experience in Enlightenment modernity as the center of political subjectivity.

Like the embodied vulnerability that is at the core of vexed receptions of Baartman's body and Beyoncé's choice to not represent her body, this book highlights a state of material risk, and the ways that Enlightenment modernity has misrecognized black women's vulnerability as a necessary, tolerable, and/or inevitable burden. I want to mark these vulnerable states not as the exceptions but the rules of civil sociality in modernity—but not end the critical plot in the naming of the injury. This study seeks to alter the plot of subjection as a critical teleology but not as a fact. Instead, I argue for a reading practice that engages Patricia Williams's (1991, 433) terms of "distance and respect" as organizing principles around political change—terms that resonate with the uncertainty that appends the fractured, partial archive of black women's embodied experience in modernity, their "mystery," in Kimberly Juanita Brown's (2015) formulation.

This phrasing also echoes a tenet of humanistic interpretive methodology: critical distance. Here, rights are conceived not as a cure but through an affect and effect of inevitable misunderstanding, a formulation that refuses the cloak of personhood as equally distributable. Instead, "distance and respect" imagines that all things, including people, are worthy of distancing from our own desires and exercises of individual power as much as possible. It is, of course, depressing and risky to think outside the terms of personhood as rights-bearing within the legacy of black lives and their relationship to property. Following Moten's (2003, 2008) continued interrogation of the possibilities of objectness and objectification, this imaginative reorientation can stop seeking a recognition of humanity, which as Patricia Williams (1991, 412), among others, argues has been a "dismal failure" for black political gain. To claim the ground of black politics on vulnerability is to embrace the possibility of abjection (alongside Darieck Scott [2010]), vulnerability, precarity, codependence, and intemperance—of feeling, acting, and being—as the center of black scholarship and political theory.[19] It is to unmake race heroes in favor of uncertain and impermanent alliances, coalitions, and desires—some of which might make us wince in their seeming unrelation to "freedom" as we have come to commonly understand and reify it, all of which are and will be dangerously imperfect and impure.[20]

This book is then a call to look at representation and culture not for a cure but for a question. As this introduction sketches out, I, along with other scholars in the wake of Hartman's (2008) "critical fabulation," retain the possibility of representation not with an attachment to getting black feminism "right" but with a commitment to staging different questions that ask us what "the changing same" or "repetition with a difference" mean, constitutively, about black feminist critical practices of looking, reading, and interpretation (Butler 2016; McDowell 1987). Patricia Williams's (1991) theory of political understanding based on the recognition of not just difference, but distance, undergirds an interpretative practice built around incompletion, the assumption of misunderstanding, and the impossibility of understanding, seeing, reading, or knowing in full that is echoed in Hartman's powerful call to responsibility and care for the vulnerable body in black feminist study.

I reckon with these early black women celebrities in their own diasporic frames, reading moments of their eruptive visibility that have made plain the cultural genres and performances of law and rights for what they are—fictions in their own time and beyond. Instead of trying to correct the record, to place these figures in the order of things that we already know about the failures of law and rights in relationship to race, I look to the ways that these infamous bodies reimagine the contours and content of the political in their own time, but most significantly beyond it, in the ways that they inhabit and transform the imaginable limits of political being and living in a patriarchal, antiblack world. I don't do this to fetishize life but to think of black women's living and representational practices around that living as political labor. This is a question of reception, but also of the temporality that I signal in my use of the word "early" in this book's subtitle. I use "early" not because these figures are, arguably, the "first" black women celebrities in the modern media frame, and not because they strictly function as the "before" of the amply studied "after" of twentieth- and twenty-first-century black women celebrities and performers, though their historical moment and import are significant to excavate. I use "early" to denote a political orientation, to write these figures out of the corrective histories that find them tragic, belated, and passé, their politics and histories always too dated or too late, even in their contemporary moment. This book revisits their histories to trace genealogies of critical attachment and desire, imagining these early black women's embodiments as doing the hard and vulnerable work of proliferation and plenitude, altering interpretive practices across law, literature, and public culture.

Baartman and the other four figures of this book embody the paradox of Hartman's (2008) call—representation with a simultaneous recognition of its impossibility (and the implicit black feminist externalization of those cultural politics: living through what seems unlivable)—through their vast archival presences. The cultural and critical field continues to return to these figures because, in their celebrity, they are archived: because of their fame, they are archived; because of their archives, they have fame. These figures are, in all problematics of the terms, *objects*, accessed endlessly through the print and visual cultures that conjure their very individual existences in and beyond their lifetimes.

I organize the chapters historically not to give an unbroken sense of political hegemony or teleology of each figure's times but to disrupt this "calculus" of value, in Hartman's (2008) terms, and the imagined scenes of repair in the corrective histories that follow. Each figure reemerges most saliently at flash points in diasporically specific shifts in racial-political discourse; it is the premise of this book that early black women celebrities are revisited to reinterpret and represent blackness in a configuration that challenges, expands, contests, or aligns with the rights debates of that moment. There is a clumping effect, of course, of cultural representations that hew toward the complicated but expected lines of their respective progressive political contexts. But these repetitions are also understudied components of these oft-told political histories, ones that show how significant the front of culture is to the negotiation of politics (Fanon 2004). Moments emerge that push against stories commonly told of particular eras and movements (like the unexpected pathos and glamour of Phillis Wheatley in former Black Panthers' Minister of Culture Ed Bullins's 1976 play), that suggest other ways to engage black political subjectivities, particularly gendered narratives and embodied histories. To trace the constant return to these figures and to place those returns next to the most important, visible, public struggles for rights, freedom, and black liberation of their time is to take seriously the possibilities and the limits of corrective histories. As I reread the more contemporary moments of their reimagining, I also generatively renegotiate these figures' historical contexts and their past critical receptions to trace alternative sites of black feminist political imagination. The chapters then revisit corrective histories of both racism and racial justice to track new ways of charting black political history's present, and possible black feminist futures.

To engage in these deep and long histories is to engage unevenly—I take up only a particular aspect of representations of these iconic figures. The goal, then, is not comprehensive coverage or definitive analysis of each celebrity figure and her corrective history but to think about historical reuse as a political and cultural strategy in relationship to black feminist thought. This project looks at and in the sphere of cultural production as a site of political meaning making—both reflective and constitutive—that interacts with and exceeds legal, formal, and official genres and regimes of public politics.[21] Most of the texts this book covers are authored by black women, but I also seek to decouple a naturalized connection between black women as cultural producers and black feminist reading, and the book includes cultural producers and critics—including myself—who are *not* black women as part of its critical conversations about the field. Following duCille (1994), I disrupt the anthropological gaze that expects and demands only sociological attachment from its nativized sources and hence gives over the field to black women seemingly out of deference but in effect abandons black feminist thought as only needed and important to black women themselves. As duCille lays out, this caution about claiming exclusive territory is an uneasy one, and that ambivalence suits a project that focuses on public lives of black women that also engender much debate across difficult affective terrains, like Beyoncé and Baartman's intersection. The first chapter begins with an interrogation of black women's celebrity and its relationship to fantasies of freedom, with freedom standing as the foundational concept and aspirational goal of both liberal humanism and black politics. Each subsequent chapter takes on an aspect of freedom and rights: the romance of freedom and/as consent; the fiction of freedom through contract; the adventurous desire for civic engagement; and the lure of sovereignty, including genres and forms of self-development, as embodied freedom discourse.

Chapter 1 focuses on Phillis Wheatley as the figure at the heart of the intersection of race, Enlightenment ideas of human rights, and the rise of the concept of freedom as the locus of meaningful political subjectivity. Wheatley is repeatedly imagined as a site of the trials and failures of freedom, yoking the invention of blackness to its relationship, even in political philosophy and especially in the formation of modern law in the West, to the domain of culture (here literature and literacy), and positing that relationship *as* the scene of freedom, so to speak. I look at the repeated representations of Wheatley in relationship to fame in order to read the work done by, through, and in the name of Wheatley's body, tying her to blackness and rights, positively and negatively. In doing so I restage this foundational figure in both the birth of the US republic and in the articulated experience of African and black subjection as a public mediator between race and rights—the first black celebrity and an origin story of Western human rights. I then trace less-recognizable routes of intimacy in Wheatley's work and her reperformances, particularly in twentieth-century drama and contemporary art and poetry, to reckon with the legacy of uncertainty and doubt as potential black feminist political methods.

If Wheatley is "the primal scene" of African American literature and the deep relationship between African American cultural representation and metrics of freedom, humanity, and rights, then Sally Hemings—enslaved Virginian and mother of Thomas Jefferson's children—is, in the true sexual Freudian sense of the primal scene, the obsessively returned-to figure, remembered and represented, via her relationship to Jefferson (Gates 2003, 1). In chapter 2, I argue that it is through the supposed contradiction between the notion that "all men are created equal" and the decades-long, scandalous (even its own time) entanglement that produced living enslaved progeny of Jefferson that we can understand sexual consent as at the heart of histories of US democracy and the violence of enslavement. Through readings of novels, poetry, film, art, and curated historical space, this chapter calls for sustained and centered attention to black women's sexuality as the base of analysis for the project of the modern democratic state and body politic, not by proving again and again Hemings's inability to consent but by imagining unconsent as the start of all political subjectivity. Hemings here, then, inaugurates the modern political subject as based in radical vulnerability rather than the ascendant ideal of a consenting agent.

Chapter 3 thinks through how fictions of consent also undergird the promise and pitfalls of contract through the labor and recirculation of Sarah Baartman, the founding figure of this introduction. This chapter approaches Baartman's legacy through representations of her 1810 trial on the validity of her labor contract, which laid bare the deeper implications of public discourse around the diminished humanity of African peoples in the law beyond the enslaved/free binary. A study of the public trial in which she appeared as a witness merges justifications that underpin colonialism and the chattel slave trade with contemporary conversations about the effectiveness of the law as an avenue for justice or achieving human rights for black subjects, particularly black women. The trial, reproduced in contemporary film, fiction, and drama, exposed/exposes the market for women's bodies that the modern West has refused either to regulate through the official protections of contract—putting women's work, in particular domestic, performative, and sex work, outside of the protective bounds of the state and yet subject to its social and sometimes criminal judgment. This chapter tracks the political, commemorative, and cultural texts that follow Baartman as well as examines the difficult critical affects around Baartman as a figure of black feminist discourse—including the fatigue of constant, repetitive, unremunerated critical labor. As the field confronts the failure of cultural, social, and legal forms to imagine better representational practices that can escape the teleology of Baartman's corporeal fate and cultural reception, black feminist thought finds itself negotiating a fragile way deeper into rather than out of seemingly negative critical feelings, including fatigue.

Chapter 4 moves from the critical exhaustion of overexposure to trace narratives of citizenship and civic desire—black, colonial, national, postcolonial, and empirical—through Jamaican nurse and hotelier Mary Seacole. Seacole, a celebrity and memoirist in the 1850s who has achieved a resurgence of attention in post-Thatcher Britain, challenges static narratives of racial, national, and colonial belonging for a black feminine subject, particularly in the way she is deployed around various racialized ideologies that limit black women's personal and political mobility. As the first and only figure in this book whose routes do not run directly through enslavement or indentured servitude, Seacole sits at a precarious moment of transition for black women's celebrity and affirmative intimacies with the state. Through her relationship with and against Florence Nightingale, a white feminist icon who refused Seacole's inclusion into her nursing corps in the Crimea, Seacole's political life is reanimated in a contemporary Britain desperate for antiracist rebranding through public and political commemorative acts. At the same time, she is remobilized in Jamaica and its diasporas as a figure of global ambition and capitalist success. Seacole and her adventurous afterlives remap the boundaries of black civic participation through the tensions between imperialism, multiculturalism, transnational feminism, global capitalism, and cultural nationalism.

In Chapter 5, I conclude with Victorian-era celebrity Sarah Forbes Bonetta and her inhabitation of multiple and conflicting genres of sovereignty in her day and in her newly emerging corrective histories. Thought to be of royal lineage in Africa, she was kidnapped from her home as a young girl and brought to Dahomey, where, in 1850, she was "given" to an emissary of Queen Victoria. She was "adopted" by Queen Victoria, becoming her goddaughter and living as an upper-class woman of English society. Her presence is recorded and unearthed largely through a series of photographs showing her in full Victorian dress. Her proximity to sovereignty in the forms of royalty as well as debates around colonial, native, and gendered autonomy are taken up with pride and with trepidation in the contemporary moment of her historical recovery, with visual art and fiction centering on Bonetta revealing the anxiety and intense labor involved with investing in autonomy, self-development, and self-determination as key features of black freedoms. Bonetta and Seacole, like Wheatley, Hemings, and Baartman, navigate institutional intimacy with whiteness and capital consumption as critics interpret their contemporary recoveries into corrective histories of inclusion and imperatives to use blackness as a repair to historical racial injury.

These chapters trace the specter of freedom and the presence of vulnerability in the afterlives of rights, moving through genres of the political and cultural: the fantasy of freedom in the face of risky, fleeting feelings of affiliation and the tenuous intimacies of community; the romance of securitization from embodied risk from the raw, open vulnerability of feeling across difference; the fiction of representational cures through exposure or refusal that collapse into the exhaustion of relentless critical labor and performance; the heroic adventure narratives of citizenship rights and inclusion that occlude the unruliness of personal and political desire itself; and the coming-of-age development narratives of sovereignty, self and otherwise, when wholeness and progress are consistently punctured by feeling badly, wrongly, and incompletely about both history and the duties of black feminist political protocols. Collectively, these figures also sit at the threshold of the Afro-pessimism movement, even as they push on the stakes of charismatic figuration (as formulated by Erica R. Edwards's 2012 critique) and political leadership in a critical time in black studies, one occupied by an insistence on death and abjection. Their histories of representation texture any historiography of antiblackness as a practice of reading rather than as an explanatory mechanism.

My reading then borrows from Nash's (2014b) "loving critique" of the field of black feminist theory in a call not to "do better" but to deeply grapple with affective analysis and interpretative desires that want so much to find the right or the wrong—the certain—reading or representation that will mark or undo or remap the political.[22] In the afterimages of Wheatley, Hemings, Baartman, Seacole, and Bonetta, this book reads early black feminist lives and afterlives as insistent on blackness's endless diversity, its ceaseless proliferation and plenitude, its ability to produce and elicit diverse ethical political practices beyond being "true and to use language truthfully," in Douglass's construction of fame. These figures embody attachments, intimacies, and recognitions that one cannot fully account for, understand, or know, in total. *Infamous Bodies* is dedicated to reading early black women celebrities and their afterlives through a frame of vulnerability and uncertainty, an interpretive practice that offers new political futures of and for black feminist study.

Chapter One

FANTASIES OF FREEDOM

A PHILLIS rises, and the world no more
Denies the sacred right to mental pow'r;
While, Heav'n-inspir'd, she proves *her Country's* claim
To Freedom, and *her own* to deathless Fame.
—MATILDA [pseud.], "On Reading the Poems of Phillis Wheatley,
the African Poetess," *New York Magazine*, 1796

In our legal and political system, words like "freedom" and "choice" are forms of currency.
They function as the mediators by which we make all things equal, interchangeable. It is,
therefore, not just what "freedom" means, but the relation it signals between each individual
and the world. It is a word that levels difference.—PATRICIA WILLIAMS, *The Alchemy of
Race and Rights*, 1991

In poet and critic Evie Shockley's 2006 debut collection, *a half-red sea*, she
finds inspiration, solace, and humor in Phillis Wheatley's eighteenth-century
poetic legacy, including an imaginative bond between the two most famous
early enslaved black women authors—one of a book of poetry, one of a Founding Father's children—in "wheatley and hemmings have drinks in the halls
of the ancestors." "those two've been / doing drinks since mark twain / was in
diapers," the poem vamps, setting Wheatley up as the founding mother of US
letters, and decidedly eschewing the tragic and formal frames of reference
Wheatley's representations often occupy. Phillis Wheatley, late eighteenth-
century African poet who was enslaved in the United States and the author
of the first book of poetry by an "African American," stands as the epitome of
black fame, even in Frederick Douglass's rigid terms, a literary celebrity in
her time and beyond, whose name and figure often signal the very stakes

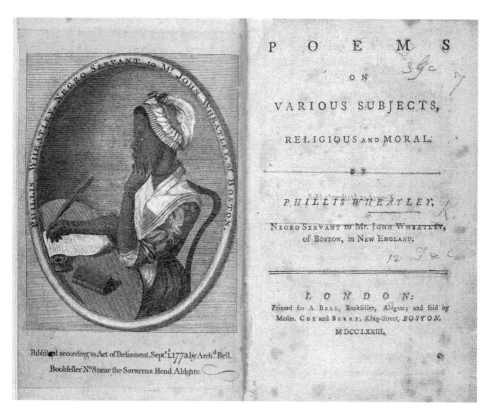

FIGURE 1.1. Frontispiece of Phillis Wheatley's *Poems on Various Subjects, Religious and Moral* (1773).

of antiracist thought as well as the fraught promises of liberal humanism. Wheatley herself and those who met with or spoke about her were compelled to reflect not just on her work but on who counted as a sentient, political subject within the newly formed concept of the democratic state. Her words and reputation circulated, as did her image, in the form of the print of an engraved portrait that graces her 1773 book, *Poems on Various Subjects*—a mark both of newly emergent markets for literary celebrity in the eighteenth century and of how significant visualizing Wheatley was to imagining her place in the emerging republic. Her race, her gender, her age, her literacy, and her enslaved status were the currency of her fame, and this frontispiece (figure 1.1) stages each of these in a single, consumable, circulating image.

I pose her portrait, and Shockley's irreverent poetic sociality between Wheatley and Hemings, as in critical conversation with the dominant fantasy of imagining Wheatley through her infamous "trial" in front of a group of white men to test her intellectual and artistic authenticity. Wheatley repeats in the cultural imagination as a multicultural representative, tragic heroine, early feminist, and example of and exception to her race since her own time. Her celebrity, re-created as and through the trial in ongoing corrective histories and representations, is deployed to confirm black women as continually injured objects and resistant if compromised agents. Her portrait, repeatedly ascribed to African painter Scipio Moorhead, is assigned to visually represent Wheatley as well as to represent a critical desire for black art to represent black political community.

The interplay of these genres of fantasy around Wheatley—the trial and the portrait—unevenly refracts the tension between her timely emergence on the scene of the American Revolution and her representational reemergence at other moments of crisis for considering black political life and futures. Through the art and criticism of and on Wheatley—her own poetic work and letters, Harlem Renaissance–era children's theater, Black Arts movement performance, contemporary art, and poetry, to name the major sites I touch on—I suggest a way to examine critical attachments to Wheatley, finding in repetitions of her story and likeness a way of rethinking black women's infamy and its relation to fantasies of black freedom. In particular, I focus on two critically ignored plays, one written in 1932 by white National Association for the Advancement of Colored People cofounder Mary White Ovington, and the other in 1976 by prolific Black Arts movement and beyond playwright Ed Bullins. Both plays were written and produced in the waning days of galvanizing political and artistic movements, ones that had, if they weighed in on Wheatley at all, often found her politically lacking.

Instead of focusing on historical and political certainty, my exploration of creative and critical reperformances of Phillis Wheatley's name and likeness centers on a method of reading the political through and with uncertainty. This method of reading suggests a black feminist epistemological orientation to the political that not only critiques what has come before in the name of rights—particularly the emphasis on the political horizon of freedom—but a politics that emphasizes vulnerability and interdependence as viable visions for black study. I read through Wheatley an imperative to interpret generously and generatively through loss, rather than taking death and mourning as the critical end point of black feminist reading and political practices.

Phillis Wheatley is the recurring figure, the "repeating body," "The Changing Same," that inaugurates and keeps alive the powerful link between black expressive culture and the political (K. J. Brown 2015; McDowell 1987). For over two and half centuries since her emergence on the colonial US and British literary scene, hers has been the name on the pens of the likes of Thomas Jefferson, James Weldon Johnson, writers June Jordan, Alice Walker, and Amiri Baraka, as well as Karla FC Holloway, Henry Louis Gates Jr., and an enormous swath of African American, eighteenth-century, African, early American, and classics literary studies scholars. She stands as and for what Lisa Lowe (2009, 106) calls the "thematic importance of literacy to black humanity," and Gates (2003, 1) dramatizes as "the primal scene" of African American letters, but also represents the collapse between cultural production and access to the category of the human—with that "access" becoming the very grounds on which one could lay claim to legal, political, and embodied freedoms.

Wheatley stands as the first black celebrity in the modern construction of blackness as a question about the relationship between race, rights, and the human. For Wheatley, this publicness manifests in the form of the trial—in her time, through individual and private tests of authenticity that were then made public, as well as public debate about what exactly her literary skills proved or disproved about the capacity of black subjects to "earn" the status of free citizen. That she wrote in the physical and philosophical midst of the American Revolution, with attention from public political figures that included the Founding Fathers, only cements her legacy—her infamy—as inevitably tied to the political discourse of freedom, a conversation in which she participated through her poetry and letters as much as she became the object of its scrutiny.

As Joanna Brooks (2010, 18) powerfully argues, "It appears that the Gates legend of the "Trial of Phillis Wheatley" has drawn at least some of its commanding imaginative power from its resemblance to familiar scenarios of knowledge production and academic professionalization, the experience of the individual mind on trial before a panel of powerful and distinguished judges, and an academic model of individual accomplishment, public proving, and elite authorization as the pathway to publication, as well as the role of gender and race especially in structuring these interactions and opportunities." Gates is not alone: Nellie Y. McKay uses the Wheatley trial legend as a framework for exploring the devaluation of African American literature and literary scholarship in her 1998 essay "Naming the Problem That Led to the Question 'Who Shall Teach African-American Literature?'; or, Are We Ready to Disband the Wheatley Court?" as does Holloway (1995) in her provocative twinning of Anita Hill and Wheatley. That Wheatley never, historically speaking, experienced such a live event is a testament to how the very frame of the black woman's body publicly on trial has gripped visions of the political, at least in part hinging on the gendered assumption of horror at the forced publicness of a girl's body being coerced from the privacy (and constructed innocence) of childhood or domestic life—a deep fiction that enslaved girls and women's lives already and always upend.[1]

I tease out the more sexualized strains that undergird this fiction, a strain that reverberates in Shockley's own decision to align Wheatley and Hemings, to illustrate how significant the terms and genre of fantasy are for the ways that freedom and unfreedom are imagined in black political imagination and in the political imagination of blackness—discourses that hinge on fame, infamy, and the visible presence of blackness in the public sphere. I use fantasy here, specifically, as a different take on the future-orientation of Robin D. G. Kelley's (2002) more utopically oriented "dreams"—fantasy as a psychoanalytic term that functions alternately as a resource, a relation, and as desire. More contemporary critics such as Anne Anlin Cheng (2011) link fantasy to melancholy, to an attachment to how structures of power and belonging operate through the axis of race, whereas feminist theorists such as Elizabeth Grosz (1994) and Claudia Tate (1998) recognize fantasy as productive desire, recalling Patricia Williams's call for proliferation and Tate's own hermeneutic of plenitude (and the critical discussions of desire I reference in the introduction and chapter 4 of this book). For Joan Wallach Scott (2011), fantasy becomes a way of understanding the intellectual life of gender and feminism, as it operates in mutable ways across time and space. Fantasy, then, embeds vulnerability. It is a fiction, not wholly controllable or intentional, and yet it provides a frame, many frames, for interpretive practice as itself a desiring act of projection, longing, resource, and sociality. It leaves room, as well, for feelings and objects in excess of the traditionally or appropriately political—for the uncertainty and even unpredictability of desire as an embodied, nonrational drive.

Gates characterizes the trial as the primal scene—which, in Freudian terms, is an event that psychically haunts, unavoidable yet unaddressable, and always already a preoccupation. It is also a sexual scene, an aspect that my emphasis on desire and embodied vulnerability suggests, and one that I address in the gendering of Wheatley and, more fully, in my chapter on Sally Hemings. As Paul Gilroy (1993, 152) notes, black literary production "was first enlisted in order to demonstrate and validate the humanity of black authors." But it is also imagined through Wheatley as a deeply gendered, intimate violation. Wheatley's imagined frail black girlhood on display, literally and/or metaphorically in front of an all-white propertied male panel of judges, is part of the varied and understandable critical desires around Wheatley and her inaugural authentication of black humanity through black cultural production. Naming these desires as such may create a pathos for what has come before in Wheatley studies as well as a nimble skepticism about any historical, moral, ethical, or political claims to the best or most accurate "use" of black women as public, political subjects in a quest for freedom.[2] This post–Black Arts movement fantasy of the trial, of the criminalized yet innocent Wheatley, comes from her specific historical trajectory of being rendered as both the ruse and the scapegoat of black freedom, as in James Weldon Johnson's and Baraka's calls for the sonic masculinist sound of resistance against her feminized, formal lines that I discuss in a brief history of her reception.

Weighing in on Wheatley in her day meant weighing in on the race question, putting black bodies in their public places by turning her into either an exception that proved the rule of racial order or an exceptional example who transcended her race altogether (Felker 1997, 81–83). From Thomas Jefferson ([1785] 1999), who claimed "Religion, indeed, had produced a Phyllis Whately [sic], but it could not produce a poet," to George Washington's ([1775–76] 1931, 361) naming of her as "a person so favoured by the Muses, and to whom Nature has been so liberal and beneficent in her dispensations," the public discourse surrounding her work always centered around her exceptional status as black intellectual and artist. "Simultaneously exalting and domesticating her talent" (Cima 2006, 480–81), both modes of locating Wheatley also shut down more nuanced or complicated reckonings with the emergent community of free blacks in the north and their dominant modes of literacy—speeches, sermons, and newspapers. They also reveal Wheatley as a savvy reader and marketer of her own work, and of the political climate of "freedom" that she wrote within (J. Brooks 2010; Slauter 2009; Wilcox 1999).

"Freedom," of course, is a sticky term, one often interchanged with terms such as emancipation, abolition, and liberation in black, black feminist, ethnic studies, and feminist theories of freedom. Jefferson's "life, liberty, and the pursuit of happiness" haunt freedom's frame in both their ephemerality as political values and in their material insistence on the individual and the pursuit of property in ways that exclude women, African American, and nonwhite peoples of the era explicitly. Poststructural theory and critiques of neoliberalism have questioned not just the history but the ongoing utility of freedom as a form of political relation. Foucault (2008, 63) argues that "Freedom is never anything other—but this is already a great deal—than an actual relation between governors and governed, a relation in which the measure of the 'too little' existing freedom is given by the 'even more' freedom demanded." As Mimi Thi Nguyen (2012, 10, 7) has compellingly written in her work on the moral economy and material violence of Western expansion in the name of freedom, "Foucault stops just short of addressing at least one problem of the dual character of freedom as the development of capacities and the intensification of power . . . [that] has ever operated as a global-historical project of modernity hinged upon structures of race and coloniality, and through which liberalism's empire unfolds across the globe through promises to secure it for others." In other words, freedom as relation transforms from Patricia Williams's "currency" to a weapon and a resource, an ideal and a justification in the name of and as an attack against those defined outside of its limited frame. Freedom is a problem, in Thomas C. Holt's (1992) terms, that is created as much as it is stymied by the promise of the law and the state, a term that "levels difference" in the cutting description by Williams (1991, 31) in this chapter's epigraph.

In black and feminist studies, a clear critique of freedom appears in works that redefine but still attach to the imaginative terrain of freedom through the history and experience of enslavement and systemic, institutional, and embodied oppression. In the wake of Orlando Patterson's landmark 1991 work on freedom as a concept that emerged in its fullest form as a Western value only through its stark relief with the figure of the slave, scholars such as Neil Roberts (2015) have articulated black freedoms based on fugitivity and marronage, and feminist scholars have called attention to the masculinization of freedom discourses, including Nancy J. Hirschmann's (2003) contextualization of choice and Shatema Threadcraft's (2016) recent pivoting of black freedom toward the embodied experience of black women.[3] Following in the footsteps of Harriet Jacobs's ([1861] 1988, 60) qualifying "something akin to freedom" (her description of "choosing" a white man who was not her master as her sexual and reproductive partner), feminism has theorized freedom as a difficult and always qualified process and promise, a "constant struggle" in Angela Davis's (2016) terms, and a more radical political orientation than one can properly imagine in Linda M. G. Zerilli's (2005) formulation of its "abyss"-like quality of uncertainty and unknowability—a formulation this book follows in concept even if it does not locate those qualities exclusively in the terminology or methodology of freedom itself. Davis qualifies freedom as not just a constant struggle but in many ways as a moving target, while C. Sharpe argues that "bearing freedom" is a multigenerational act, a tension between subjection and survival (2010, 26). This philosophy is historically echoed in Natasha Lightfoot's (2015, 224, 2, 20) work on the aftermath of legal freedom, which she deems "incomplete freedom" that "entailed material distress and personal uncertainty" and often "still reified the troubled forms of freedom embedded in" empire-led emancipation.

Between freedom as an impossibility, a ruse of the state, a "paradox" in Patterson's more recent terms (Scott 2013), and freedom as adaptive futures as-yet-unknown, stands the figuration and almost immediate circulation and refiguration of Phillis Wheatley as the symbol of black freedom's necessity and its constant state of becoming, of proving itself in the Enlightenment modernity era. If emancipation has figured the terrain of legal freedom in the most material sense, and liberation has taken on the tenor of a spiritual break with bondage, this Wheatley-esque freedom has been the terrain of the social and political imagination—sometimes claimed quite literally, as with arguments such as Anthony Bogues's (2010) claim that freedom is imaginative labor, or as when Ralph Ellison (1952, 14) claims freedom as "knowing how to say what I got up in my head." Langston Hughes, in his essay "200 Years of American Negro Poetry" ([1966] 1997), writes that Wheatley "wrote herself to freedom"—both a material and an imaginative claim. Wheatley as a figure shows that politics has been fought on the terrain of black cultural production even during revolutionary American times—redating Richard Iton's (2008) compelling claims about black culture's relationship to black politics, and the ways that definitions of freedom and black humanity have long relied on black celebrity and hypervisibility. Toni Morrison (1992, 37) takes this up in her analysis of enslaved presence in Herman Melville's *Benito Cereno* in her larger diagnosis of the ways that enslaved humanity was displayed as "surrogate selves for meditations on problems of human freedom, its lure and its elusiveness." In *Beloved*, Morrison ([1987] 2004, 191) plays with a different, more embodied version of black feminist freedoms: "not to need permission for desire—well now, that was freedom."

My interpretations of Wheatley's work, her reception, and her representations wrestle with Morrison's fantasy of freedom as a kind of desire without consent or authorization as I confront those critics across this expanse of black political-literary authorship who have found in the portrait and work of Wheatley a denial of black freedoms—analyses that seek to regulate not just interpretation of black texts but black desire itself. James Weldon Johnson's (1922, xxvii) sensitive account of Wheatley's poetry calls for a reading of Wheatley against the project of African American literature as "agonizing cry," as does Baraka's 1962 (2009, 124) talk about her "ludicrous departures from the huge Black voices that splintered southern nights with their *hollers, chants, arwhoolies,* and *ballits.*"[4] Wallace Thurman (quoted in Gates 2003, 46) excoriates Wheatley with the claim that "Phillis in her day was a museum figure who would have caused more of a sensation if some contemporary Barnum had exploited her," in a description that aligns the nineteenth-century history of racist display with Wheatley's compromised feminine publicness, confirming the hermeneutics of suspicion as the major frame for black women's celebrity/public visibility. Wheatley's formal verse can seem very far from the protocols of the Black Aesthetic, and the related political iterations of black nationalism, and so it stands at odds with the political life that emerged through and from that expressive culture in the post–civil rights era.[5] In these discourses, Wheatley is either squarely placed in opposition to what is imagined as the black political imaginary, or recovered into a recognizable version of it.

Uncertain Visions, Fantastic Corrections

This impasse defined the post–civil rights pushback by black feminist and literary critics to return to Wheatley as resource—for fantasies of freedom and beyond. It is no accident that this fantasy of a primal scene is articulated in the face of Baraka's and James Weldon Johnson's calling-out of Wheatley on her lack of African American "pride" and "huge[ness]." This scene is a confrontation with whiteness and also ideal masculinist formulations of black freedom. Gates points out an assumption of black literary traditions of masculine participation and modes of literacy in his re-creation of the trial as the dominant public genre of black self-making—public, contested, bearing the burden of proof of humanity, of cultural and hence political value, for black women. Wheatley is then on trial as both slave and author, pupil and chattel, example and exception, or as early Americanist Eric Slauter (2009) has characterized the debate around her authorial authenticity, imitation and invention.[6]

These fantasies are not to be found in spite of Wheatley's visibility on the scene of freedom, but as the very impetus behind her "It" factor, as Joseph Roach (2007, 8) identifies it in eighteenth-century celebrity and beyond, as "the power of apparently effortless embodiment of contradictory qualities simultaneously. The possessor of It keeps a precarious balance between such mutually exclusive alternatives . . . waiting for the apparently inevitable fall makes for breathless spectatorship." Wheatley's celebrity status, both in her contemporary moment and in her twentieth-century reception within and outside of the African American literary canon, brings to visibility the gendered and racialized labor that the "effortless embodiment" wills into "breathless" being. She embodies the tension that *is*, in the Foucauldian terms above that Nguyen (2012) teases out, freedom. Wheatley encapsulates the ways the black female body in the spotlight in the post-rights (civil, individual, human) era has been imagined: criminalized, vulnerable, precarious, performative, resistant, exception and example, victim and hero, victim as hero. The imagined performance of Wheatley's body (and body of work) is the site (Tillet 2009) and scene (Hartman 1997) of black political work on freedom—a poet (and poetry) that somehow acts as the example of, exception to, and the hinge on which the relationship between race and the political possibility of rights is evaluated. It is from this mapping of critical fantasy that I move back to a visual index of Wheatley's relationship to black political production—the fantasies of black resilience, black respectability, black self-authorship, and black artistic and political community augured in the circulation of her uncertainly authored portrait. This collective set of fantasies, read together, can begin to offer a diagnosis of the problems of existing Wheatley critique, but also to coalesce into different trajectories for political desires and critical ends, approaches that hinge on the use and possibilities of fantasy rather than correcting and certifying their course into the confines of freedom.[7]

Uncertainty appends to the engraving of Wheatley's portrait, which though much discussed in recent historical work on Wheatley, stubbornly refuses have its authorship confirmed, even as it is frequently attributed, with an asterisk, to fellow African artist, painter Scipio Moorhead. As various art historians, most notably Gwendolyn DuBois Shaw (2006), have noted, there is no evidence to support this claim, and, in fact, no extant work by Moorhead exists.[8] What we do know is that Wheatley included a poem to Moorhead in her 1773 book, "To S.M., a Young *African* Painter, on Seeing His Works." When critics, historians, and artists go "Looking for Scipio," as Slauter (2006) puns on Isaac Julien's 1989 art film *Looking for Langston*, as the artist and author of Wheatley's frontispiece, her not-quite-self-presentation to the world, what is also laid bare is a critical desire to reckon with Wheatley's political meaning in a sphere of recognizable and comparable blackness. To do so is to look for a "currency," in Williams's terms above, a value that reaches beyond Wheatley's status as black literary fetish object for white readers and patrons, and to imagine her working life and its afterimages as liminal spaces of black freedom, in their own time and through to the current day. Through the unascribable origin of the engraved portrait, I trace how uncertainty works through these corrective histories and how that uncertainty both adheres to and critiques critical desires around black freedoms.

We might then reimagine this portrait of Wheatley as the primal scene of black humanity, one that projects outward into (historical) fantasies of freedom and beyond. In the "idea and image of freedom," Jasmine Nichole Cobb (2015) notes, black visuality has been key to the slow project of remaking blackness into recognizability in white civic culture, frequently through what is now deemed respectability politics. Wheatley presciently stands at this border in her portrait—as one of the few black subjects of the time to leave a self-represented paper trail seemingly outside of the mundane data collection that defined the biopolitics of the state, especially in regard to enslaved life. Wheatley and the portrait—particularly the will to name its uncertain author as a fellow African in the United States—also represent a critical desire to read "a cutting figure" to use art historian Richard J. Powell's (2009) designation of black portraiture, into the Wheatley frontispiece, and to place her in the context of revolutionary rhetoric and burgeoning women's authorship in the New World.

Such focuses on vision also append to the current Wheatley moment: that of the historical-literary investigation into Wheatley's work and context. This is, in many ways, a welcome turn, but not one to mistake for a search for or answer to the "true" Wheatley. History, too, can be a teleology of freedom, here performing it through recovery and repair. This historical Wheatley, while highlighting alternate routes to thinking about her political and cultural community, also underscores uncertainty as a major mode of *knowing* Wheatley.[9] The move toward historicizing Wheatley—the dominant mode of studying her in the twenty-first century—can act as representative of desires for a more just world, a recovered history of the eighteenth century that can restore her agency as a black feminine cosmopolitan subject, and Africa as a site with its own specific and coterminous histories, identities, and formulations of modern identity in and from this era.

This returns us directly to Wheatley's portrait and its uncertain origins. The issue of portraiture in eighteenth-century literature is one of ambivalence, as Helen Deutsch (1996, 17–18) puts it in *Resemblance and Disgrace*: portraiture "poses problems of truth and 'truth to life,' of identity conceived as visual stasis rather than narrative movement, of original subjects and faithful representation, that consume both Pope and his reading public." This same ambivalence trails Wheatley and Wheatley criticism, perhaps even more so when the question intersects with narrativizations of race and racialized subjectivity. Wheatley's own portrait, which emphasizes her in the act of writing (holding a pen) and her frail, youthful appearance, also attempts to "encapsulate and make graspable the elusive body. Thus portraiture as a metaphor permeates the fabric of eighteenth-century society and spans its polarities," as Marcia Pointon (1993) articulates in *Hanging the Head*. Wheatley's portrait then both marks the act and the site of corrective histories—the question of her authentication as human displaced by a claim to the certainty of shared black humanity.

To desire critical company in bondage and for freedom is the understandable affective pull of antiracist and feminist work. To place Wheatley in historical context here is also an attempt to relocate her from the racial loneliness of the imagined trial, to give her a history that both acknowledges and moves beyond the encounter with whiteness: her potential African, Arabic, Muslim, black, and even girlhood identities.[10] The slippage between the authority of the archival work that can, indeed, flesh out these details of belonging and that of the wishful thinking/looking for Moorhead's work to represent her body and body of work reveals these critical impulses for racial recognition and political resistance—of performance of black freedoms—that the contemporary moment can recognize. But as in the Shockley poem above, and a Kerry James Marshall painting I discuss below, the impulse for those connections to be historically true—to be accurate and representable in their full relationality, rather than speculative or openly fantastic (unbelievable)—can occlude a more nuanced discussion of how critical desire operates when representing Wheatley and other early black celebrities.

Looking at and for Wheatley is a then a complicated act of critical identification. The frontispiece may have been drawn from visions of Alexander Pope and abolitionist women of Europe at the same time that it is a first—the first woman illustrated with her written work—that would start a trend among female poets and eventually African American women writers as an authenticating gesture (Shaw 2006). Rather than code the poem or portrait, or the realm of art/culture, as resistance, the image points to the ways that cultural forms, their malleability and uncertainty, allow for an articulated vulnerability of interpretation to the publicness of the black body without reinscribing a totalizing model of reading for agency/submission. Following Serpell's 2014 investigation of the imperative of uncertainty in ethics of reading and the production of contemporary literature, as well as recent anthropological investigations of the value of uncertainty in Limor Samimian-Darash and Paul Rabinow's 2015 collection, I argue not for uncertainty as definitively radical, resistant, or risk-proof (i.e., not as an interpretative or political cure) but as a reading modality that exposes desires, both positive and negative, rather than relying on already known critical outcomes. What endures in rereadings of Wheatley, then, is the exposure of the labor of interpretation and the unavoidable risk of misrepresentation that goes into being a black woman speaking subject producing through the projected fantasies of race in the antiblack sphere of Enlightenment modernity.

Wheatley, as viewed through her portrait and her writing's sense of herself as black celebrity, is, as several critics of her contemporary reception argue, uncannily aware that she will be misread, a double-consciousness that is less about her strategic appeals or vision of herself than of her letting go of that certainty of meaning and of control of one's circulation or even labor. Wheatley's work revels in that vulnerability of the page, of print, of "deathless fame"—knowing all too well the precarity of the fantasy of being entitled to embodied existence brings in her own sphere and beyond. It is that vulnerability—here as interpretative uncertainty—that also marks both the hope and the impossibility of identifying Wheatley's portraitist, hence destabilizing the search for nonwhite agents of freedom in the eighteenth century, a quest that reveals the limits of the archive even as it deeply and creatively engages with its contents.[11]

That Wheatley herself was immediately placed or displaced in the literary marketplace according to her very visible status as a black author is without question. As critic Phillip M. Richards (1992, 172–73) argues, Wheatley stood as a "test case," a "racial oddity." Wheatley's public role as celebrity because of her supposed singularity seems to have not been lost on her, nor is it lost on those who revisit her figure. Her image, even more than her poetry, continues beyond her to mark her body as a site of black labor, the combination of Africa as the site of cultural identity, London as the site of capital/commodification, and the United States as the site of the trial of black humanity, all in uncomfortable conversation—an uneven transcontinental intimacy, in Lowe's (2015) terms—with each other. Wheatley had no luxury to disassociate textually or publicly with her race, as Gay Gibson Cima (2006) convincingly argues about not just her work but her book tour in London. In Wheatley's eighteenth-century world, these competing fantasies emerge. The transcontinental Wheatley is African, and this very portrait is used to ascertain her facial features and claim her geographic and ethnic/linguistic belonging on the continent, for instance. As critics remain wary of these processes of recovery, of turning to Africa as authenticating a pure blackness that freezes the continent as always already in the idyllic past, at the same time this historical turn to Wheatley's origins gives depth to the other worlds that Wheatley began in, other trajectories of black life and labor in addition to plantation chattel slavery that are significant to illuminate in order to undo the discursive bounds of agency/submission. The globalized Wheatley travels to London, marking her and the labor of black celebrity as cosmopolitan. Wheatley's African and European sites also invoke the "romance of diaspora," in Yogita Goyal's (2010) formulation, here echoing work on Harlem Renaissance authors in Europe, where blackness becomes a different kind of racial commodity—an exotic fetish. The uncertain frontispiece portrait invites/includes/contains these desires, the wish to do more and do better in service of a more just history and world, and also the knowledge that completeness will likely always be partial/failing, like freedom—a fantasy.

Kerry James Marshall's (2007) own imagined portrait of Moorhead—in the imaginary midst of painting his own self-portrait with a sketch of

FIGURE I.2. Kerry James Marshall, *Scipio Moorhead, Portrait of Myself, 1776* (2007).

Wheatley from a slightly different angle than the frontispiece portrait in the background—*Scipio Moorhead, Portrait of Myself, 1776* (figure 1.2), stages just such desires and longings for recognition, performing fantasies of black knowability in an archive that both claims and refuses that metric. Marshall's painting refuses the scene of live intimacy, proximity, and collectivity between black artists, instead offering the practice of black art as a means to "picture freedom" where it lies, in the materials at hand rather than the understandable projection of black corporeal solidarity. In this sense, Marshall's portrait of Moorhead keeps alive the uncertainty of authorship even as it demands

FIGURE 1.3. The Phillis Wheatley monument, by Meredith Bergmann (2003), part of the Boston Women's Memorial.

attention to the fantastic possibilities of transhistorical black collaborations, to what was lost to time and a history of structural racism that doesn't allow us access to the artist's possible work. To return to Slauter's (2006) looking for a Scipio reference, encounters with Wheatley's portrait and the uncertainty around it are cast by Marshall and others as an alternative primal scene for African and American studies methodology—a representation of the critical desire for identification, for a claiming that is not just archival but also allows for fantasy. Marshall's self-portrait self-reflexively projects the contemporary moment, not to close the Wheatley "case" but, in projecting himself as Scipio, to offer such visible yearning that the work represents and argues for alternative critical desires other than truth and recovery—unbounded circulation and interpretation, proliferations and plenitudes.

The portrait of Wheatley is reinterpreted and recirculated in our own time as a memorialization to Wheatley in a Boston statue (figure 1.3), or in the numerous children's books depicting Wheatley's visage and narrative of triumph, many of which contain the word "freedom" in their titles (figures 1.4, 1.5, and 1.6). The shift to recovery in academic circles comes at a time of a commitment to

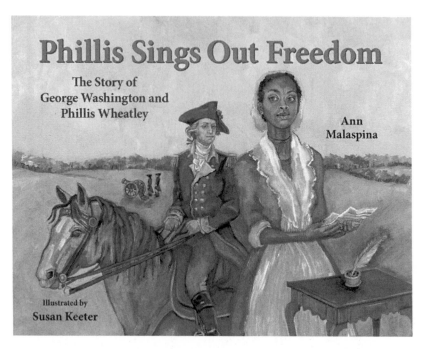

FIGURE 1.4. The cover of children's book *Phillis Sings Out Freedom: The Story of George Washington and Phillis Wheatley*, by Ann Malaspina, illustrated by Susan Keeter (2010).

FIGURE 1.5. The cover of *Phillis's Big Test*, by Catherine Clinton, illustrated by Sean Qualls (2008).

"multiculturalism," meaning that Wheatley, as the most famous black woman of the revolutionary period of US history, becomes the subject of many freedom plots, such as children's books that focus on Wheatley's triumph over adversity—with adversity representing the system of chattel slavery, and triumph being the achievement of emancipation through authorship. Here, reinterpretations of her portrait abound in illustrations, emphasizing not just her writing body but her girlhood—nearly all recovering the seriousness of her expression in the portrait. Wheatley's gaze remains off-center, never directly addressing the reader but looking determinedly off-stage. Her historicized femininity in full dress and bonnet allows for respectability, yes, but also identification with the hypergendered world of children's literature. Her story, like her image, rests on the tension between her vulnerability as young girl and her fit within the genre of children's literature that emphasizes the progressive possibilities of overcoming adversity. Rendering Wheatley into an American Girl doll–like figure, then, these texts seek both to take her girlhood seriously and to commodify it in the generic—and gendered and raced—conventions of children's literature, the most direct, didactic form of "corrective history" in circulation beyond monumentalization and memorialization.[12]

Following in the footsteps of black girlhood scholars Marcia Chatelain (2015), Nazera Sadiq Wright (2016), and LaKisha Michelle Simmons (2015), and Robin Bernstein's (2011) critical reevaluation of the nineteenth century as predicated on notions of racial innocence, I must also note that the young adult literature regarding Wheatley offers complex emotional renderings of freedom plots as adolescent coming-of-age stories, where Wheatley's troubling of her own fame and trajectory takes center stage. Robin S. Doak's *Phillis Wheatley: Slave and Poet* (2006), Afua Cooper's *My Name Is Phillis Wheatley: A Story of Slavery and Freedom* (2009), and Ann Rinaldi's *Hang a Thousand Trees with Ribbons: The Story of Phillis Wheatley* ([1996] 2005) mark complicated representations of Wheatley's interiority in the face of the imagined trial as external test. Rinaldi, also the author of 1991's *Wolf by the Ears* on Harriet Hemings, includes the rhetorical click bait "Celebrity or Slave?" on her book's back cover, showcasing in the young adult generic formula a clear opening for reckoning with the unresolved tensions between desire and political subject formation that do not need to end on triumph but instead are allowed, like much of YA fiction, the space to dwell in uncertainty. But perhaps most startling in this canon is the 1949 biography of Wheatley written by Shirley Graham (known after 1951 as Shirley Graham Du Bois, W. E. B. Du Bois's wife, in most historical circles). In one of a series of biographies on notable African Americans, Graham dramatizes the trial as if it were a school test, complete with Wheatley's nervousness about recalling "*anything* she had been reading the past days. Her throat was dry and her mind seemed a blank" (102). The trial concludes with John Hancock's declaration "You are a good American!" (106). But despite this rendering of her authenticity trial as high school exam, the book ends on the chapter entitled "'Tis Freedom's Sacrifice," documenting the economic consequences of the war for free blacks and describing Phillis's eventual death through the prism of her poetry, letters, and newspaper archives, which shows her intent to continue writing. Ending on Wheatley's last published poem, "Liberty and Peace," Graham mirrors Wheatley's letting go of her last material possession, a shawl (168), with a renegotiation of—and perhaps resignation to—the terms of freedom itself. In the poem, peace and freedom are aligned as are acts of sacrifice and "spread." Wheatley becomes a martyr to the United States and its overvaluation of freedom for Graham's narrative, while still refusing to let go of her interior ambition, her desire not just to write, but to publish. Her insistence on the publicness of her labor, of making her writing visible and famous even as her flesh demands more urgent attention, strikes the last chord for Graham. "Phillis Wheatley is dead!" (168) exclaims the last line of the narrative before presenting her poem without further comment. The fame of her writing, as well as her embodied, vulnerable form, becomes her emplotted teleology, even as Graham invokes freedom as the recognizable frame.

Corrective histories can also be traced in the way Wheatley's visual legacy is shaped into respectability politics in the early twentieth-century Phillis Wheatley clubs, offshoots of the YWCA, for example, or settlement houses—spaces of social containment and reform (figure 1.7). Wheatley's name is used as an organizing symbol of black middle-class civic participation and uplift projects. But it is also used as a sign under which to agitate for collective resources for and by black women political subjects under cover of political infrastructure. While respectability politics is one name for such a political formation, to dismiss the ways that black women, in particular, accessed and had access to the public sphere through feminized culture is dangerous for collective diaspora politics. The reperformance of Wheatley, then, is also a performance of critical desire rather than an endpoint of *evidence* for Wheatley and for other black artists who perform their subjection and their freedom in the very same act of making texts—she is, of course, celebrity and "slave." Such visualized desire cannot solve the conundrum of black freedom in Enlightenment modernity and its aftermath, but it can be the basis for rereading Wheatley into other more vulnerable trajectories of the black political, emphasizing uncertainty rather than a teleology of freedom, individual or critical.

Wheatley's Black Celebrity as Methodology

If "the refusal of the payoff of visibility" (Phelan [1993] 2003, 19) remains a vexed issue for black feminist history cultural criticism, Wheatley's ([1834] 1988, 114) poem to Moorhead, "To S.M., a Young *African* Painter, on Seeing His Works," takes up this ambivalence from the site of visibility itself—"On Seeing His Works." As Helen Deutsch and Felicity Nussbaum (2000, 18) so aptly note in their introduction to *Defects*, the conflation of eighteenth-century authors and their bodies in the period was one of a "fetishization of difference, [and the] need to know difference through envisioning." Not only does Wheatley's address to Moorhead mark the absence of other black women

FIGURE 1.7. Phyllis Wheatley Club, Buffalo, NY. Courtesy Everett Collection Historical/ Alamy Stock Photo (1905).

writers in her cultural sphere, but it is also an attempt to connect language and vision, the poet and the "painter," to the limits of racial subjection, and to the impossible search for black freedoms. The first section, the six-line sentence that begins the poem, crystallizes this focus on the figuration of artistically producing bodies in the line of black and eighteenth-century public vision in the drama of fame:

> To show the lab'ring bosom's deep intent,
> And thought in living characters to paint,
> When first thy pencil did those beauties give,
> And breathing figures learnt from thee to live,
> How did those prospects give my soul delight,
> A new creation rushing on my sight?

Rendering "breathing figures" is both about representing others and representing the labor of the artist—"to show the lab'ring" bodies' "intent" and "thought." Wheatley lays claim to the possibilities of such a public vision of black expressive labor. Black cultural work itself is a subject made visible and not reduced to the frame of freedom/unfreedom in her work.

The following fourteen lines of the poem dwell on the price and prize of such creative visibility—that of "fame" and "immortality." Wheatley's production of text mirrors acts of visual production. She turns the artistic process into one of religious proportions, where the labor of writing/painting exceeds or transcends their own material bodies even as it is grounded in their *work*, the intimacy between artist and her/his art. Wheatley's poetic concern is often about the afterlife of objects, texts, and bodies, how they will circulate after the moment of creation or death, but here it is the role of both production and reception that is in question:

> Still, wond'rous youth! each noble path pursue;
> On deathless glories fix thine ardent view:
> Still may the painter's and the poet's fire,
> To aid thy pencil and thy verse conspire!
> And may the charms of each seraphic theme
> Conduct thy footsteps to immortal fame! (1998, 114)

Black cultural work, then, is neither a retreat nor quite an imaginative rebellion in real time that some have read Wheatley as performing. It is a practice that imbues fame and constant visibility, not freedom from the visibility of blackness. Wheatley's eyes are on her fellow black artist here as much as and in relation to artistic labor's possibility both to represent and to bring the artist "deathless glories" and "immortal fame." Wheatley, as recent scholars have noted, is surely a savvy reader of the rising market for the consumption of art in the eighteenth century, and the possibilities for black artists that this "democratization of fame" (to quote Leo Braudy 1997, 595) can bring. Her Chaucerian and Popian heroic couplets, usually associated with epic and narrative poetry, here in short form, evince a naked desire for her and Moorhead's epic fame, for black artistic "immortality," recognition, and renown.

Racial celebrity, then, is what separates Wheatley but also what compels her, and perhaps her contemporary critics. This very celebrity through the literary is what is considered excessive and inauthentic, though, even to nineteenth-century critics such as Douglass, who excludes her from his heroic definition of worthy fame. It seems that Wheatley's celebrity, as well as her "affiliation" with other white celebrities of the time, is an uncomfortable proximity (Felker 1997). While her intimacy with the public print culture of the United States and England offered her, to quote Jacobs again, "something akin to freedom" as well as, eventually, technical freedom, it is not the leveling of difference that the currency of freedom seductively offered to her. Instead, Wheatley's work suggests freedom might be displaced in political thought with a critical eye toward the uncertain labor of cultural production and reception. It is in this same vein that Wheatley ([1934] 1988, 153) ends one letter, to Native American preacher Samson Occom, with an "I" who is writing consciously at the site of rights and freedom: "How well the Cry for Liberty, and the reverse Disposition for the Exercise of oppressive Power over others agree—I humbly think it does not require the Penetration of a Philosopher to determine." She speaks of slavery's unsustainable contradictions with the American Revolution as surface, obvious points of contention, not work that requires her particular labor to unearth, understand, or to produce critique around, and suggests that her own work does not deny or dissemble this critique but assumes it, and she self-consciously considers her own work to be able to do something with, from, and beyond that understanding.

The continued attention to "the obedience of black women's textual bodies" (Cima 2000, 472), including Wheatley's, suggests a relationship between the text and the body of the icon that cannot be ignored, even by Wheatley herself in her letter to her friend, free black woman Obour Tanner. Wheatley's body was known for its frailness, her constant state of illness, which is referenced in several letters and by several critics. It is this frail body that also distances her from Baraka's ideal cry for black freedom—it is not representative of poor black southern labor that is suggested as authentic by certain strains of black cultural criticism. Instead, it is a fragile body, one seemingly suited to a life of print culture. The referent to her frailness, coupled with the reference in this particular letter to Obour Tanner's sickness, suggests a concern with black women's bodies and their limits, which in turn questions equating the problem of representation with the problem of black freedom. She writes, "I am very sorry to hear that you are indispos'd, but hope this will find you in better health. I have been unwell the greater part of the winter, but am much better as the spring approaches" (1988, 178). These struggling bodies test the limits of ideal representations of black womanhood, both from black and white sources, on the auction block, in the field, in Africa. They throw into relief both the lure and the lore of Wheatley's femininity in the portrait, one repeated in the children's book illustrations: what it means to be and become and perform as a palatable commodity to whiteness that is nonetheless not reducible to that white reading of, and opening for, a black woman celebrity.

Wheatley appears on the cover of her text as a slight, engraved presence in profile. Her weak body seems to engender her as irrevocably feminine in contemporary circulation, but her proximity to failing health, to a threatened body-politic, seems to inform her work as an act of both epistemological and ontological ambivalence. Even with this body, Wheatley travels, she promotes, she does readings, she does the work of the circulating texts. She is performing something different than freedom/unfreedom, in other words. Her health was the supposed reason given for her "publicity tour" of England, a tour that confirmed that her body was both sellable, knowable, and readable to the anglophone public sphere for its cultural labor (Isani 2000, 260). It is her visibility as "a freakish, strange anomaly" (Cima 2006, 493) that drives the consuming body of eighteenth-century England, where "the London reading public is invited to read the poems not because of their intrinsic worth but because their very existence as the work of a Black woman makes them sufficiently novel to warrant perusal" (Wilcox 1999, 14). Wheatley's body then circulates through an always already failing, inadequate, and fleeting visibility, one defined by and through vulnerability to the white gaze but also by the intimacy of shared precarity and knowing critique, a living through rather than against the polity of the time. This version of reading Wheatley, too, is a constructed fantasy of freedom, but it is one that imagines political attachments and the critical desires they demand in a differently embodied frame, one grappling with the material conditions of black women's embodiment as not that which prioritize escape to freedom, but as the labor of deliberate thought, of artmaking, and of crafting a public persona through art.[13]

These readings of Wheatley's portrait and verse, her own fantasies of black cultural production in 1773, echo in Wheatley's recirculation among late 1970s and 1980s black feminist authors June Jordan and Alice Walker (1983, 243), who in her title essay to the collection *In Search of Our Mothers' Gardens* speaks of Wheatley's work alongside her mother's own survival through aesthetic production by claiming her as "my heritage of a love of beauty and a respect for strength." Poet Margaret Walker inaugurates this reimagining of Wheatley as not just black feminist hero but nuanced, embodied author of beautiful writing in her NEH-funded 1973 Phillis Wheatley Poetry Festival celebrating the bicentennial of the publication of *Poems on Various Subjects*.[14] This festival was attended by Alice Walker and June Jordan, who presented work there alongside Lucille Clifton, Paula Giddings, Audre Lorde, Sonia Sanchez, and Nikki Giovanni (Luckett 2018, 186). This festival led to their work in the following decade on Wheatley as both titular "miracle" in Jordan's ([2002] 2006) essayistic and poetic terms and as black feminist progenitor in her vulnerable combination of delicate eighteenth-century verse and intellectual strength as an enslaved person under a microscope in her day and beyond. This combination is also the legacy carried over in Shockley's poetic fantasy of Wheatley as both entrapped in binaries ("bio/autography [or, 18th-century multiculturalism]" in 2006's *a half-red sea*) and as "that thin young chick who / looks and snaps like a whip" in the poem that opens this chapter, realigning the frail body with the power of Wheatley's sharp prose work, rather than opposing them. These twentieth-century reinvestments in performing Wheatley beyond a Black Aesthetic frame of freedom allow space for desire and embodied vulnerability in their fantasies of black political life.

Performing Interdependence

Cultural adoption of Wheatley both conforms to the race rhetoric of the times but also takes surprising, uneven directions as African American writers struggle with an enslaved intellectual and cultural past that can be "usable" for their political present. In the 1890s, at the heart of the post-Reconstruction debates between Booker T. Washington and W. E. B. Du Bois, the first YWCA geared toward black women, named Phyllis Wheatley (*sic*) clubs, sprung up across the nation. These clubs, largely geared toward education, labor, and respectability, yoked Wheatley with ambition, propriety, and youth (see figure 1.7). Mary White Ovington (1932) offers a different didactic lesson for the political set of the time in her children's play *Phillis Wheatley*, at once representing Wheatley's proximity to the Founding Fathers and ideals of freedom, rights, and the human, and representing a more quotidian sphere of black womanhood that exposes the imagined ambitions and desires of Wheatley and the way that dovetailed with scripts for female respectability. Ovington, a white woman, was a founding member of what is now thought of as the bastion of respectability politics, the National Association for the Advancement of Colored People (though in its time, it was too radical for Booker T. Washington's political strategies, for instance). In her short play *Phillis Wheatley*, Ovington stages Wheatley's letters to Obour Tanner. Dramatizing their friendship through an imagined in-person meeting, the play in many ways anticipates the critical turn that Tara Bynum (2014) makes in her work on Wheatley that imagines the connection between the two women as key to renegotiating Wheatley's work and legacy, as well as the dynamic imagined in Shockley's poem between Wheatley and Hemings.

Ovington's play, a prescient vision of black women's friendship—think *Waiting to Exhale* but set in the Revolutionary-era United States—foregrounds Wheatley's desired proximity to the Founding Fathers and stages an imagined "live" conversation between Wheatley and her free black woman friend Obour Tanner, with whom Wheatley had a long written correspondence history. Tanner comes for a visit as Wheatley both waits to hear back from George Washington about her poem to the general and decides on marriage to John Peters, here imagined as a ne'er do well whom Tanner warns Wheatley about. The play then exposes the imagined ambitions and desires of Wheatley and the ways that they departed from but also dovetailed with scripts for female respectability and black freedom.[15]

In the play, Wheatley, newly freed and still attending to her sick former master, impatiently waits—and drinks a bit of wine—with Tanner while they are attended to by an older, still enslaved, black woman. The play clearly emphasizes Wheatley's privileged status following publication and the trip to London. The pair discusses George Washington's delayed possible responses to her poem, as well as Wheatley's trip and her growing fame. Ovington does not shy away from marking Wheatley's historic reputation as based on white recognition, nor does she refuse Wheatley's desire for and excitement about that recognition. In other words, she represents Wheatley's creative and professional ambitions, not as examples of black unfreedom or false consciousness but as a site of black women's interiority.

If the waiting for Washington plot remains the mostly offstage conflict for the all-black cast (in the list of characters preceding the play, Ovington notes this specifically), conversations involving Wheatley's fame and her future dominate its central action, particularly the limits of her future as a free black woman in Revolutionary-era New England. As Wheatley's former master lays dying, unseen and offstage, the crisis of the play is that Wheatley's fame will not materially sustain her outside of her enslavement, and her employment as an author, will, in fact, make it so that Wheatley cannot make a living otherwise doing the domestic labor that is available to her. Ovington stages Wheatley's marriage with John Peters as necessity, as a compromised choice in the face of Wheatley's technical freedom, and as an emotional folly. In the last sequence of the play, this comes to a head as Tanner speaks frankly to Wheatley about her future husband, her mortal fate, and her immortal fame:

> OBOUR: I will say naught more. (*Changing her tone and going to Phillis and putting her arms about her affectionately*). But you love him, Phillis, and I love you and I can see naught ahead of you but sorrow.
>
> PHILLIS: (*Shaking off her angry mood and responding to Obour's affection*). This is all moonshine. We are like two children building castles in the

air. John Peters has not asked me in marriage and never may. I am just Phillis Wheatley who has written a little verse, and will be forgotten before the grass is green above her grave.

OBOUR: No Phillis. Your people will always remember you. A little girl, once a slave. Later to have her verses printed in London town. To write lines to George Washington and to receive a letter of thanks from his hand.

After this exchange, the stage directions call for the sounds of a parade of revolutionary soldiers including General Washington, the sounds to which "the girls listen, then run to the window" to wave. Ovington's play is then an unexpected tragic romance and feminist interpretation of Wheatley's biography—including her short postemancipation life—as well as a treatise on the state of racial citizenship based on Wheatley's public celebrity.

Ovington's play incorporates both a more radical black feminist critique of marriage as well as a focus on the significance of friendship and epistemological understanding between black women, and a Du Boisian focus on the talented tenth, as Wheatley wants to sit with George Washington as he winces not. As Ovington herself is dramatized in Saidiya V. Hartman's *Wayward Lives, Beautiful Experiments* (2019), the white social reformer wavers across her own radical sense of herself as eschewing white feminine social norms and her attachment to normalizing black "intimate lives," "this anomalous, yet beautiful, world" of black genders that she witnessed, translated for white audiences, and documented as an outsider sociologist. Ovington's play doesn't so much wholeheartedly celebrate black community here—the excoriating portrait of John Peters as a shady businessman and Phillis's tragic downfall suggest the complicated world of black intimacy imagined for Wheatley by Ovington—as much as she stages and champions the mundane, domestic world of Wheatley, even as extraordinary emplotment exists at the margins of this space. That the black intimacy so sought after with her portrait's attribution to Moorhead already exists through evidence in the more quotidian letter exchanges with Tanner that mention having a cold, suffering from asthma, and being received by royalty in England in the same space, for instance, suggests a different pitch to political desires for Wheatley, ones centered not only on publicness but on authorship, agency, and the possibilities for love, loss, health, and distance (J. Brooks 2010).

Wheatley's fate hinges not on her freedom from enslavement, but on her unfreedom from marriage, from the marital domestic work required of a body in increasingly failing health, and also her more difficult bonds with her dead and dying enslavers, as well as with her long-distance free black friend. Ovington stages limited options for freed black women, whether servants or poets, without white patronage. The plot played out is not the marriage, though its doom is foretold by Tanner, but instead in the intimacy with Tanner as the vehicle of Phillis's self-construction. This teleology, spelled out explicitly by Ovington (and further interrogated in this book's third chapter on Sarah Baartman and the bounds of marriage and labor contracts), exists in complicated relation to the fantasies of freedom that undergird Wheatley's celebrity, fantasies that aim for the resolution of vulnerability and uncertainty as political aims.[16] While the performed relation between Tanner and Wheatley could also be read as mirroring the ascription of Wheatley's portrait to Moorhead in its romanticizing of black community, the dramatization of their letters into embodied performance, along with the tense representations of Betty the servant and John Peters, complicate such a one dimensional formation. Black women's friendship doesn't save Wheatley—instead, it offers a new frame in which to imagine, reperform, witness, and interpret the inequitable interdependencies of fame and the domestic labor of enslavement and of wifedom that contextualize Wheatley's production.

Phillis Fantasizes the Political

If private and public intimacies merge in Ovington's reimagination of Wheatley's politics, Ed Bullins, Black Panther and Black Arts movement prolific playwright, revels purely in Wheatley's publicness. In an opening critical frame for a review of the 1976 production, a *New York Times* critic (Gussow 1976) asserts, "Children's theater is seldom used, effectively, to educate or to inform. The goal is usually entertainment. When writers of children's theater contemplate significant events, such as moments in the nation's history, they tend to glamorize or to condescend. Ed Bullins is an exception." Recalling the above conversation about children's and young adult literature's devotion to Wheatley as a subject, my discussion of Bullins's play connects "glamorize[d]" entertainment and black political subjectivity beyond negative critique. The aesthetic and emplotted foil to Ovington's play, *The Mystery of Phillis Wheatley* is conspicuously focused on Wheatley's celebrity. Bullins's play is part morality tale, part *Christmas Carol*, part Afrocentric funeral ritual, a performance that reckons with Wheatley's celebrity in her day, her tragic circumstances and death, and her resurrection and even immortality—and revenge—through her continued fame. As such, Bullins does not just toe the line of Baraka, denying Wheatley's aesthetic legacy as outside of blackness. Instead, Bullins offers a different, difficult tragic romance plot—this one between Wheatley and her audience, including the Founding Fathers—where Wheatley as literary and political celebrity triumphs even as Wheatley's enslaved body is not long for the mortal world.

The Mystery of Phillis Wheatley, then, is a biographical play/allegory/"musical parable," according to the *New York Times* review, of the slave trade writ large, with characters, including Wheatley; Wheatley's husband, John Peters; the Wheatley family; villain "Captain Diabolical," described in the playbill as the "Symbol of Slave Trading Forces"; and the Emcee/Narrator, "Lord Africa," described as the "Spirit of African Liberation." Lord Africa brings Wheatley back from the dead in a generically Africanized funeral rite to experience her life with constant reassurances during traumatic events that she will both experience more and worse fates at the hands of Captain Diabolical throughout her actual/material life, and that all will be made up for, to her and to the world, with her fame and celebrity. In the *Times* review of the play, critic Mel Gussow (1976) claims that Bullins's "iconoclastic" vision of Wheatley is "as a kind of wild child, discovered and misused by civilization," perhaps missing some of the pleasures that Bullins's Wheatley takes in her fame, as well as the promise Bullins's narrator sees in that celebrity, as the reviewer rushes to read Wheatley as a tragic dupe because she is not being constructed via recognizable freedom plots.

The fixing of Wheatley's story to that of political discourse—specifically, freedom, democracy, and rights—is directly named here, in several occasions in the play, sometimes ironic in its investments in its currency and sometimes seeming to embrace the possibilities of their value, especially as they are carried on through black expressive and political culture:

> WHEATLEY: My place is back in America; there is a revolution brewing there, and I have to be part of it; that is my place to be. I am Black, I am African born, yes, but I must be an example to all future Black generations that find themselves lost in the wilds of America, and I must sing in my small voice that we are Americans too—among the bravest, among the strongest, among the most worthy native sons and daughters to be found. (Bullins [1976] 2004)

These lines at once expose the US state's ideology of freedom under chattel slavery and self-consciously invest in feelings around freedom's political promises, via the body and body of work of Wheatley.

The labor of her celebrity and the reperformances of her body, as well as continued word of her fame, are the undergirding that enables the fantasies of collective black identity and national inclusion outlined above. But Bullins's posturing of the celebrity body of Wheatley beyond tragedy, and also beyond recognizable black political heroism, troubles these identifications, as does his choice to have Wheatley's book tour in London take up much of the staging of the play. Here, Bullins stages not just an altruistic Wheatley but one inhabiting the role of celebrity with style, desire, and ambition:

LORD AFRICA: (*presenting*) And now ladies and gentlemen of nobility and note—MISS PHILLIS WHEATLEY!

(PHILLIS sweeps in like Diana Ross to the applause of the guests. SHE is surrounded and the object of attention.) . . .

JOHN PETERS: (*plays Lord Mayor of London*) A true Black pearl, or I'm not the Lord Mayor of London.

PHILLIS: I only hope that I may prove worthy of your consideration, my Lord.

JOHN WHEATLEY: (*plays Earl of Dartmouth*) Well said, well said, Lord Mayor. And even more so you, our dear Phillis: I, the Earl of Dartmouth, am ravished by your charms and bearing. I am your faithful servant.

(THEY ALL bow and curtsy repeatedly.)

PHILLIS: (*overwhelmed*) Thank you. Thank you, one and all.

JOHN PETERS: I request a toast. A toast for Phillis Wheatley, the first Black princess of poetry!

GUESTS: TO THE BLACK PRINCESS OF POETRY!!!

Here Bullins begins to imagine and perform other networks of political and racial belonging for the narrative of Wheatley, beyond that of confrontation with the Founding Fathers and communion with other black artists. The Founding Fathers in particular are the oppositional but also aspirational center of the play's conflict, but Bullins's embrace of Wheatley as black royalty also prefigures the iconoclastic investment in Sarah Forbes Bonetta, adopted goddaughter of Queen Victoria and subject of the final chapter, and more recent turns to "black girl magic" (witness, for example, the coverage of Meghan Markle, or the political and cultural deification of Oprah and Beyoncé). In this vein, *The Mystery of Phillis Wheatley* imagines an opulent world of individual desire and lush commodification as a site of pleasurable identification, rather than a rejection of Wheatley's blackness. Wheatley's freedom comes, perhaps unpalatably for those of us trained in the aesthetic and political protocols of the Black Arts movement, in the form of her objectification, as do any future freedoms she augurs.

To read this scene, then, and this connection between Diana Ross and Wheatley, is to imagine not just another black radical or black feminist fantasy of freedom, but fantasy itself as a scene of political formation, one whose trajectories may not lead to or even desire freedom, but to acts of uncertain yet desired recognition and uncomfortably couched intimacies. If the will and desire and right to freedom, in Wheatley's own words in the letter to Samson Occom that was made public in her lifetime, do "not require the Penetration of a Philosopher" to discern, then her work and her afterlives might take up other questions of political life and of racialized reading that take seriously the ongoing state of vulnerability that both opened and foreclosed Wheatley's material life and the fantasies spun from it.

Bullins's reference to Diana Ross invokes not just her own illustrious celebrity but also her turn in 1975's *Mahogany* as a fabulous fashion model who must choose between her man—who literally represents civil rights activism and political leadership—and her own dreams of an international fashion design career. If the teleology of the film, like Wheatley's early death, must conform to the conventions of post–civil rights politics (i.e., anything outside of purist politics equals death/the death of the race), the film and this reference can also be read against the grain of inevitable Black Arts political ends and sympathetically differ from the feminist fantasies of subjection and agency that followed. The pleasure of Wheatley's entrance, likening her to the exuberant and iconic image of Ross as Mahogany that was present in the minds of the audience for the play at the time, points to the tension of defining the political against and through black women and black feminine gender performance, and the pitfalls of not taking into account deeply gendered concerns in black feminism about mobility, ambition, and professional, personal, and sexual desires that may be at odds with the political mores of Bullins's time.

This interjection of an iconic figure of black culture, black femininity, queer desire, and crossover success in the 1970s into the "primal scene" of black freedom, be it of her trial for Gates or her funeral for Bullins, fictive though they may be, exposes not just the violence done to black women's bodies across the two centuries between Wheatley and Ross, but the way that black women's navigation through those both "terrifying yet also exciting" worlds, to quote Amber Musser (2016, 171) on the tensions in Kara Walker's "A Subtlety" exhibition, could be the very basis of a conception of "the political." Black women's navigation through those worlds also afforded pleasure, joy, desire, and mobility. Bullins may not have intended to highlight such alternate political pathways, but the context of the post–civil rights literary-political-cultural landscape leaves Wheatley's star turn in *The Mystery of Phillis Wheatley* open to interpretations beyond politics as usual. Bullins's obsession with Wheatley's death and fame suggests the ways that Wheatley's infamous body has always been yoked to the political discourse of freedom, but also foregrounds the importance of her proximity to death. Her own short life and, as J. Brooks points out, her traffic in commissioned elegy are traits that are not rehabilitated or repaired in her celebrity but embodied in it—a set of politics based on intimacy with triumph and also grief and the precarious temporality of embodiment represented in her letters with Tanner and in Ovington's play, as well as in the joy of Wheatley's *Mahogany* moment in the work of Bullins.[17] That Wheatley's legacy has so often been staged (several other plays from mid-twentieth century to today center on her and her trials[18]) renders the precarious figure of Wheatley—her body, the means and ends of her authorship, her standing in African American literature and politics at any given point in her long public history—as the central history of modern political thought, not as its exception.

Wheatley's very repetition refuses, or defuses, her exceptionality or her fixedness. The 1970s was a dynamic time when the rise of human rights discourse took off, as Samuel Moyn (2012) documents, but it did so in the face of the constructed failures of Western-installed leaders of African decolonized states as former colonial powers extracted resources and came up with the modern system of national debt in which they held their former colonies. It was also a time when media representations of minoritarian subjects were on the rise, as was a nascent, postracial, neoliberal "war on drugs" that led to a mass incarceration movement. Nothing about Wheatley, or Wheatley's moment, is static, even in Bullins's allegorical morality play. She is a "racial icon," in Fleetwood's (2015a, 4) formulation (and Ross is, in fact, Fleetwood's case study), one whose image "can impact us with such emotional force that we are compelled: to do, to feel, to see" in sometimes unpredictable ways, much as the 1970s period begs us to reimagine the tenets and tactics of previous freedom dreams that relied heavily on the transformation of the formal political sphere. Bullins foregrounds Wheatley's relation to the Founding Fathers, yes, but imagines her celebrity as political labor in its own fragile, personal modes of interrelation.

Conclusion

These key sites of Wheatley's visibility and the infamous bodies that haunt narratives of her life and work then ask about, in the titular words of poet and essayist June Jordan ([2002] 2006), "the difficult miracle" of black art and black life's persistence in the face of white supremacy. But though Jordan still imagines that persistence to be by and for the goal of freedom (in the vein of #blackgirlmagic), she, too, suggests alternative political fantasies at the end of her sonnet for Wheatley when she says, "Your early verse sweetens the fame of our Race." In thinking about the legacy of Phillis Wheatley in the black imagination, then, Wheatley's fame is always bittersweet and necessary, even as she herself remains unthinkable in whole, unknowable, a "miracle" at once requiring *and* transcending "proof," marking the impossible question that poet drea brown (n.d.) asks in her poem "flesh memory: an invocation in cento": "what does a victorious or defeated black woman's body look like?" In thinking about the legacy of Phillis Wheatley in black imaginative culture, this question invokes and critiques the problem of the poles of freedom infamous black women are frequently shoehorned into in their very visibility—a visibility that leaves them vulnerable as in open to injury but also open to interpretation and their own interpretative practices.

Brown's poem, like Bullins's play, stages a "mystery" and its interchangeable medieval performance designation, "miracle," indeed, a set of all-too-familiar cultural myths performed. Wheatley and her afterlives reimagine a political struggle recentered on vulnerability and need—a reorganization of politics that doesn't fetishize the masculine public sphere of the political as the only legitimate encounter with power at the expense of the falsely quarantined private sphere, or the dismissed feminized public sphere of celebrity culture. My interpretation of drea brown's poetic question becomes twofold, then: What do we critically do with individual figures, icons like Wheatley, in new and supposedly better representational economies of freedom? And when we, as critics, invest in the enduring, repeating texts of Wheatley, does freedom, however recontextualized, emerge as the only possible trajectory of black study? If we instead center on Wheatley and her representational uncertainty, what do we do with and about representational economies of "victory" and "defeat," of freedom's cast as war and conflict? Brown herself, in her chapbook of poems on Wheatley, *dear girl*, that focuses on the scene of her Middle Passage, imagines something existing in between the relentless repetitive injury ("*waves and waves on waves* / devolving without end" [2015, 24] and "moments of warmth and benevolence" [29])—or not in between, exactly, but in both temporalities simultaneously. Freedom is not the horizon that Wheatley represents or falls short of here; instead, she inhabits methods of reading for and through proximity, intimacy, and care through violence and vulnerability.

> there is always already urgency
> to piece in place what has not
> been said I am talking about
> scouring graves plunging
> in hopes something will float (25)

Brown writes of a kind of practicality about living and writing in the wake that is not void of the pleasures of writing or of being, itself, with a different tenor but a similar range to Shockley's poetic conversation between Wheatley and Hemings. Brown even imagines "mercy" as a June Jordan–inspired figure not of maternal love, exactly, but of a combination of circumstance and straight talk: "had I come another time girl / you would already be gone," even as she acknowledges that "nothing will be your own" in Wheatley's world (31–32). In brown's formulation, "owning" oneself might not be the political goal critically desired of the political, much as Wheatley's authorship collapsing into Hemings's issuing of Jefferson heirs in Shockley's poem refracts the many complicated attachments we might have to agency and self-expression.

This chapter has argued that fantasies of Wheatley and her celebrity legacy can point to black intimacies and uncertainty as politically viable politics instead of focusing on the horizon of freedom as a litmus test for the use of and engagement with black women's history. In reframing our critical desires around Wheatley, we can bring fresh dramas of black being and feeling to the scene of the political—and allow those performances of the needs and desires of black women as its very foundation. The constant histories Wheatley generates point to the generative place of fantasy for and in black women's political subjectivity, and while imagining Wheatley, as she imagines herself, into the discourse of freedom is one site of that fantasy, I have also traced other routes for the political life of Wheatley, approaches that critique notions of racial collectivity even as they perform attachment to black life and art, methods that, like Hartman's call for historiography, imagine a black feminist theory that is always and already rooted in the impossibility of representation to repair or cure even as it revels in the labor of black expressive culture and its infamous, unpredictable receptions.

Chapter Two

THE ROMANCE OF CONSENT

SALLY HEMINGS, BLACK WOMEN'S SEXUALITY, AND THE
FUNDAMENTAL VULNERABILITY OF RIGHTS

The romance is not saying that they may have loved one another. The romance is in thinking that it makes any difference if they did.
—ANNETTE GORDON-REED, *The Hemingses of Monticello*, 2008

If the definition of the crime of rape relies upon the capacity to give consent or to exercise will, then how does one make legible the sexual violation of the enslaved, when that which would constitute evidence of intentionality, and thus evidence of the crime, the state of consent or willingness of the assailed, opens onto a Pandora's box in which the subject formation and object constitution of the enslaved female is no less ponderous than the crime itself or when the legal definition of the enslaved negates the very idea of "reasonable resistance"?
—SAIDIYA HARTMAN, *Scenes of Subjection*, 1997

A beautiful young woman sneaks through a hallway to his door. Or he sneaks to her small room. He has been teaching her to read, or she has been tending to his wrist injury. This is all she knows, or she does not understand what she is getting herself into. It was love. It was rape. She is his "mistress." He is a rapist. So repeats a performance that again and again is rehearsed in the circulated narratives about Thomas Jefferson and Sally Hemings: the scene of sexual consent. It is surely a version of Saidiya Hartman's (1997, 87) foundational formation of "the scene of seduction," or the rendering of enslaved black women as both legally incapable of/outside the realm of consent and as always already consenting sexual subjects for white men, and part of what historian Emily A. Owens (2015) refers to as "fantasies of consent." Following the previous chapter's claims about the vulnerable, world-making capacity of fantasy, I trace here how the question of consent—was their relationship rape, coercion, a business transaction, a convenient arrangement, or love?—is crucial to the representations of the Jefferson/Hemings relationship, and the crux of understanding not just this individual coupling but also Jefferson's ideals of individual freedom and the base of democratic rights.

If Wheatley's ultimately chaste primal scene evokes the specter of intellectual and embodied violation of black women and girls by white men as the inaugural tension of black freedom and the burgeoning Enlightenment scene of human rights, then dwelling on and imagining the sexual encounter of Jefferson and Hemings becomes the on-the-nose Freudian scenario for collective democratic freedoms. This constant peering in upon the Founding Father and his enslaved "concubine" (the historically accurate if unfulfilling term for Hemings's position in Jefferson's home and life, and the term their son uses to describe the relationship, as discussed later in this chapter) marks the relationship as the specter of national origin that haunts the development of the liberal humanist subject, as well as another "first" for African American literature—the first novel published by an African American, William Wells Brown's *Clotel; or, The President's Daughter* in 1853, is a story about the progeny of a fictionalized Sally Hemings and Jefferson.

Sally Hemings was infamous in her day as well as in our own, but she exists in the historical record as an ephemeral presence: the subject of local gossip; the known mother of those who carried Jefferson's DNA; the daughter, sister, mother, and laborer of those whose lives are well documented around her. She also exists as a keening absence: there is no record of her official position in her house and little documentation of her physical and emotional life besides a list in Jefferson's farm book of the children she bore, a few words about her in extant letters, and the brief testimony to a newspaper reporter by one of her sons after emancipation. Yet her afterlives in the US imagination are highly visualized, speculative fantasies of desire, both of white patriarchal desire and an attempt to locate black women's agency in sexuality under enslavement. As the open secret—a term coined to think about the way queer desire operates in modern culture as both taboo and yet widely practiced (Sedgwick 2008)— that undergirds US discourses of freedom, Hemings's popular circulation in her own time through the present renegotiates the fundamental definitions of freedom. Through local newspaper accounts of her day, novels such as Brown's *Clotel* and Barbara Chase-Riboud's *Sally Hemings* (1979), films such as *Jefferson in Paris* (Ivory 1995), the drama of Anna Deavere Smith (2003), the artwork of Carrie Mae Weems (1999) and others, and contemporary black women's poetry, Hemings's (un)consent figures enslaved sexuality not as the exception to the concept of freedom but as its founding principal of operation and circulation, "the text upon which democracy stands and modernity forms" (K. J. Brown 2015, 11). That is to say that the historical and international debates about the who, what, and why of freedom function on the level of Hemings's open secret: obscured, contested, coerced, illegible, and always speculative, pushing toward a romantic fantasy while constantly confronted by more difficult desires for political resistance and corporeal consent.

This chapter holds two simultaneous conversations/analytics. The first is a reading of these repeated representations of the scene of consent between Jefferson and Hemings, like the fictional trial for Wheatley's authenticity, as sites of what I call the romance of consent, with romance denoting both the genre of the novel/fiction in total and the focus on a romantic love plot that figures agency, individual choice, objective truth, and sexual desire as always and eventually in alignment with each other (Goyal 2010). The romance of consent and the figure of Hemings herself undergird the foundation of freedom, returned to repeatedly as a site for working out the promise and the failure of human rights within a US formation. At the same time, I recast this historical and cultural obsession with Hemings and sexual consent as a way to join with a growing chorus of black feminist scholars who heavily critique critical reliance on discourses of agency and resistance that offer little in the way of understanding the complexities of black women's positionality in the history of sexuality in the Americas, or how we might reorganize and reimagine political desires with this history as their center. A group of black studies scholars have contributed to this critique of sexual agency and its vestigial attachments to liberal humanism and its construction of legal personhood through and against the unfreedom of black subjects—as well as the black nationalist celebrations of what they see as obvious/direct/violent rebellion under a masculinist frame of action/agency.[1]

Hemings's enduring representational legacy here stands as both a transhistorical case study to offer a genealogy of the formation of consent as a legal/civic category and as a way to read against the grain of consent as agency for a black feminist genealogy of the political. This chapter imagines a critical universe and discourse where Sally Hemings is figured as the central political subject of black feminist thought in the way that Harriet Jacobs, for instance, has been in recent years. Hemings, though, figures as a compromised subject who never exists in the realm of self-representation—strategically or otherwise—in the archive, and so is both wholly imagined and historically contextualized in every iteration. She is a celebrity who exists in and because of erotic speculation around enslaved womanhood. If Wheatley's "trial" is imagined as one with a necessarily impossible verdict, and that uncertainty acts as a generative fantasy for black feminist political thought, one might also imagine Hemings's representations as a terminally unfixed scene of seduction—terminally "ponderous," in Hartman's terms—as they both undergird and undo liberal humanist politics. A focus on Hemings asks us, pushing on Sara Clarke Kaplan's (2009) formative work on Chase-Riboud's novel on Hemings, to unmake the link not only between consent and erotic love but also between consent and the political subject. This chapter then puts black women's sexuality at the center of intellectual theories of the political, not as its exceptional or marginal subject.[2]

Valuing Consent; or, What's in a Name?

The contemporary debates about Sally Hemings hinge not on the question of did he or didn't he have a long-term sexual relationship with a black woman. Nor do they rest on the question of are they or aren't they the children of Thomas Jefferson who bear the Hemings name; all but the fringes of right-wing culture (and some of Jefferson's relatives) now accept as fact that Jefferson fathered children with Hemings. Instead, the contemporary question of Hemings is about consent—did she or didn't she consent to her sexual relations with Jefferson? Think pieces in *Teen Vogue* and other venues make this starker: Jefferson was a rapist (Blades 2017). We need to call Jefferson a rapist. Op-eds in the *Washington Post* echo this as they critique the use of the word "mistress" as a qualifier for Hemings's relationship to Jefferson, even in recent articles about the restoration of "Sally's Room" at Monticello (Danielle 2017; Sullivan 2015; Krissah Thompson 2017).[3] This connotation of a consensual, amoral, extramarital relationship is also in the outrageous sequence of revelation in the tour video at Monticello, which as late as June 2017, when I last viewed it, claimed that "many historians now believe" in the Hemings/Jefferson relationship but swiftly followed that information with the qualifying statement that Jefferson's wife, Martha, had been dead for many years before his relationship with Hemings started. These attempts to domesticate what Owens (2015) refers to as the "ordinary violence" of enslaved sexual relations evidence the reason for these concerns over naming Hemings and the reasons that historians go back and forth about the appropriate terminology for those enslaved women in long-term relationships with their white male masters— with Annette Gordon-Reed (2008) and Brenda Stevenson (1996) working through the historical "accuracy" of the term concubine for Hemings and her peers, though not without long explanation and some critical reflection.[4] As Gordon-Reed (2017) has weighed in, "a number of news reports as well as comments on social media discussing the plans drew the ire of many readers because they referred to Hemings as Jefferson's 'mistress' and used the word 'relationship' to describe the connection between the pair, as if those words inevitably denote positive things." This heated debate does more than police linguistic options for discussing black women's sexuality within enslavement. It points to the very limits of the conceptualizations of consent inherited—or not—around sexuality, sexual economies, and sexual violence (A. D. Davis 2002; A. D. Davis and BSE Collective 2019; Owens 2017).

Stevenson (2013) deploys the term *concubine* to think about long-term sexual arrangements between white men and black women during enslavement, a word that manages to incorporate the controversial terms of both the consent-assuming, durative name "mistress" and the assumed powerlessness of "rape victim."[5] These debates about naming the relationship between Hemings and Jefferson engage with and can also be located within the obsessive US appetite for imagining and representing Sally Hemings's desire(s). As Kaplan (2009, 774) so compellingly argues in her reading of Chase-Riboud's novels surrounding Hemings, these conversations have "served as a vehicle for and reflection of the production of knowledge about the meaning of racialized sexuality within slavery, the charter of historical and contemporary Black subjugation, and the conditions of (im)possibility for the articulation and recognition of Black subjectivity within the United States." Kaplan's own consideration of the novel as a site of a renegotiation of social death is the jumping off point for my discussion of Hemings as a limit case of "liberal humanist force" when trapped in the discourse of false dichotomies that such naming projects produce (778). Kaplan argues that under the terms of social death, it is only by disarticulating the erotic (what she terms "erotic love") from free will that one can begin to come up with a representational language to understand the work of Hemings as a figure and as a text, a contention that dovetails with both recent work in the field of black erotics and longstanding questions of black women's historiography. This chapter then attends to the ways Hemings's historical and cultural presence—and present legacy—is made and unmade through narratives of racialized sexual desire and critical assumptions about the possibilities of her political subjectivity that obscure how she—and racialized sexual discourse—is made legible through these desires. Hemings serves not just as agentic "threat" (787) to liberal humanist formations of dominance and resistance, but as a generative figure for what lies beyond those categories' undoing.

What becomes clear in looking at representations of Hemings are the tense overlaps as well as disconnects that make up the social fabric and context of (un)consent: how individuals have been differently hailed into institutional identities and rhetorics of violence, coercion, protection, threat, favor, and fear, often in conflicting or shiftable ways.[6] Scholars have done much to document the "widespread and obvious," in Stevenson's (2013, 101) words, forms of "sustained sexual contact between an enslaved woman and her master," as well as the less obvious routes that sexual terror and negotiation operates through and in outside of enslavement's strict bounds.[7] This collective work on black women's sexuality speaks to the links between conceptions of injury and articulations of radical vulnerability as the heart of how political life is conceived. To take a page from the powerful work of anthropologist Sameena Mulla (2014) in *The Violence of Care*, the enforced narrative of the violence of rape engages certain languages, temporalities, and affects and refuses others, even as one can see sexual assault in terms of other temporalities than before/after the event, other than as the most significant trauma that can be brought on a woman. "Rape" itself is an event and terminology of liberal humanism, the carceral state, and biopower, or as Emily Owens argues, consent "has frequently sutured the freedom of some to the unfreedom of most" (2019, 148) in the history of black women's sexuality as well as in antiqueer sexual moralism (Fischel 2016). What does it mean to bring representation to Hemings and her sexual "scenario" with Jefferson, to borrow the language of performance scholar Diana Taylor (2003), to think about an event with rough scripts that also plays out with a difference?[8]

The project of renegotiating Hemings and her significance to black feminist thought then begins at the point of what Christina Sharpe (2010) calls "monstrous intimacies"—where scenarios of unconsent are assumed as the basis of "all modern subjects" even as its costs are "largely borne by and readable on the (New World) *black* subject" (3). This chapter explores how shifting analysis of the allusions, depictions, occlusions, and eclipses of the "moment" of (un)consent that have come to define the life and afterlives of Sally Hemings might not operate in service of finding her or her experience of her sexuality a better, fixed name. This chapter instead seeks out critical space for "desire, solace, and material comfort" (Stevenson 1996, 183) as well as the mix of what Ann Laura Stoler calls "tense and tender ties" (2001) within the confines of sexual terror. In doing so, this work does not conflate false consciousness with non-consent (S. Wells 2017) nor seek resistance, but instead views the vulnerability of unconsent as a terrain that can reshape the limits, possibilities, and definitions of the political subject as authored through the work of early black women's celebrity and a genealogy of black feminist thought.

FIGURE 2.1. James Akin, *A Philosophic Cock* (1802), a political cartoon of Sally Hemings and Thomas Jefferson. Courtesy of the American Antiquarian Society. ˙

Reproducing History, Reproductive Histories

Here I trace in brief the narratives and alibis produced around Hemings as a means to assume, occlude, and displace the role of consent in the drama of Hemings and Jefferson's entanglement. Though historians are not the first to imagine the scene of Hemings and Jefferson's relations/relationship, they are in some ways the first front in the debate surrounding Hemings's presence in Jefferson's world and the significance of her imagined or invisible consent. The first thing to note, in terms of archival presence/evidence, is that the Jefferson/Hemings entanglement is not and never should have been news to twentieth-century historians. News of their relationship, beyond undoubtedly the oral transmission of gossip around their progeny in eighteenth- and early nineteenth-century Charlottesville, was even confirmed in print, first in 1802 in a Virginia newspaper by political reporter James Callender during Jefferson's campaign for presidential reelection. After this, a series of political cartoons, bawdy ballads/poems, and news coverage followed, giving Sally Hemings her most enduring presence in the form of racist nicknames—most notably Dusky Sally. Frequently sexually explicit, they clearly assume Hemings's consent as a given—or rather, as beside the point in a civic culture that did not allow for the possibility of black women's unconsent, as Hartman (1997) so painstakingly outlines and others have examined. Hemings is, for instance, a hen in one political cartoon, following Jefferson's cock around the farm (figure 2.1). There is the obvious racist association between African American–identified peoples and animals here, and Jefferson, too, is made bestial in his pride but also in his sexual appetite for Hemings's dark-skinned, enshadowed "hen" following him around the yard.

As Gordon-Reed (2008) has argued, of course, it is Jefferson's long-term association with Hemings—the number of children, the duration of their connection that can be mapped through these births, and the fact of his continued unmarried status—that rankles, suggesting that it is not the one-off event of rape or sex with Hemings that debases Jefferson but his very durative, obviously affective attachment to a mixed-race woman rather than to a white woman. Here, it is Jefferson's consent to be emotionally and socially connected to a black woman, in the form of his unbroken, long-term entanglement with Hemings, that threatens to expose Jefferson's political and moral weakness—one that always exists as part of his public persona simultaneously with his legacy as the author of the Declaration of Independence and purveyor of manifest destiny.[9]

As Gordon-Reed (2008) suggests, the rule of *nullius filius* that was applied to enslaved women—their children are, legally speaking, the children of no one, as they are not allowed to legally marry—makes Hemings's children suspect in the eyes of the law for the very purpose of forwarding racial inequity and rampant sexual abuse through enslavement. The proof, then, is set on legally visible grounds that structurally marked the high likelihood of master-enslaved entanglements; the documented confirmation from a perhaps ethically compromised but ambitious and accurate reporter James Callendar, who most surely was repeating common knowledge in Virginia of rumors printed earlier about Jefferson and who had perhaps seen Jefferson's children at Monticello; in the fact that Jefferson never publicly denied the existence of his relationship or children; in the documented farm book that shows that Hemings's children were all conceived within a month of Jefferson's returns home to Monticello and never conceived in his absence; in the fact that all were named after Jefferson's family and not Hemings's (as documented thoroughly in Gordon-Reed's

The Hemingses of Monticello); in the unthinkable circumstances that Hemings and their children continued to live on at Monticello through the scandal and beyond; in the bare fact that Sally Hemings is the only enslaved member of the household whose labor and movements appear to be wholly undocumented by the data-and efficiency-obsessed Jefferson; in the common knowledge that their children were the only younger persons informally or formally freed during Jefferson's lifetime or in his will; in the equally well-known fact that Sally was not formally freed but was able to walk off Monticello with her freed children at the behest of Jefferson's estate with no repercussions; and in the face of Madison Hemings's oral history in 1873, transcribed by an Ohio reporter, that confirms his paternity and offers a family history. Though all of this is documented, we are to understand that there existed reasonable doubt for generations of historians as to the truth/evidence of said relationship between Hemings and Jefferson before DNA confirmation.

To boot, though it is documented through partus sequitur ventrem that master relationships with enslaved women were the norm in the South, it still becomes unthinkable that this relationship occurred. Joseph J. Ellis (1997) even suggests, pre-DNA, that he doubts the relationship because Jefferson's sexual desires existed on a more rarefied plane—this despite his wife's near constant state of pregnancy during their marriage, a condition that from the first threatened and eventually took her life. And though there is absolutely no evidence of Hemings's relationship with any other white man, many of these same historians assumed her consent as freely given—or again, beside the point—to a range of Jeffersonian white male relatives, which could explain family resemblance and even DNA while denying Jefferson's ability to consent to a relationship with her.

I belabor the point of the evidence uncannily put together by legal historian Gordon-Reed and others to emphasize that "open secret" is a term that could operate here only through a white patriarchal imaginary, one that creates and demands archival silence around enslaved sexuality even as it enacts law and manages rights (or lack thereof) that directly acknowledge, address, and manage the existence of mixed-race peoples. (Though technically the legal one-drop rule would come at the turn of the century, at a state-by-state level, it was in practice from the antebellum period.) It was no secret to the community of laborers at Monticello, but the fact that their informal or formal testimony was entirely disallowed by law and by custom made it so that information circulated through black subjects meant, legally and in the white public sphere, nothing "official." Like the law that refused the enslaved the right to testify at trial (a law born of the intimacy between the enslaved and their masters and then reverse-engineered to pathologize black trustworthiness, a gendered and racialized paradox about the relationship between private intimacy and trust and public/structural negation of that very set of relations) this refusal of enslaved testimony as history similarly refuses the very intimacy of enslaved/master relations, the very intimacy that made enslaved life so precarious for those closest to whiteness, like the entire Hemings family, and the kinds of intimacy through proximity and endurance that make the idea of any individualized scene of consent nearly impossible—and politically idealistic, at best—to imagine.

I track this to explain how the scene of (un)consent for Hemings and Jefferson was both visible and refused in its own time and for centuries afterward—and still is among Jefferson's white descendants and white nationalist conspiracy theorists. But, in fact, in conversations that deny adequate evidence for the relationship's existence, Hemings's sexual consent and/or her inability to even have access to that category based on her status as property is never broached. Jefferson's own assumed morals and character are brought up as evidence against the claim, which might for some be a tacit acknowledgment of the moral impossibility of gaining noncoerced consent from an enslaved woman, but also reads as a way of denying that anyone as "good" as Jefferson would need or want to take a black or mixed-race woman as his concubine. And even in acknowledging begrudgingly the possibility/likelihood of the affair, explanations are often wholly unconcerned with Hemings's consent, reproducing enslaved black women's sexuality as a commodity that is assumed to be willingly negotiated on some kind of open market of lifestyle favors and takes as a given that proximity to white men is the most desirable/protected position to be in. This line of thinking in turn assumes Heming's equality or even power over Jefferson, despite her being fifteen years old at most when their sexual relationship began (a different age of consent at that point in time but nonetheless thirty years younger), the youngest half-sister of his deceased wife, and part of a large extended family enslaved at Monticello. Other explanations rationalize the relationship as a result of Jefferson's own vague Enlightenment-inspired views on necessary sexual release that basically make Hemings into another technologically advanced device or invention at Monticello after a rumored promise to Martha on her deathbed that he would never remarry. As Kimberly Juanita Brown (2015, 39) notes, if Hemings "did not exist, she would have to be invented." For mainstream historians before and immediately after Gordon-Reed's first 1998 book and the DNA evidence's conclusion, Hemings's consent is particularly invented, as a given or beside the point—or, as B. R. Burg (1986) compellingly argues through structure as well as content, Hemings never crosses the threshold of "family" in white patriarchal imagination. Considering Clare Hemmings's (2011) construction of stories that matter—in the context of interdisciplinary academic fields and their narratives of formation, change, and meaning—it is important to note the language of history here and its plots for miscegenation and sexual coercion: denial, refusal, shame, minimization, aberration. I rehearse these invented narrative forms for Hemings to trace in how consent looms as the crux of investment in Jefferson and the imaginary of Jefferson's United States—and how the specter of his life as a slaveholder must be set off as an irresolvable contradiction, somehow acknowledged but bracketed as an impossible economic/social situation of its time (despite Jefferson's own uneven history as a proponent of abolition and despite the fact that many before him freed their slaves upon death, such as George Washington himself, even if they could not imagine their own lives outside of slave ownership and the benefits of existing on the labors of enslaved people). Somehow forced labor and lack of consent in the form of slave ownership can be understood, but the bridge that is too far to cross is the question of sexual consent—and a sexual investment/desire in blackness, even within the context of coerced black labor. As filmmaker Ken Burns repeats in his interview with Anna Deavere Smith (2003), which is staged in her play *House Arrest*, "He owned her!"

Rather than an outer limit of US citizenship, then, the question of sexual consent can be reconfigured as the very foundation of liberal humanist rights. Here I follow Hartman (1997) and others who have compellingly argued that black unfreedom underwrote white freedom (coded as just "freedom"). While it is a foundational claim that consent is what republicanism (later in the form of democracy) offered beyond the monarchy—consent to be ruled, rather than having no "choice"—that very construction was underwritten by its glaring exceptions in modernity's construction of its others: white women, who were to be ruled by their male relatives (by biological inheritance) or spouses (technically by consent to transfer said power, and, by extension, a patriarchal logic that went unchecked in other racialized scenes), and enslaved peoples, who were denied consent by a range of management techniques that defined racial difference as outside of the adult human paradigm of the Enlightenment white male. Black women and men existed outside of consent in the way they used their bodies or how their bodies were employed and deployed by others, unless they were found criminally liable for their actions. But with *partus sequitur ventrem*, black women's bodies had another level of unconsent; their children, too, male or female, were to follow in their status of unfreedom—hence they could reproduce unconsent. The entire enterprise of chattel slavery, as well as the modern imperial nation-states it produced in the name of liberal humanist individualism as a doctrine of inalienable rights, is underpinned and underwritten by this nonconsensual reproduction—of bodies, of labor, of the discourse of biological difference at the very site of biological genesis.

This is the crux of Hemings's difficult and mythical position in white and African American imagination: she alternately stands for the unimaginable limits of whiteness, the horrific antiblackness that defines the United States, and the romance of inclusion in the founding system of rights—the transcendence of race through the romance of consent, both in her own time and at other key moments of political reckoning.[10] But it is also important to document here, in a transition from historical stories that matter about Jefferson and Hemings to fictional/narrative scenes of consent, that there is another register that exists alongside of and that emerges from some of this open secret documentation, this refusal to see or register black women's unconsent as the foundation of offering up individual rights to white men: that of the romance of this contradiction. The romance at the heart of rights discourse itself is a temporary story that can be retold and refashioned until it reaches its impossible ideal. Before Gordon-Reed's own investment—but also canny disavowal—quoted in the epigraph about the historical evidence for a loving, affective, long-term relationship between Hemings and Jefferson, there was Fawn M. Brodie's (1974) *Thomas Jefferson: An Intimate History*. Brodie's bestselling biography engaged psychoanalysis as a way to legitimate the overwhelming evidence of a sexual relationship between Jefferson and Hemings. Using the language of love and romance alongside the formative affective narrative relationship with enslaved people and labor that Jefferson was so attached to, she renarrates the historical evidence denied so extensively by her white male peers. Derided as an amateur and particularly singled out for her investment in theories of psychoanalysis that defied historical methodology, Brodie was accused of unprofessionalism for her suggestive reassessment of Jefferson and his legacy. But her book sparked a cultural movement toward white public acknowledgment of and fascination with Jefferson and Hemings within the genre of sexual consent—the romance. Post-Brodie, Chase-Riboud (1979) wrote her novel, Merchant-Ivory produced *Jefferson in Paris* (Ivory 1995), and CBS aired the television movie *Sally Hemings: An American Scandal* (Haid 2000). Brodie's biography, invested as it was in individualized psychobiography, turned the tide and interest in the entanglement, interest that assumed Hemings's individual consent.

Of course, as I turn to these fictional stories we tell, I keep in mind the inevitable backlash to these romance narratives that efface and assume enslaved women's sexual consent, no matter how difficult it is represented to negotiate, especially in that these romance narratives emerge post–Black Arts movement (as opposed to *Clotel*, for instance), in a country that is at once orchestrating resegregation through neoliberal means and grappling with the failures of formal civil rights. I engage both impulses here—the pitfalls of the romance genre for telling Hemings's story as it represents the scene of consent, and how some representations may complicate this narrative genre and its perverse relationship with sexual consent and female agency, both individual and collective.

Fantasies of Freedom as and from Consent

Brodie's 1974 biography, the first to posit an enduring, monogamous, and loving relationship between Hemings and Jefferson, was more than a bestseller; it was the inspiration for the boom in Jefferson/Hemings representations for the remainder of the twentieth century. Artist and historical novelist Barbara Chase-Riboud published her first romantic novel on the families in 1979 after reading Brodie, followed by her 1994 novel on Harriet, their daughter, after rediscovering William Wells Brown's *Clotel*. Merchant-Ivory, the period-piece Oscar-bait arthouse producers, used Brodie's materials to launch the narrative film *Jefferson in Paris* about Thomas Jefferson's time in France in the 1780s, featuring romances with the married Italian-British Maria Cosway and the start of his affair with Hemings. Young adult novelist Ann Rinaldi published *Wolf by the Ears* in 1993, also about Jefferson's daughter Harriet Hemings, followed by Barbara Hambly's (2007) *Patriot Hearts* (about a range of America's First Ladies), Steve Erickson's (1996) sci-fi thriller *Arc d'X*, and Stephen O'Connor's (2016) *Thomas Jefferson Dreams of Sally Hemings*, this "love" story between Jefferson and Hemings endures in narrative fiction and cinema across the late twentieth century and into the twenty-first century. The scene of consent remains the primal scene of US identity formation in these iterations, up to and including the refusal to represent the scene of consent in the narratives centered on daughter Harriet Hemings. In this section, I move from the historicist fervor over this designated romance into the fictional narratives used to imagine the scene and its contexts as strategies of both containment of sexual desire under the rubric of consent/unconsent and some more radical disavowals of such a scale, even as sexual desire, racial terror, pleasure, and other affective terrains are still accessible.

In Freud's theorization of the primal scene, it is the real or imagined encounter with the sexual congress of mother and father that shapes the maturing self. While acknowledging the literal impossibility and normative claims of psychoanalysis that rely on monolithic and mythic family structures, this is an apt construct for the United States' relationship to Hemings and Jefferson entanglement as a founding national scene that is both the object of fascination and denial, of spectacle and of occlusion, in public culture. In a country founded in and through white supremacy and antiblackness, naming this sexual scenario the primal scene of national identity poses a number of challenges to normative liberal humanist claims to freedom and rights as the foundational values of the United States. The years-long and torrid debate about proof of the Hemings/Jefferson relationship functions in terms of this primal scene characterization, which also oscillated between "real" encounter and "fantasy" encounter in Freud's own time. This debate foregrounds the way that Enlightenment thinking acts as an obstacle to political imagination—as a way to forestall interpretive acts in favor of the labor of evidence that the very structures of enslavement and its archival practices deny. When one is not afforded the rights of citizenship, marriage, or paternity, as it is defined by the state, how can one begin to show up "on the record," especially when that record and the definition of proof renders you, specifically, invisible? Of course, such an analysis of the limits of evidence and proof also demands critical interrogation of the desire to claim evidence as a limit—or to end analysis with acts of historical completion that declare an end to the story with the word "rape," rather than the beginning of inquiry that starts from the terrain of unconsent.

If the primal scene as such hinges not just on the trauma of experience but on the act of interpretation, then the encounter between Hemings and Jefferson can be read as the primal scenario that grounds discussion of black feminist subjection, much in the way Frederick Douglass's (1845) fight with Covey in his *Narrative* comes to undergird so many discussions of black (male) subjection and freedom. As outlined in the first section, the fixation on black women's sexuality as *the* site of their subjection—and the potential site of agentic redemption—haunts the politics of black feminist thought through genealogies of sexual violence and political activism. To argue that sexual terror defines black women is to both call out white supremacy but also imagine it as the most significant limit—the most shaping quality of the self and the subject—to black feminist politics. To imagine, as one article puts it, "the rhetoric of miscegenation" (Burg 1986) as the foundation of black feminist subjection is then both material in an evidentiary way and salient as the plot point or primal scene that is endlessly repeated and/or fantasized about through affects of hope, terror, political impossibility, and political change. As Joan Wallach

Scott (2011) has argued about the generative possibilities that have come out of the seemingly incompatible discourses of psychoanalysis and history, "fantasy," as a narrative and/or aesthetic act of imagining beyond generic and disciplinary realms, even for a moment, can make visible heretofore unthinkable, or unspeakable, questions about methodological practice.

This not only echoes back to the previous chapter's arguments about Wheatley and attachments to freedom, but also marks the ways that, again, the sphere of celebrity culture does meaningful political labor at the level of political imagination. To name the Hemings and Jefferson scene as a primal one is neither to praise nor condemn black feminist practice to the scene's existing interpretative limits, but instead to consider how critical desires around this sexual scenario might engage, like Douglass's fight scene, with "genres of the human," following Sylvia Wynter (2015) and Alexander G. Weheliye (2014), that are both recognizable and as yet unnamed or unthought in liberal humanism. It is also to claim, for black feminist thought, the founding national myth of subjectivity *and* subjection—to have the archival, affectual, and political uncertainty of black women's sexuality sit at and as the vulnerable center of US civic imagination (Tillet 2009).

Hemings's (un)consensual sexual representations track in five terrains: as the always sexually willing black woman (harkening us back to Patricia Hill Collins's [2000] controlling images of Jezebel, available to any and all white men who visit Monticello), an animal who "breeds" with whomever (as noted in Burg's 1986 article on the rhetoric of historians pre-DNA on Hemings's reproductivity); as the impossible-to-desire, invisibilized enslaved subject, not worthy of historical mention because she, as referent, cannot exist in the visible frame of Jefferson's sexuality (if he even has any, according to some historical denialists); as the romantic partner/love object of Jefferson who transcends race; as the pedophilic victim who represents enslaved women's primary definition through sexual violence.[11] The fifth strain represents the empowered slave woman who "negotiates" a sexual contract with Jefferson to improve her lot—part victim, part shrewd agent of redress, in the mode of Michel de Certeau ([1984] 2011) and his theory of quotidian acts of self-making, as employed by Hartman (1997) and Jenny Sharpe (2003) on their work on black women's sexuality. These representations are in many ways reimaginings of Madison Hemings's 1873 narrative as told to an Ohio newspaper. He gives a slim answer as to how Sally negotiated her children's future freedom as a condition of coming home from France, where she could have claimed her freedom if she never returned to the United States: "the treaty," as he refers to it, a clever way of thinking, even then, of sexual contracts between sovereign entities, and the ways that legal rights alone cannot account for the totality of black women's sexual and political subjection or freedoms (Hemings 1873).

These categories of representation also map the ways that sexuality is at the heart of cultural formations of black women's subject(ion): as their constitutive reason (black women's aberrant sexual desire marks them as subjects of and to enslavement); as they are "ungendered" and altogether left out of the realm of existence (in the visualization of white/free sexuality as pleasure); as the transcendent route to freedom (yoked to interracial "love" here); as impossible to experience under the definition of sexual violence and trauma that deauthorizes the supposed agency that sexual pleasure requires; and in the fifth version, as a commodity to barter with in order to gain a slightly "better" version in the hierarchy of social death, whereby one is always assumed to want to escape "the field" to find leisure and leniency/safety in more intimate proximity to whiteness (a fallacy long critiqued by black feminist historians).

One can see the first genre of Hemings in the early nineteenth-century representations of Hemings after their affair was exposed in 1802 during Jefferson's second presidential run. As mentioned above, ballads referenced "Dusky Sally" and cartoons imagined her as a hen following Jefferson's "cock" around a farm. Some historians and Hemings denialists, too, engage the language of Hemings as a "breeder," or the sexual entertainer of multiple members of Jefferson's male relatives without any question. Other denialists, while not taking up Hemings's children's paternity in alternate theories, simply deny the possibility of her attracting Jefferson's white desire at all, as if black women are indeed "ungendered" in the eyes of white notions of sexuality, not only as proper object but as objects who even have sexuality to speak of; reproduction is rendered as largely separate from sexual acts as anything other than ungendered mechanisms of production, not desire (Ellis 1997). Then there are those imaginings of the romance between Jefferson and Hemings as challenging to and transcendent of the bonds of slavery and the desires between races— positing their coupling as forbidden, unthinkable, and hence transcendent of racial bonds even as it displays liberal humanist acknowledgment of enslavement's racist structure. Novels such as *Patriot Hearts* and visual narrative renderings such as the Merchant-Ivory film *Jefferson in Paris* and the miniseries *An American Scandal* have trouble getting out of this genre in their investments in Jefferson as a complex but morally recoverable Founding Father.

It is on the fifth strain of representations of Hemings, though, where this section will focus. I will not be exhaustive in my readings of these narratives as I'm also interested in the nonemplotments of Hemings's consent as places to negotiate a different politics of black women's sexuality and political subjectivity.

But, to quickly reference some of these emplotments, one can begin with *Clotel*, which imagines the relationship between Jefferson and Hemings as one of cast-off desires that motor the plot of the sale of Jefferson's enslaved daughters (a historical fiction), and which ends by reaffirming the primary significance of choice of marriage partner as the ultimate right and means to progress (for women).

In 1853 William Wells Brown published the first novel by an African American, *Clotel; or, The President's Daughter*. Here, in the antebellum United States, a half-century since the "gossip" of Sally Hemings hit white print culture and well before the 1873 testimony of Madison Hemings, comes the founding novel of African American letters, focused on Jefferson's "daughter," Clotel, emerging from a (historically inaccurate) myth that Jefferson and Hemings's daughter was sold into slavery. Clotel is identified as Jefferson's daughter, explicitly. Building off of the long trail of African American history, mostly oral history, passed down among generations of African Americans regarding Jefferson and Hemings's open secret, *Clotel* doesn't so much traffic in the secret part of the Hemings/Jefferson liaison—it is clear, open, and matter of fact about its existence—as much as it explodes, to borrow a phrase from Ann duCille (2000, 443), "the DNA of African-American" history, literary and otherwise, as a genealogical line that does not run in the same narrative strain as (white) US history, with its disappearance of sexual and racial injustice but also its absolute insistence on the impossibility of evidence for said violences even as it defined the very terms of archiving practices and official documentation to excise them from view.[12] The plot, with its emphasis on the failures of traditional marital protections for enslaved women and the inevitability of interracial sexual life under enslavement, foregrounds generations of sexual and reproductive entanglement that hinge on unconsent. Even its genre of romance does not transcend or eclipse this, as it renders the lack of protection for black women's sexual, romantic, and physical lives as the tragedy of the novel—and of US history. Romance alone—love, even—between white men and black women is treated not as transcendent but inadequate without not just consent but the *right* to marry that Brown clearly delineates as protective of both moral and physical vulnerability. *Clotel* treats the right to marriage as an exercise of romance, respectability, and rights.

Clotel has been discussed as engaging with and upholding models of respectability and the cult of domesticity, clearly rendering sexual enslavement—and its implied nonconsent—a fate equivalent with or worse than death, given the suicidal choices of Currer and two other women in the narrative. Many of those black women living out the romance—the fantasy, in Owens's (2015) terms—of consent in the narrative have their own fantastical narrative of sexual choice as freedom, liberation, or protection undone, largely by the complicated set of laws governing black rights, enslavement, and partus sequitur ventrem. One could argue, then, that *Clotel*—and black respectability politics/strategies themselves—argues for abolition as the only route to ensure black women's respectability through its protections of their rights (under marriage, of course) as citizens that then ensures their sexual consent is meaningful. By this, I mean to reverse some of the logic of respectability criticism that would think about African American literary appeals to true womanhood as appeals for rights that merely trade on the affect of women's particular vulnerability and value against and through virtue. Instead, it is the right of consent that is being undermined in particular for black women, as women, as sexual consent—or consent to marriage under respectability logic—is the only form of power allowed under coverture.

But one might also argue that *Clotel*, as a long-tail document that entwines "the DNA of African American literary history," as duCille (2000) calls the novel, with the founding history of the United States through the woeful tale of the figure of Clotel (and Currer, the Sally Hemings surrogate), also centralizes black women. By subject, here, I do not mean the rights–bearing, ideal individual inexorably moving toward freedom as the focus of African American literary tradition (à la Frederick Douglass) or the project of US democracy. Instead, Clotel is a part of a genealogy that doesn't fetishize the consent of the subjected citizen/slave nor the rights-bestowed emancipated slave/citizen as the base of inquiry for African American political thought or US citizenship. The circuitous route of its plots—some containing consent, sexual and political, in traditional forms and then failing, others not and then succeeding, and most unevenly weaving in and out of the space that consent marks as a pole/marker of agency—offers a view of self-making in the context of systemic, diasporic movements and modes of gender, race, and capital that does not hinge on individual resistance or submission, and perhaps not even the minor key of redress. Instead, *Clotel* offers mixed histories where the fate of the individual and collective body, represented through the complex experience of black women as subjects and objects of desire and subject to/objects of cultural and civic law, does not adhere to that existing map, that teleology of cause and effect, of submission or autonomy. In *Clotel*'s world—indeed, in its alternative historiography of the United States writ large—the map of blackness (and antiblackness) exceeds these liberal humanist frames, even as it never questions the circumscription of black women's bodies through sexual and political discourse. What other existences, subjectivities, pleasures, and plots are available, it seems to ask, not beyond consent but given that consent is not even on the table?

More contemporary narratives' focuses on the primal scene of sexual negotiation tend toward an inevitable emphasis on black interiority—on giving Hemings "more" than her sexuality even as they repeat the initial sexual encounter as her primary site of self and symbolic meaning. Romance, then, as genre and narrative, seems to both define and defy the rational liberal humanist subject in the time of enslavement and in the ways the history of enslavement is made/written/invented in reemplotments of the era and ongoing event/time-horizon of slavery (Warren 2018). Kaplan (2009) interestingly suggests a pattern of evoking Hemings to work through these entanglements through genre-bending narrative representations of her and Jefferson's relationship in her reading of Chase-Riboud's *Sally Hemings* (1979) and *The President's Daughter* (1994). Here she displaces romance as the main genre for an investment in the neo-slave narrative form as the post–civil rights era's most salient genre of African American literature par excellence, and points to that genre's renegotiation of the meaning of chattel slavery to US and African American national identity and imagination in the specter of Enlightenment modernity. Apart from Ashraf H. A. Rushdy (1999), Kaplan (2009), and Salamishah Tillet (2012), Chase-Riboud's *Sally Hemings* is a little-discussed and infrequently praised book that fits uneasily into the neo-slave narrative genre in its assumed emphasis on field work, violence, rape, resistance, and escape.[13] It is in this slippage, between genre expectations and the figuration of Hemings within this genre, that Chase-Riboud finds room to displace consent and choice as the markers of freedom in the liberal humanist mode.

Chase-Riboud's post–Fawn Brodie novel on Hemings tracks her long life with and beyond Jefferson's but spends nearly half of its length in Revolutionary-era Paris charting the start of their entanglement. Far from suggesting that Hemings entered into an arrangement with Jefferson to secure a more privileged position within enslavement for herself, Chase-Riboud charts the generations of mobility built into Hemings's life as the child of her mother's own relationship with her master and the half-sister of her master's wife, as well as the inherent limits and distinct vulnerabilities of such proximity and intimacy to white family and the rule of enslavement. Hemings is, after all, a third-generation "concubine," and Chase-Riboud does not dwell long on the site or scene of Hemings's consent to the initial sexual encounter as a pressing mystery of their coupling. But the scene Chase-Riboud sets is interesting in that she imagines (as would others following her) the lead-up to the coupling involving the intimate twinning of Hemings's growing financial and intellectual autonomy—her receiving wages (historically documented) and her learning to read (totally imagined)—and her recognition of her capacity to claim freedom in France. In this sense, the novel mirrors the arc of the neo-slave narrative and slave narrative genres, with a growing conflict between the revelation of enslaved subjectivity and the push toward "freedom" through access to the privileges and rights of personhood. But rather than stage these revelations from the space of violence or its threat, *Sally Hemings* imagines it from a space of comparative or escalating privileges that blood, racial order, and mobility within enslavement might afford. And, of course, Hemings's story is not a march toward freedom, though the book is framed and interspersed with Hemings's post-Jeffersonian life as a free woman of color in Virginia, having never left the immediate vicinity of her home of Monticello in the rest of her days. In this way, the book offers a complicated vision of freedom within and outside of enslavement, displacing the idea of emancipation as the inauguration of choice and consent by offering a vision of arcs that do not neatly fall into such teleologies.

This thwarted romance with freedom and emancipation runs in parallel and intersecting lines with the "romance" between Hemings and Jefferson. Hemings is fourteen years old and away from all family but her brother James in France, where she lives in close proximity—the same house—with the widowed Jefferson, among far fewer laborers than at Monticello. She and James are the only enslaved people in the French household. Chase-Riboud stages this context as one of inevitable sexual transgression, as Sally has few options but to be "seduced" by France, freedom, growing intellectual and personhood parity with "Master" Jefferson, and her adolescent sexuality. Chase-Riboud presents her only other encounters with her sexual body as unwanted verbal and physical assaults by house staff (again, repeated throughout other narratives). The actual moment of consummation is one marked by anticipation and inevitability, for both Sally and the reader—both of whom "know" what is coming based on familial and US history, respectively. Relegating sexual consent to a noncentral role in negotiating "something akin to freedom," Chase-Riboud not only uncouples the presence of erotic pleasure and romantic love from freedom/unfreedom polarities, as Kaplan (2009) argues; she also imagines such conditions of unconsent as the normative and quotidian economies of enslaved labor.

While Hemings talks to a white census taker whose obsession with her frames the novel, Chase-Riboud's novel has her omniscient narrator lay out this terrain of negotiation as such: "It would have been more fitting, she thought, if, instead of exchanging thoughts, they exchanged pleasures. This would have been much more acceptable than what they were doing; for thoughts, feelings, and memories were all a slave, or an ex-slave, had to call her own. Even Thomas Jefferson had bowed to that rule. He had loved her as a woman and owned her as a slave, but her thoughts had always remained beyond his or anyone's control" (38). A passage like this one suggests a more straightforward melodrama of agentic self-presentation as black feminist politics than the rest of the novel engages with, however, as critics Tillet (2012), Kaplan (2009), and Rushdy (1999) have noted. This neo-slave narrative novel subverts the conventions of the neo-slave narrative genre, as it is not a text that builds toward legal freedoms. It does, though, yoke reciprocity of pleasures to the sexual labor of black women, rather than assuming black women's pleasure cannot be part of what is exchanged under enslavement, and even in the terrain of unconsent. It also refuses to yoke sexual pleasure to interiority, instead attaching it to structural power, a "rule" that Jefferson, not Hemings, "bowed" before.

This pairing of pleasure and power does not, however, easily translate to the kind of empowerment through sexual labor thesis that historian Marisa Fuentes (2016), for example, remains skeptical of in some newer work in black feminist history. Or, at least, the power play switch is one in keeping with the rules, scripts, and history of enslavement as centered on black women. Hemings, for Chase-Riboud, is a knowing player in the entanglement she sees as inevitable long before the act itself, when, "I felt around me an exploding flower, not just of passion, but of long deprivation, a hunger for things forbidden, for darkness and unreason, the passion of rage against the death of the other I so resembled. . . . Thus did Thomas Jefferson give himself into my keeping" (102). Here, pleasure and death are intertwined with acts of ownership ("keeping") as well as grief, care, and intimacy. The next section will explore some of these ways of thinking of Sally Hemings that, following Sarah Jane Cervenak (2014), wander and weave between these representational and narrative poles, imagining perhaps other ways of doing and thinking politics that spring from wells of the deep, durative, and conflicted work of black feminist theories of black women's sexuality.

Memorializing Consent

Emplotment of the scene of consummation—a scene void of consent in the initial entanglement—has its limits. In the post-DNA era of Sally Hemings's figuration, the genomic, too, intersects with race, embodiment, and pleasure—not just in that it figures the consequences of sexual acts themselves. For

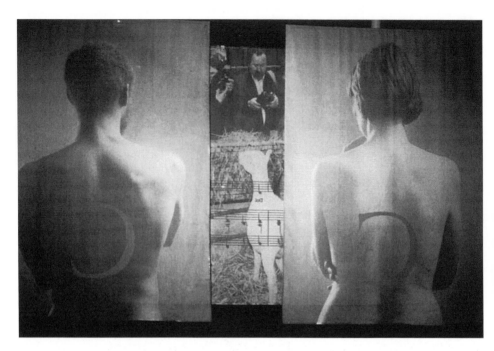

FIGURE 2.2. Carrie Mae Weems, detail from *The Jefferson Suite* (1999). DNA backs in installation, here with the RNA sequence imaged on adult human backs, like a brand.

instance, in Carrie Mae Weems's *The Jefferson Suite*, she prints semi-translucent black and white scrims that hang from the ceiling with a range of raced and gendered naked backs cut off just by the tailbone, with large red letters that represent different nucleotides of DNA and recall both slave brands and marks of whippings while the nakedness alludes to sexual desire (figures 2.2–2.6).

There is one single scrim with a staged photo of an actor playing Jefferson writing at a desk while looking at an actor playing Hemings in a dress with her back exposed, standing at the far end of the photograph. Other scrims reproduce photographs of Dolly, the cloned sheep, the scientist Charles Darwin, a ticker tape parade on Wall Street, the United States Capitol dome lit up at night, a duo of violinists in an orchestra, and a woman and a baby, among a few others (1999).

Here, Hemings's sexuality isn't so much elided as it is genealogized under the name but also beyond the frame of Jefferson and his metonymic representation of US national identity. The naked backs, the scene of Jefferson at work while Hemings is also, presumably at work in her role as his sexual partner, and the labor of science are all linked through the body, but also deeply

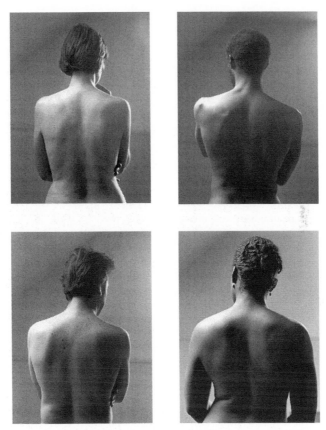

FIGURES 2.3–2.6. Carrie Mae Weems, "DNA Backs," detail from from *The Jefferson Suite* (1999).

through analogous if unequal terms of reproduction: photographic, capital, sexual, scientific, historic, ideological, cultural. It is the repeated image of the differentiated but naked backs that coheres the installation—sites of desire, sites of feminization, sites of vulnerability, figures of romance that evoke sexual pleasure and intimate proximity without exposing the taboo parts of the body actually involved with reproduction. It seems clear that Weems's work here is not claiming consent for Hemings—far from it—but nor does she claim the sexual labor of Hemings as devoid of pleasure, even connecting it to the production of classical music that "suite" references as well as several of the panels, and the valence of suite as "an interior, private space" (K. J. Brown 2015, 9). Jefferson, yes, is always identified as the "orchestrator," as are the big business capitalist interests in vulnerable bodies and scientific innovation. But the piece also suggests that such acts and such reproductions contain elements of pleasure and non-self-authored production of the meaning for the work.[14]

Calling on us to think with, under, and beyond the skin—in the blood, in our ears, in the microrealm of the gene, and across unclear juxtapositions— Weems's Hemings is at once in the center of and one strain of the racial imagination that Jefferson so desperately marks and that Hemings unmarks or must make and unmake in her retellings. Her body is source and resource; laboring and leisuring; object and subject; commodity, the means of production, and the coproducer of a sprawling set of social meanings and histories. Here, Hemings is connected, literally, to the stuff of life, DNA, for better and for worse. More than embodying contradictions, Weems's installation insists on less of an up-down, social-death-or-sexual-pleasure model, with its walk-through design acting as a way of experiencing multiple stories of Hemings and her legacy across these binaries. The pieces stage the significance of Hemings's sexuality to understanding not just a chronic lack of agency for black women but the ways that the uneven terms of enslavement and social death also created complicated, unpredictable strains of US experience, at the cellular level. The beauty of the photographs, or of the classical suite, scientific innovation, or the sexual event is in many ways like the scrims: ephemeral, unnamable, tied to the senses, undocumentable—sublime, perhaps. And yet the pleasure of looking both names the audience as complicit and defies the kind of proof that Enlightenment modernity insists on for the fiction of imagining race and sociality as narratives of progress.[15]

Though the decentering of consent can be read as a way to get around the foundational nature of black women's sexuality to concepts of freedom, sociality, and civic participation, or as a way of engaging respectability politics (whereby Hemings is only recoverable as the victim of assault or as the all-but-marriageable love object), we might also consider the ways that black women's sexuality through unconsent may be rendered present, though not necessarily through mimetic representation or emplotment of its usual routes through and in the body. A strategy of reading sexuality without bodies—a scene of (un)consent without sex—offers us a way to recalibrate/resequence thinking about the centrality of arguments about agency and black women's subjectivity to not just include sexuality, but to imagine sexual desires as places to renegotiate the very conceptualizations of freedom, where proving and disproving agency is not the end of the question of political and social "life."

I move here to the structural, in particular, to think about pleasure apart from the mimetic representation of bodies, to get at something more like the spatial in thinking through the in-between-ness of Hemings's subjectivity

FIGURE 2.7. Todd Murphy, *Monument to Sally Hemings* (2000). Photo by Andrew Shurtleff. This sculptural representation of Hemings stood in a visible location in the geography of Charlottesville, Jefferson and Hemings's hometown.

and how that uncertainty hinges on interpretation of the consummation of her and Jefferson's bodies. Space, in some ways, gives us a different scale than the individual-as-representative-of-the-collective mode of interpretation that shapes so much of the questioning of black women's sexuality and black political thought and action (McKittrick 2006). Space moves us away from the singular time and scale of the event without erasing contexts or bodies, instead resituating the view, the lens. Artist Todd Murphy, in 2000, staged a piece on top of the Charlottesville Coal Tower, *Monument to Sally Hemings*: he erected a steel frame on top of the structure, which can be seen from town, and draped it with a flowing white fabric (figure 2.7).

One might wish to read this as an abstract figuration of Hemings—and it is, to be sure, or can be read as disembodied but still enfigured (by the suggestion of a dress/a body) representation of Hemings. But one can also imagine it, and the constant figurations of Hemings, as structure, as architecture. Just as the dome of Jefferson's intellectual vanity project, the University of Virginia (an institution meant to reproduce other white male property owners in his own likeness), can be seen from his architectural vanity project, Monticello, the public figuration of a monument to Hemings is similarly suggestive of that which, materially, the enslaved built in and for the United States just as surely as Hemings is, in K. J. Brown's (2015, 29) phrasing, "a veritable industry of memory."

It is also a monument to commemorate violence and to make enslavement visible in a way that Monticello and UVA are still struggling to incorporate into a landscape of pastoral beauty, pleasure, and leisure that attempt to simultaneously narrate and marginalize enslavement as the producer of white male genius and freedom. But the translucency of the fabric, like the scrims in Weems's installation, also suggests beauty, sex(uality), and pleasure in what one cannot quite keep or document, in what one cannot prove, know, or restore, even as it is always already the constant backbone, the constant material, of intellectual imagination around black women's history. Murphy's piece is then both historical and counterhistorical. In many ways, it is about the difficult history of sexuality that Hemings's presence brings up—enervating, dangerous, ravishing, ephemeral but also undeniably material. It has endurance and frailty built into its structure—its story is not one of event but of duration and of the duration of difference in the narration of human genetic material, material structures, built space, and urban design and development.

The architecture of Monticello, too, offers us this material space in which to contemplate other forms of black women's sexuality. In early 2017, the Monticello Historical Association went public with its restoration project of what they purport to be Hemings's room, one that was literally made into a bathroom in the monument to Jefferson that receives thousands upon thousands of visitors a year. The actual decimation of this room by preservationists, who wanted to disappear evidence of both enslavement and the Hemings-Jefferson intimacy in order to preserve white bloodlines and somehow the antiracist character of the slave-owning but not slave-siring Jefferson, is laughable in its irony and in its transparently racist and misogynist motives, let alone its abjectionist replacement of the history of enslaved women's sexuality with the site of human waste relief. But with the announcement of this restoration, coming up at the same moment of the historic opening of the Smithsonian National Museum of African American History and Culture and various monuments to America's slave and racist past across the country, Monticello also traffics in its own version of corrective history, one that imagines that inclusion, proof, and evidence will displace the damage done, so to speak—even as DNA evidence has coalesced in articulations of, in the language of the Monticello docents, "the foundation's belief" that Jefferson was the father of Hemings's children. The historical site trades on the materiality of proof, of evidence—and is left with questions of how to represent in ways that balance, in Hartman's terms, the necessity and the impossibility of representing the history of a figure like Hemings even as it introduces new tours and a "Slavery at Monticello" mobile app that foreground the ample testimonies of enslaved people and the industry of enslavement on the mountaintop. Monticello chose to project Madison Hemings's words about his mother on the wall—at once visualizing evidence and insisting on its ephemerality, echoing Weems's scrims and Murphy's fabric. The projection is, after all the excavation, still a scrim. The curators also choose to throw the question of rape into crisis by representing it as a crisis— the word in quotes, designated as such to self-consciously mark its difficulty and the dissent around how to label the entanglement. Sure to enrage many, what Monticello now offers is a stark occupation of the space of Hemings's stripped-down maybe-room and always secondhand story.[16]

More recently, Monticello has sought to build up both physical and historical architecture around enslavement at Monticello, staging the Mountaintop Project to solicit ideas on how to best memorialize the enslaved lives at Monticello, as well as offering the "Slavery at Monticello" app that includes oral histories of enslaved descendants. It would not be difficult to problematize either these structures or their presumed markets, as they characterize Hemings as a "Domestic Servant and Devoted Mother" with an icon of a hearth and an opening sketch of a woman in a head wrap holding an infant that uncomfortably recalls mammy images. They also use Jefferson's handwritten account of her children from his farm book and a photograph of her descendants to represent her in the absence of her representability, begging the question of what scholars who are invested in black women's sexuality might make of the site's "historical" bedroom/public bathroom/restored monument as a space for black feminist studies to sit in, as a space where black women's enslaved sexuality can be deeply considered as an event of rape/unconsent and an enduring campaign of racial terror (which it undeniably was), and also as a space where other political desires and subjectivities might reside—those of vulnerability, risk, care, ambition, and other affects that can entrap and free, resist and submit, and that we, as critics, cannot necessarily assume to recognize at either pole. What does it mean for Hemings to be rendered consumable at these sites that have struggled to make her presence visible, in the diminutive forms made available—a room, an app icon—that are necessarily incomplete, partial, and politically unsatisfying?

Chase-Riboud (1979), in her novel, reconstructs this space for Hemings as a room routed through the private stairs that lead her to Jefferson's chamber—the space of his bed but also his desk—as a space of privacy, memory, reflection, feeling. She introduces the room in a chapter about its construction that begins with an epigraph from "founding mother" Abigail Adams (1776): "I always had a fancy for a closet with a window I could more peculiarly call my own." Not a plea for Woolf's whole room or her push for the labor of writing, Adams and Chase-Riboud seem to suggest a map of women's subjectivity and desire that hangs in the shadow of women's sexual labor, not as repudiation of it but as a space that also includes leisure and self-contemplation. Chase-Riboud imagines Hemings requesting rather than being remanded to "hidden" space:

> "I should like you to design . . . to build a room for me." I went on quickly, before he had time to respond. "A secret room adjoining yours where I may pass to and from without crossing the public hall where anyone who happens to be about may see me," I said. There was not a servant or member of the household who did not know that only I had access to the apartments of the master. I was mistress of his bedchamber and his wardrobe. His premises were forbidden to all, including his daughter. Yet I felt naked every time I had to enter by the public hall, always full of people: visitors, workmen, servants, relatives. It would be so easy to find me a little space of my own somewhere. I longed for the shadowed recesses and the vast apartments of the Hotel de Langeac with its endless attic rooms, secret corridors, unused apartments. Here, every space was occupied by slave or master. Twenty servants ran in and out of the main house, not counting all the other people, and even once a horse. . . . I recounted all this without stopping, as if I would run out of courage before I ran out of breath. (205)

Designing a space where she is neither "slave or master," Chase-Riboud places Hemings's desire squarely in the realm of the open secret—seeking not to shield others or herself from existing carnal knowledge but to imagine the unimaginable, to squarely inhabit a built space that could exist alongside the impossibly visible and improbably unspeakable life of enslaved black women's sexuality. A plea to be recognized and unrecognizable, this speech act does not to live up to ideals of bestowing upon Hemings political agency within individualistic liberal humanist privilege, nor does it repudiate some of its pleasures.

Chase-Riboud clearly does not place the scene or the site, only recently rematerialized at Monticello, as either feminist triumph or the pathology of false-consciousness. Instead, the room conjurs not so much escape or agency, but respite—a third space that is neither resistance nor submission:

> There I waited, accumulating my account of hours. My small treasures from Paris filled the room: the onyx-and-bronze clock, my Paris sofa and bedstead, the copper bathing tub that Joe Fosset had copied for me, my chests full of dresses I never wore, my linens, my bolts of fine silks and cambrics, my books, my guitar. There I was free, solitary, away from the multitude of the mansion. I savored entering his inner sanctum by my own stairway. Only in my official capacity as slave and mistress of his wardrobe did I enter by the public hall on the ground floor.
>
> Only after he had built the miniature stairway to my room did he discover to his dismay that the two new wings of his mansion had no stairs at all! He quickly ordered John to add a stairwell to each wing. It was barely wider than my own—a mere two feet across—and had to accommodate not only the bulk of his masculine company but the hoopskirts of his females. I thought of the great stairway at the Hotel de Langeac, that monument of rose marble I had fled down that March morning eight years ago. Only my secret room, with its passageway and tiny staircase, resembled the great houses of Paris, and it linked us to the past. Soon our private existence would give way once again to the demands of the public and of power but, for a while at least, I was safe, happy, hidden, and loved. (209)

Despite its status as built space, the room offers temporary refuge but not permanence of meaning, or even architecture. To claim love, pleasure, privacy, sanctuary, and solitude within the confines of enslaved existence not as resistance or agency, but as gifts that are deeply interwoven with the literal structures of plantation life and labor is to claim social death and sexual pleasure—even sexual "freedom"—as overlapping rather than always antagonistic structures. There is never a completion, for Hemings or for Monticello, as it was and is constantly being rebuilt, restored, expanded, redesigned.

This representation of Hemings's desires, appended to this imagining of the built space of Monticello, embraces the dangerous associations with concubinage—the negotiation of special privileges that may allow one a better or separate life than that of the "multitude" of enslaved laborers in exchange for sexual autonomy, as well as the ever present threat of such a contract, the ever-encroaching "demands of public and of power" and the quotidian domestic labor of enslavement that occupies Hemings's daily life at Monticello. The novel and perhaps the space of Hemings's room locates these limits—tangible and intangible—as structures of daily life that exist inside of and as constitutive of love and pleasure. They recognize Hemings's sexuality as encompassing all of what is and also what is possible, acknowledge her desires as including but also exceeding hailed notions of freedom and subjection from her own participation in liberal humanist life.

As Tillet reads in her "Black Girls in Paris" (2009) article and chapter (2012) on Chase-Riboud's representations of French relations to blackness during enslavement and colonialism, the novelist's view leaves room for romantic readings of transcendence—where France codes for a space of liberal humanist freedom and also where the Hemings/Jefferson "love story" stands in for late twentieth-century liberal reimaginings of miscegenation as a site where racism is/can be transcended, where love, as affect and narrative, can conquer the deep structures of racialized violence and dehumanization, including economic sanctions. But one must wrestle with Hemings's options as a limited set. Freedom in France gives her a life of uncertain labor in a space where she knows virtually no one, where she abandons her kin and natal connections for the uncertainty of free labor and the radical anonymity of urban sociality; bondage in Monticello offers her familiarity and a support system but the constant threat of the radical alteration of these bonds through death, sale, or any other vagary of white desire or embodiment. As with Gordon-Reed's (2008) delicate excavation of the Hemings story as one of emotional connection coded as love, the novel, too, has to navigate generic expectations of the appearance of this particular affect—expectation that, in Gordon-Reed's phenomenal terms, anyone believes it makes a "difference" if it is "love." Gordon-Reed's point is to question whether love alters at all the base structure of enslaved/master sexual relations and the institution of chattel slavery. It is to posit love, like the "dresses I never wore," as a useless commodity in the market of freedom and consent, but as an instructive opening on which to question otherwise the terrain of race, sexuality, and politics in the United States.[17] Given the poles of racial discourse that imagine love and other pleasurable affects at one end and racist systems of oppression at the other, Gordon-Reed as well as Kaplan (2009), in her reading of the place of erotic love in the novel, wants to be sure that even as we tell the story of Hemings, we refuse to give the impression that we should imagine enslavement as endorsing either side of that disturbed and limited range of readings as the object of interpretive completion.

Evie Shockley's poem from *a half-red sea* (2006) cited in the previous chapter, "wheatley and hemmings have drinks in the halls of the ancestors," mines this underrepresented lacuna between love and racist abjection (as if the two are opposites) explicitly. Sally, with her "parisian lilt (25)," must field the naked curiosity of her US audience even in the fantasy of the afterlife, as "someone gushes: *i have to know— / was it love? for you and thomas? or / you? susanna?*" (26). Twinning narratives of romantic love and platonic devotion that trouble the representations of Hemings and Wheatley, Shockley imagines the two figures, inebriated and sharp, turning the language of typology on the inquirer by referring to the question as a "kind" that needs to be classified (26), like black women's bodies and the degree of racial purity needed to be classified as white. But Shockley, in having both figures ruminate on Mark Twain's own culturally overexposed narrative of enslaved subjectivity and US fantasies of freedom, does not disavow romance narratives themselves, does not spend time proving them false, but rather pauses on the refusal to learn differently, to ask differently, from them:

> sally
> always says, *you ain't got to be*
> *smart to be among the ancestors. no,*
> phillis shoots back, *just dead.* (26)

This clever Hemings, watching and advising and delighting in her heirs from a Monticello-like afterlife setting, loves to "think" on a good story, a good romance—insisting on readerly practice as agency beyond evidence.

In another envisioning of Monticello via Hemings's sexuality, Lucille Clifton's (1974) poem, "monticello," a slight four lines, offers up not the scene of consent/unconsent, but a vision of its aftermath: the genetic reappearance of "Jefferson hair." Instead of a focus on Sally's body or will, the poem takes as a given, but also a starting, not end point, the absence of anything akin to agency in what amounts to a narrative fiction born from a historical truth—"this black sally" issuing Jefferson's children. "God declares no Independence," announces the first line, making the rest of the poem appear to be a non sequitur, a localized, colloquial three lines following philosophic decree. Clifton begins with the premise of enslavement as the human condition par excellence (not the ideal, but nonetheless the precarious basis of humanity), discounting inalienable rights or individual autonomy as givens or as progress narratives of political achievement. In focusing on the "branding" of Jefferson hair, Clifton also imagines black women as the subjective center of the experience of enslavement—moving the violent value of the slaver's brand to the act of reproduction under partus sequitur ventrem. In declaring the "natural state" of this new paradigm of the human subject, Clifton suggests ways to read Sally Hemings that do not rely on the moment of individual choice or subjection as the end point, the litmus test of human capacity. Instead, she imagines sexual subjection as the foundation—the territory—of Jeffersonian thought, his home, monument and memorial: Monticello.

One can read the trace of Jeffersonian violence through the hair as the domination of white supremacist history or as the literal red flag that signals us away from the site of individual rights and bodily autonomy, instead emphasizing the enduring material of structural racism. The collective responsibility, for Clifton, is to see, to reckon with texts Jefferson leaves in his wake, as enduring and as binding as the Declaration of Independence, to be used as interpretative tool, a living comparative model that US civic myth constantly holds up to itself—the part where "we" are ruled, lifting the veil of consent. Clifton's version of Hemings seeks no truth about her as individual, but takes her cultural representation—"this black sally"—for exactly that, with no interior that the historian can access or the political theorist can theorize out of. That sounds bleak, I realize, and it is, but it also refuses a plot of progress that in and of itself assumes access to individual rights and entitlements as the answer to America's problem with valuing black women. Clifton's poem opens a door to assuming subjection and precarity—unconsent—as the normative condition of the human, rather than the ascendant ideal of rational citizen. This normalization of unconsent is not to look away from it; quite the opposite, it is to assume it as the starting point for all conversations about modern subjectivity and governance. Here, Hemings becomes not the victim but the central subject (in all valences of that word) of the United States, the underpinning of the national imagination. Clifton opens the door to that precarity as the foundational unit of analysis, the public intimacy that marks subject and object relations in the violence of modernity, and from which further analysis must spring, not end.

Natasha Trethewey's (2012) poetic visits to Monticello with her semi-estranged white father in "Enlightenment" offer us another critical representation-without-a-teleology of the difficult intimacies that mark social-sexual life in the United States. In fact, the poem takes pains to mark the ways that looking for definitive evidence extends the racist base of Enlightenment thought to its experiential ends:

my young father, a rough outline of the old man
he's become, needing to show me
the better measure of his heart, an equation
writ large at Monticello. That was years ago. (159)

Taking the simultaneous acknowledgment and elision of enslavement during a tour of the estate house as a moment to mark the painful intimacy between white father and black daughter, Trethewey's lyric suggests that the analytic that assumes enslavement and not Enlightenment as a US ideal brings with it a host of affective and critical relations, including the more standard ones of trauma, anger, and denial. But in not assuming the recognition/nonrecognition of consent/unconsent as the end point of discussions of race and rights, Trethewey also imagines a temporality that endures, unevenly, between subjects—an intimacy that also includes humor, pathos, guilt, quietude, and change (Quashie 2012):

Imagine stepping back into the past,
our guide tells us then—and I can't resist
whispering to my father: *This is where*
we split up. I'll head around to the back. (160)

Trethewey's poetic architecture allows for difficult relations that are not prescriptive, but it is also rooted in a history where agency is not in question, because it is not present, and hence not *the* question to ask of black women's intimate relations or their political trajectories. She begins, along with other artists and authors, to imagine what a post-consent Hemings representation might look like, what forms it might take—something that Monticello itself has taken into its aesthetic projection of Hemings's room—an actual projection of words on white walls past a vague bust of a female form that could be read as refusing a "side" *or* as honoring the uncertain, competing, and likely destroyed historical evidence of Hemings's presence by refusing to fix her representation into permanence and proof.

The rise in white public acknowledgment of Hemings's role in Jefferson's life comes at a time when institutional change seems also to be wrestling with and incorporating difference—writ large as race, gender, and sexuality beyond white, male, and straight identities—into their own visible representations. As we've seen, that acknowledgment engenders Hemings's presence as one that demands certain disciplinary responses and narrative constructs—namely, imagining the romance of consent, even in its negation, in order to retain the hold of core US values of freedom and Enlightenment, and naming the violence of rape/nonconsent as a tactic of resistance and redress to the invisibility of black women's agency in institutional life. It is to romance that poet and critic Evie Shockley (2011) turns first to understand, again, the structure of Jefferson's words, life, and home:

> you
> named your home in a romance
> language spent 40 years
> constructing it and the myth
> of yourself (23)

Paired structurally with words from the Declaration of Independence, "dependencies" is a rumination on the facts of Monticello and the intricacies of the stories it tells about the dependencies of not just enslavement, but word and action. In other words, she focuses on Jefferson's agency rather than Hemings's, writing around the impossible verb—"had"—of their relations:

> i hear you had
> sally hemmings I hear you
> and she had
> six children (24)

The poem traffics in the parlance of gossip, of romance, even as Shockley's stark, simple verb "had" marks not the crux of the poem but part of the backdrop, the basic if not passive dependencies of writing/making the history of enslavement. Narrative history, fiction, and film have complicated the critical terrain, representing the moment of sexual consent or lack thereof as both a crucial but also not the only plot available to consider Hemings's legacy and recurrence in civic myth. Forms such as poetry, art, performance, and architecture have been, for this book, one place to look for representations of Sally Hemings that break even further from centering consent in both civic political myth and in analysis of black women's sexuality, while at the same time retaining focus on the deep violence done to black women's bodies by and through the democratic republic and its discourse. The public intimacies of these forms attempt to represent Hemings both as intimately imbricated into the fabric of national identity and as a laying bare of black women's foundational and transformative presence as both the material victims but also the conceptual founders of Enlightenment modernity. These modes of representation help us reread and refigure Sally Hemings without fetishizing consent or unconsent as the center of personhood or claims to rights/freedom.

Vulnerable Life and Futures of Black Feminist Thought

In a 2002 *Saturday Night Live* skit, Robert DeNiro, costumed, plays a smitten Thomas Jefferson attempting to ask Maya Rudolph's Sally Hemings out on a date. "What time do you get off of work?" he asks, to which Rudolph deadpans, "Um, never," followed by a full laughter from the studio audience. As one of many, many representations of this founding US "couple," but one of the few humorous ones, the skit takes liberties with historical accuracy (including Hemings's age and the fact that she was known to Jefferson for her entire life) in order to call forth the uncomfortable "scene of seduction" and its simultaneous discursive formation as a romance/courtship narrative and a story of enslavement that refuses the myth of consent. Sally's unconsent is mined for present-day humor—the irony of enslaved life and cross-racial romance coinciding in seemingly obvious dissonance to the presumed liberal humanist audience of *Saturday Night Live*—giving the audience the opportunity to recognize that narrative's continued presence in contemporary constructions of desire and sexuality by playing on De Niro's own very public celebrity romances with black women. But the skit also foregrounds the rocky ways the scene of un/consent is manufactured and repeated—how few the genres are that consider so fully the impossibility of consent without the arc of tragedy, or the triumph of romance.[18]

This chapter has asked what happens when we more deeply consider Hemings in definitions of black politics and black political subjectivity. If we, as critics, can imagine these representations of Hemings as a site for critical desires to find different attachments for thinking through black women's sexuality and black feminist thought, then, we might imagine, also, the materiality of so-called social death as the given mythic construction of all liberal subjectivity (not just its underpinning). If consent is no longer the vanishing point of freedom dreams, in other words, but a radical temporariness in considering both pleasure and subjection, then the care that it includes, follows, and fills in the gaps in between might be part of a politics organized around black women's political and material needs. Developing such a politics was the radical goal the Combahee River Collective named in its manifesto, a statement that stands as the contemporary of Chase-Riboud's narrative and Brodie's psycho-biography of Jefferson. In other words, repair might suggest fixing not the broken fiction of the system that is, but instead the acts of responsibility—institutional, aesthetic, and affective—that acknowledge and follow the uneven distribution and inevitable continuation of violence, risk, terror, pleasure, happiness, safety, privacy, solitude, and even death. It is to see vulnerability as the precarious conditions of living and being a political subject.

I argue this point not to delay or deter the practical politics of making a better world for racial and gender justice that redistributes both risks and pleasures, but to think of Hemings as a racial icon whose compromised position might augur a different way of organizing intersectional political imaginations. To this point, let us consider two very pressing feminist issues of the day through this lens: movements for consent, particularly Title IX/Campus Consent politics and the Black Lives Matter movement. Much has been made of the "loophole of retreat" of the garret in Jacobs's *Incidents in the Life of a Slave Girl*, and Katherine McKittrick's (2006) field-changing reading of the garret's geography of black womanhood in many ways defines the way that black feminist studies might want Hemings to resist within her limits. Can she escape? Hide? Do anything to leave her sexual oppressor while still, somehow, claiming intimacy with her family and children? While Jacobs strategically games the dictates of the politics of respectability, I remain cautious around critical attachments to her acts of resistance that wind up reifying only those who "fought back"—solidifying definitions of "real rape" and real resistance that rest on masculinist and militarist notions of individual agency, violence, and bodily autonomy that, as Jacobs's story itself suggests, deny the kinds of sociality and personhood women under enslavement and beyond can enact. Praising Jacobs's balancing act—a version of the superwoman myth of black women's resilience where she has it "all," with "all" being physical resistance as well as dedication to/sacrifice for her family—could be balanced by claiming Sally Hemings in her room as a complicated figuration of the limits of solely organizing around consent as a political goal. As Walter Johnson (2003) argues, every pleasure or joy or connection experienced by the enslaved is not and cannot be redress or resistance. But organizing around consent perhaps leaves us with overdetermined readings, and overdetermined questions of agency or submission, while reading with a starting premise of vulnerability offers a route to deconstruct the radical ways that the politics of liberal humanism and the politics of respectability have always had the disciplining of desire—particularly libidinal desire and illicit pleasure—placed onto the most vulnerable bodies. This we certainly hear in exhortations for women not to drink on campus, but one might also counter that the disciplinarianism of the campus refuses, as Jennifer Doyle (2015) argues, that much of what we call "sex" is lacking full or clear consent. The arc of campus discipline as feminist justice is thus understandable but also engaged in the very frames of the carceral state that not only disavow black bodies' rights but put the cure of punishment on display as a way of marking social safety that is almost wholly a lie to the precarity of women, especially low-income and nonwhite women, in everyday life.[19]

Similarly, Black Lives Matter, largely organized by queer and trans women of color, has also faced criticism in the form of gender politics, with many imploring us to #sayhername to discuss black women who have been killed by police in a representationally reciprocal act of recognizing harm. Though Black Lives Matter has steadfastly refused the discourses of respectability and singular leadership in finding good or better victims to uphold, they have also engaged in the understandable fullness of victims' lives as fathers, mothers, sons, and other kin arrangements that bestow value in black humans' connection to other humans, in the afterlives of feeling and mourning that such victims produce as well as in their affective productivity—someone loved them, someone found value in them. That so many victims are torn down at trial and in the court of public opinion because of their human desires—for money,[20] for mind-altering substances, for bodily safety (think: "but why did he run?"), for clothing choices—gives any feminist pause, as many of these discourses of dismissal similarly hang on the bodies of women as sexual assault victims. The construction of black women's bodies as always already on the verge of death and mourning might shift, then, not toward the disciplinarianism of law and proof (although it would keep both strategically in sight) as its ultimate pole, or to the limit of physical death. It might turn, instead, and as black erotics scholars have done, toward vulnerability, risk, and mutuality as its major narrative of the political, understanding that those, too, encompass violence and death. It might risk incompletion and impurity as its terrain (Brody 1998). It might imagine Hemings as its generative primal scene.

Rhetorics of (un)consent are one of the ways women and those with feminine embodiment have learned to live with and through radically vulnerable embodiment, some of which is strongly narrated through unconsent/force (sexuality under enslavement), and some of which is strongly associated with ideas of choice/risk (sexuality/pleasure and free will).[21] As black women's bodies seem to only become politically visible (and viable) when they approximate the violence and death done to black male bodies, or when the sexual abuse, violence, and terror of racialized violence to black women is held as their constitutive property of difference (their version of death-death), one might recast gendered social death as something that is posited not just through the eyes of white ascribers but in the eyes of black political thought. Such characterizations reinforce "real rape" myths that elide what it means to live under a system where consent is beside the point, what it means to live in a rape culture, codified by law or exceeding legal definition or recognition.[22] Marking the sexual terror and trauma under which black women's sexuality is constructed, we must also seek to mark the work of Sally Hemings as labor—not to valorize her role but to think about sexual consent within a system where consent to labor of all kinds is impossible, especially for enslaved workers, as well as the valorization of "free wage labor" that, in fact, still engages in myths of liberal humanist choice without offering many resources, alternatives, or protections.

Corrective histories of Sally Hemings then expose—intentionally and unintentionally—how sexuality and sexual consent are at the heart of the social contract: the right to marriage, the right to bodily autonomy, the right to work. To read Hemings's representations through this lens is to read all the ways that black women are left out of these rights and protections via enslavement, marriage, prostitution laws, and, in fact, rape laws. These rights and protections not only exclude black women in the eighteenth and nineteenth centuries under slavery and often beyond emancipation, but also enforce definitions of displayed virtue, physical force, verbal resistance, and other proofs of nonconsent that demand women's bodies be operated without pleasure at all cost lest they be considered always already inviting pleasure—their own and others. It is a pull that resonates today in the affirmative and campus consent movements. And yet many of these shifted narratives rely on the same tropes—trauma, injury, victimhood, black women's bodies as sites of subjection but not of subjectivity—again and again. Though deeply controversial (and in Kipnis's work, dangerously dismissive of any and all feminist concern with bodily safety or patriarchal hierarchy), feminist critics of Title IX and campus consent movements such as Jennifer Doyle (2015), Janet Halley (2016), and Laura Kipnis (2017) might serve as cautious jumping-off points for thinking about the inflexibility of feminist thought. These critiques, merged with the work of black feminist historians on sexuality, might push us to articulate a politics with a different emphasis on how representation operates as a corrective and within corrective genres. Maybe the narrative of rape itself, and making sure bodies stack up in tragic generic formation, might be questioned as the *sole* feminist political strategy around sexual assault.

As Ann duCille so provocatively interrogated the rise of black feminism nearly twenty-five years ago, black feminist thought might pause before making "black women" into "a kind of sacred text . . . a hot commodity that has claimed black women as its principal signifier" that positions black feminist scholars as disciplinarians and native informants "in which it can be readily validated only by those black and female for whom it reproduces what they already know" in a way that "both delimits and demeans those discourses" of black feminism (1994, 78). The critical cruel optimism of rehearsing the injury in the same way and hoping for a different effect is one that contemporary black feminist critics are returning to interrogate. As Erica R. Edwards (2015, 151) argues, "Black women's desire in cultural texts [acts] as, indeed, living text for a dying nation: as a potentiality that has been set to work both for the survival of the global state and for the survival of those abandoned by, or abandoning, or living in reckless abandon within the state." As the sign of "both premature death and surplus life" (142), black women's sexuality is the under-acknowledged center of the symbolic economy of black political life—and here I argue, all political life. Acknowledging black sexuality studies—particularly black feminist histories of enslavement alongside black erotics' willingness to dwell in abjection (A. D. Davis 2011; Scott 2010)—at the center of political inquiry shifts to claim black women not as the sacred sign of subjection but instead as the model for a political life that assumes vulnerability as its initial state, assumes the "impasse" (Berlant 2011).

Sally Hemings offers us this as icon, as figure: the way ambition, desire, pleasure, and bodily autonomy do not always look, and cannot be made to look, the way the best liberal humanist case would. She exists beyond repair, turning politics into "regard for another's fragile, mysterious autonomy" (P. Williams 1991, 432) and "an embodied enactment of mutual care and subsistence" (Edwards 2015, 160). In Chase-Riboud's (1979, 208) construction, this Sally Hemings "had long ago abandoned myself to that particular joy of not being responsible for oneself. I had struggled against everything that surrounded my master and was hostile to me. I had overcome the fearful disgust which his situation as master and mine as slave inspired in me." A critical practice of vulnerability, of assumed unconsent and the embodied living done within that assumption, asks how political theory might live and feel through an abandonment of liberal humanist subjectivity as master of the self, articulating black women's sexuality as the fragile state of possibility from which to build politics on, not against.

Chapter Three

VENUS AT WORK

THE CONTRACTED BODY AND FICTIONS OF SARAH BAARTMAN

"Business is booming / and I am not loved / the way I want to be"; this is the blunt assessment of the narrator of Morgan Parker's 2016 poetic version of Baartman. I move here from the oversaturated domestic imaginings of Hemings within a largely US democratic frame (with important diasporic excursions to revolutionary France) to perhaps the most globally overexposed figuration of black women's sexuality—and sexual subjection—Sarah Baartman. I trace Baartman's representational legacy to think through black women's political subjectivity in relationship to the promise of contract, perhaps the most fundamental legal tool of the modern nation-state and the object of Parker's above ambivalently resigned narrative affect. If democracy promised consent to be ruled as its ideological political foundation, contract was the postemancipation tool, as historian Amy Dru Stanley (1998) notes, meant to bring this register of consent in line with democratic practice. Both free labor and marriage are transformed by the affective force of contract as an agreement between equals regarding both divisions of labor and corporeal and financial protections—a language and a metaphor that the 1873 description by Madison Hemings of Sally Hemings's return to Paris with Jefferson, without the force of legal contract, as "the treaty" begins to evoke.[1] Madison Hemings's construction of sexual, reproductive, domestic, and affective labor between enslaved and enslaver as under the metaphoric guise of contract suggests contract's power not just through law but through custom—it acts, then, as Karla FC Holloway (2014) so suggestively proposes, as a fiction that defines and sutures the delicate relationships between race, gender, sexuality, and rights in the duration and wake of enslavement and the ongoing project of capitalist colonialism.

In early nineteenth-century England, a new performance sensation was entertaining scores of Londoners. She was Sarah (Sara) Baartman, better known as the Hottentot Venus. A Khoikhoi woman born in rural South Africa while it was under Dutch colonial rule, Baartman was brought to England to be exhibited as an "exotic" specimen of black African women's bodies. She performed strategically unclothed for the masses, to the outcry of abolitionists and others concerned with the dehumanized portrayal of African-descended peoples in the West. Though not technically enslaved (slavery was outlawed in Britain, but not its colonies, by 1810), Baartman created controversy during her own short time in England and France in her liminal status between enslaved and free as contracted performance labor. Her performance acted as a lightning rod for the charged racialized debates of the time over abolition and British national identity, resulting in a trial surrounding her possibly imprisoned body. The furor over her display in her own moment indeed prophesied how Baartman would become the cultural reference point for all black women's bodies—particularly their representation as radically different than white women's bodies—for decades if not centuries to come.[2]

This chapter pivots its focus on Baartman's performative legacy to the imprint of the criminal case brought against her employers/enslavers/captors. Shortly after Baartman began her London performance in 1810, a court case electrified London newspapers: a group of abolitionists convinced a British court to serve a writ of habeas corpus—charges of false imprisonment—to Baartman's "managers," one of whom was her enslaver in Cape Town. At issue in this case was whether it was possible for Baartman to truly consent to an employment contract with those who had so recently held her in bondage in what is now known as South Africa. Baartman's location at the border of legal recognition—neither enslaved nor a recognized citizen as a black African woman in England—was one that abolitionists of the day exposed as a gray area of labor contracting, one that threatened to undo the promise of emancipation itself as law, as a contract by the state with a group of nominally free citizens.

Baartman, the ur-subject of black feminist theorizing around sexuality, is central to the formation *and the critique* of the power of contract to produce something like equality or equitable relations in the contemporary world. Legally free on British soil, Baartman stood and stands as the test case to the limits of the labor contract within the context of emancipation in a radically inequitable social, political, and economic sphere. Unlike Wheatley's imagined trial, which has dominated and limited definitions of black freedom, the neglected scene of Baartman's "trial" questions not her body of work, à la Wheatley, but rather her ability to consent to her particular performative labor across South Africa, England, and France. What lure did contract hold, and does its discourse still hold, for black political life in these diasporic territories? What are the postcontract possibilities for imagining Baartman as a laboring, desiring, and desired subject in the political field of black feminist studies? In this chapter, I turn to creative reimaginings of Baartman in the arts, in public culture, and in law, in order to explore the ongoing, exhaustive, and exhausting critical desires and attachments around Baartman in black feminist studies. This exhaustion in many ways hinges on the inhabitation of Candace Jenkins's (2007, 16) "doubled vulnerability" of the respective threats to and possibilities of self that racial scrutiny and human intimacy pose not just to cultural objects—Baartman and black women being watched through the veil—but to critics worrying on the limited rubrics for visualizing black women's bodies at all. These vulnerable feelings that accompany an acknowledgment of the failures of contract and of representation as reparative political sites decenter the promise of equity and instead move toward a politics of quotidian, temporary, and uncertain relationality with black feminist pasts.

The trial about the validity of Baartman's contract lays bare the deeper implications of public discourse around the diminished humanity of African peoples as a factor in law beyond the enslaved/free binary. If Baartman was constructed as unable to contract her labor in this capacity in England, what agency can or should be ascribed to her—in her own time as a public performer dependent on her body for a living wage, in her public circulation as a cultural representation of European racism in the twentieth and twenty-first centuries, and in her case's role in shaping the very discourse of what constitutes a noncoercive contractual agreement for a range of disadvantaged subjects before and in the law? This question marks a map for thinking through Baartman's difficult subjectivity in contemporary human rights frameworks; as Baartman was neither a fully consenting legal agent/citizen nor a categorically enslaved person, her case stands at the limits of what and how to consider freedom, or consensual unfreedoms, in the face of a severely limited set of choices. This chapter questions why we want to keep focus on discerning freedom or its lack as a measure of Baartman's worth as a subject in black feminist political trajectories that take up her performative case. What might letting go of the promise and structure of contract, explicitly and implicitly, bring to the field? I posit from Baartman and her artistic legacy a theory of vulnerability, of the inevitable and complicated boundedness of self-performance, self-authorship, and living an embodied life. This orientation can change what, how, and why we read the political subject in black feminist studies and beyond.

As suggested in this book's introduction, Baartman has practically become a genre in the field of black feminist studies, one that seems to demand a clarity on individual agency and humanity, restaging Baartman again and again, "bringing up the body" to determine the representation's "value" on a scale of progressive political determinism between agency and subjection even when seeking other paths to narrate this familiar set of issues. I, too, have rehearsed these critical contractual obligations (Pinto 2013), so it is in the spirit of trying to imagine critical possibilities not beyond agent/victim, but which can make visible this contract and the competing critical desires that append to Baartman's body, that I proceed. This chapter then lays bare critical attachments and detachments that may disrupt critical duties, revealing them as contractual fictions that also require consent to that which is coerced—to invest in and attach to corrective histories of Baartman as if they can bring something recognizable as justice within or somehow wholly outside of a liberal humanist frame.[3]

The excruciating accounts of Baartman's racist exhibition, classification, and study linger as exceptional stories of racial horror—horrific lived experiences of racist fictions. A study of the public trial in which she appeared as a witness merges justifications that underpin the chattel slave trade with contemporary conversations about the effectiveness of the law as an avenue of justice for black subjects, immigrants, and those involved with human trafficking. The trial surrounding Baartman's possibly coerced presence in London complicated public understandings of the relationship between colonial violence and employment for the displaced/free in emerging exploitative markets for labor that one had little choice but to participate in if one was to survive. The trial also touches on the market for women's bodies that the modern West has either refused to regulate or make subject to the official protections of contract—putting women's work, in particular domestic, performative, and sex work, outside of the protective bounds of the state and yet subject to its social and often criminal judgment. Baartman's case tested the limits of law through her exhibition and the subsequent appeals to sexual decency, abolitionist ideals, and colonial constructions of racial "otherness" based on that indelible performance. Merging an exploration of Baartman's ongoing significance to the legal concept of contract with an analysis of her cultural representations, this chapter flows through representations of her trial in cinema, drama, and fiction. It then follows the international human rights argument for the repatriation of her bones to South Africa as another scene of contract's fictional promise and Baartman's repetitions as acts of exposure and repurposing of those fictions. Finally, I interrogate the legacy of critique surrounding her visualization in black feminist studies, and imagine what kind of critical "contract" she might represent beyond the terms of freedom/unfreedom, as well as the potential of critical fatigue from these constantly rehearsed scenarios of black women's embodiment that repeat the efforts and failures to secure freedom through cultural representation and through law.

The Contracted Body

As a touchstone for thinking about the history of race as a pseudoscientific field of study and for the pernicious sexual exploitation of black women in the West, Baartman's cultural legacy stretches across continents and centuries. Noting that, as Clifton Crais and Pamela Scully warn us in their 2009 biography, Baartman lived only the last five years of her life in Europe "yet she has come down to us in history captured by the icon of the Hottentot Venus, a supposedly paradoxical freak of race and sexuality, both alluring and primitive, the very embodiment of desire and the importance of conquering instincts" (1), we might pause to think about how Baartman came to stand in for black women's unfreedom. Sarah Baartman was born in the late 1770s during an era of violent transition, when the Gonaqua segment of her Khoikhoi linguistic group was moving from a pastoral social organization to one marked by the colonialist Dutch overtaking their land. It is due to this violence that Baartman was displaced to Cape Town, where she began serving as a domestic indentured servant to families, even as her firstborn child passed away. One of her enslavers, Hendrick Cesars—now thought to be a free black man who had "made good" in the multicultural bustling trading town of Cape Town—along with Alexander Dunlop, a white surgeon for enslaved laborers, shepherded Baartman into service as a performer in London. After receiving papers to travel from the magistrate, Baartman arrived in London causing a sensation for almost a year, when she then disappeared in the provinces of England, likely due to a pregnancy, the only marker of which is her baptism and marriage certificate, most likely to Dunlop. When her exhibition failed to take off again, Baartman seems to have resumed performing among a group of other self-managed acts, until she was sold to do private shows in France with a circus owner/animal trainer, who subsequently sent her to scientist/naturalist Georges Cuvier, who documented her as an anthropological specimen in life, and then, in 1815, after succumbing to what is assumed to have been acute alcoholism, in her death.

Her remains, including organs, bones, and a cast made of her body, remained on display until the 1970s in the Musée de l'Homme in Paris, and were "repatriated" after a protracted battle between governments for a public burial in South Africa in 2002, in a plot which is now a tourist site for the free state. Not only do traces of Baartman's history and legacy remain in newspaper cartoons, ballads, and art of her own day, Baartman's reference reverberates in a slew of contemporary poetry, visual art, fiction, drama, and public memorialization—as well as the critical texts accompanying these art forms that analyze this difficult, violent, antiblack trajectory. This chapter digs specifically into a question that Christina Sharpe (2010) has asked regarding Baartman's legacy and cultural returns: What is it that Baartman's body authorizes for the various constituencies that invoke her—from early nineteenth-century British abolitionists, to the twentieth-century South African state, to critics of black feminist representation.[4] Her performance catalyzed, as critic Zine Magubane argues and which Sharpe (2010), Zoë Wicomb (1998), and Sheila Lloyd (2011) all gesture toward as well, the tension between "the right to liberty and the right to property" brewing in the rolling postemancipation modern West (Magubane 2001). This chapter turns to the space of the trial to imagine Baartman's legacy through the trope of "the contracted body" as a way of thinking about black women's labor and their status as commodities through but also exceeding the frame of enslavement. What follows is my subsequent analysis of several contemporary texts that reimagine the scene of Baartman's "trial"— Baartman being the contracted body in question and not on trial herself.

In Elizabeth Alexander's (1990) poem about Baartman, she speaks the language of contract in relation to the long critical history of black women's sexual exploitation that Baartman usually signals and the assumed project of interiority that this poem is usually marshaled into: "I left Cape Town with a promise of revenue," the narrator offers, a decidedly unpoetic line in its engagement with the negotiations of capitalism in between stanzas about "London skies" and "damask plums" (4). But all three actually tie into the contract and the relationship between commodities and markets, and agents and consumers. Those critics who have focused on the trial have noted how Baartman reigns at the limits of liberal humanism and capitalism. Christina Sharpe (2010) notes how Baartman winds up standing at the intersection of coerced consent and "free" labor in her chapter on Baartman in *Monstrous Intimacies*, with her words in the court asking her to perform the lie of this connection. In the vein of recent work by Lisa Lowe (2015), who traces the racialization of the continuum between enslavement and wage labor (as do Stanley 1998; Steinfeld 2001; and Wong 2015), Baartman exemplifies both the promise and skepticism of contract labor as a more moral, ethical, and equitable system that relies on the construct of the contract—implying free will and consent—in relations of power during the transition from chattel slavery (Friedman 2004).

But as law and literature scholar Holloway argues, the affective and representational work of contract is deeply embedded in this presumed exchange:

> A contract is a legal form of a promise. In all, contracts are deeply regulated. They are governed by the principle of consideration (the value in the exchange), by obligation, representation, disclosure, and even fairness. In fact, with this constellation of duties, the law of contract may be the one area of law that most directly incorporates and composes complexities inherent in compelling narratives. A contract may even be judged as illusory. It has all the components of a fiction. (2014, 89)

The fiction of contract transitions the terms of enslavement—with human beings as property—into consenting, equal parties without resource redistribution and with only some recourse, as the very terms they sign up for are frequently nonnegotiable. This is not to deny workers' rights as an incredibly important strain of social justice under modern history, but to say that, as a covenant, a promise, between individuals, it affords protection mostly to the moneyed entity, and affords the fiction of liberal humanism, choice, under the guise of equality for the laboring body. As historian Emily A. Owens (2017) has argued, sexual labor of enslaved women often fell into an affective contracting she terms "promises"—yoking the fictions of legal contract to the assumed fantasy of sexual and romantic love in order to think of the thorny terrain of sexual labor for enslaved black women. Baartman performed in the role of a captured "savage," even as she was living her nonlaboring life in London receiving famous visitors. Both performances of self were necessary to expose at her trial, either claiming the performance as fiction or claiming the performance as truth. The fiction of Baartman as a discrete and consistent subject who either can or cannot consent—or can possess/not possess agency—is constructed, legally, as her "act."

Contract, then, functions as both a specific material document between parties as well as a structure and a metaphor for all social relations and organization. The habeas corpus trial involving Baartman as the wrongfully imprisoned or rightfully contracted body calls attention to the fiction of the material contract in light of the context and condition of social relations in which Baartman is supposed to be able to "consent" to her labor. In doing so, it points to the ways that even surface abolitionist thought and practice questioned the apparatus of the legal contract of free labor as a fiction in the given world, as do the few contemporary critics of Baartman who, like Christina Sharpe, focus their attention on the trial. She compellingly argues that

> even as Baartman has the legal signifiers of a free subject conferred upon her by the outcome of the case, in fact she remains captive to her employer and becomes a kind of theoretical limit case that helps define the limits of freedom for the English subject. However the case could have been resolved, the freedom at issue was never Baartman's own. Had she not been viewed as a free citizen under contract in England, she would have been set free (redemption operating here in the sense of the "action of freeing a prisoner, captive, or slave by payment") on the Cape into a state of near slavery. (2010, 82)

Viewed ever in the comparative mode—something akin to free and something akin to enslaved—Baartman does the labor of a stand-in, a representational pawn, in the semantics of contract law, as surely as she labors as the representationally tragic pole of black women's embodiment.

Baartman is the "contracted body," then: an intersectional subject who constructs herself and is constructed through and by discourses of law, capital, labor, embodiment, and choice. Rather than assuming Baartman as either the victim of or the resistor to some of the more unsavory desires named under this constellation, "contracted body" suggests both a state of subjection but also the material, social, and temporal nexus where Baartman is the founding conceptual figuration of labor relations, rather than its horrific exception.[5] And, viewed in light of Lisa Ze Winters's (2016) compelling rereading of the role of sexuality in negotiating the terms of financial and labor contracts for black women in the diaspora, Baartman's role in this trial shows the perils in considering sexual contracting as only violating a moral and corporeal contract, and not considering the ways that women's negotiations of freedom— or something akin to freedom—were, in Winters's terms, necessarily private due to their exclusions from large swaths of the public, political, legal sphere. Baartman then represents not the exception to subjects under/in contract, but the paradigmatic contracted body in her less-emphasized role as the litmus test between enslaved and free labor. As I will outline below, critical rushes to locate her in either the frame of injury or agency can reinforce the promise of contract rather than expose free labor—and freedom itself—as another set of fictional social relations between "the governors and the governed," in Foucault's terms.

"The contracted body" also exposes the fiction of the social contract, as it is based upon the exclusion of certain bodies and labors from this imagined

Rousseauian contract as the very philosophical origin story of the Enlightenment modernity experiment with democratic society. Rousseau infamously argues that "man" exists, naturally, in a state of complete freedom, but that individual freedom is saturated with violence and radical vulnerability. In compromising and agreeing to a "social contract," humans agree to give up some degree of individual liberty to a sovereign body—they consent to gain a measure of security, including secured property rights for all. Charles W. Mills (1997) has infamously unpacked said contract as a racial one, one between whites to secure white supremacy. Carole Pateman (1988) exposed the social contract as well as one "between men" (also noted by Sedgwick [1985] 2016). Both Pateman and Mills (2007) and the many critics and political theorists who have followed them push on the boundaries of contract as a promise of equity and civil society liberties, whether through law, market, or custom. I echo and extend them here to think about contract as a "social form," following legal scholar Sherally K. Munshi (2018), a fiction that governs intimate and critical labor as well.

Performing the Contracted Body

Wheatley's "trial" of authenticity becomes a critical crucible for discerning corrective histories that restore a Wheatley beyond whiteness. For Hemings, this crucible is how to read the scene of consent/unconsent in her initial sexual encounter with Jefferson. For Baartman, the primal scene of interpretation is her exhibition show, where Baartman's visual performance is of enslavement and animality. Victimized by a master, a whip, and (perhaps) a cage onstage, the performance is a repeated "act" of disciplining dangerous sexuality as well as a cannily knowing performance of that imagined taboo for the crowd, embodying the very question of what, exactly, constitutes agency and choice for an individual, let alone who may "deserve" it as a group (Garland-Thomson 1997). Pivoting to representations of Baartman's trial both extends and complicates these lines of questioning. In a field of limited choice and considerable coercion, a virtually unenforceable promise of a transnationally transacted employment contract is itself a performance before the law and for the social.[6] In a field of limited options for survival and access to notions of the good life, Baartman's possible consent to a different set of radically unequal, exploitative conditions than the violent genocide and exploitation of her native ethnic group on the African continent throws into relief and possibly into crisis the fiction of contract—itself a fantasy of freedom, a romance of consent—not just to expose but also to push the watching public: Can the contracted body

FIGURE 3.1. Performance scene in *Vénus Noire*, directed by Abdellatif Kechiche (2010).

be free(r)? What is the calculus between emancipation and contract? Baartman's performative legacy confronted and confronts us, again, with this puzzle. Turning from her stage show to representations of her trial provides a different angle to examine how contemporary renegotiations of Baartman foreground the unspectacularity of quotidian dependencies, the fictions of contract and choice that everyday, gendered life is made of that take different forms but nonetheless represent the impossibility of freedom as the starting point of political life, rather than the condition to be cured.

The trial scene of the 2010 French fictional narrative film *Vénus Noire*, directed by French Tunisian filmmaker Abdellatif Kechiche (figure 3.1), provides a means to trace these narrative arcs of contract, structured through humanitarian discourse, the filmic gaze, antiracist discourse, and racial-sexual iconography as much as by the legal terms of contract. Baartman enters the court case in medias res for her imagined testimony—though she herself never made an appearance or testified in court, only in an interview at her residence, a point I will take up in a moment regarding other corrective histories—with close-ups of white male magistrates in silence before a close-up of Baartman's character as she delivers her statement in Dutch, which is then translated into English by an actor in the scene.

This corrective history, in a film meant in part to commemorate and humanize Baartman, utilizes the close-up throughout the scene to put Baartman on "equal" visual footing with both the judges/court and audience. Even through mediated discourse—translation—Baartman is played not quite stoically, but with a kind of blank affect, one maintained through graphic scenes of sex work as well as other scenes of sexual assault during exhibitions where Baartman's distress and refusal are made evident even as the film refuses to pitch black suffering in a sentimental mode. The film employs the glimpse of interiority and feeling in Baartman's recrafting, but also wishes to expose the thorny intersections between bestowing interiority and the performance of free will that coalesces in legal personhood and the act of contract. As Hershini Bhana Young (2017) has recently argued about Baartman, will and desire can be read against the grain of the archive of her experiences, but to do so is not to erase the coercive context of such performances. Too often, if/as Baartman's corrective histories perform her self-knowledge about her bodily performance and its commodity status, she is hailed as a willing participant for everything that follows in an uncomplicated fashion in front of the law, and the nation, where "even a Hottentot can find friends to protect her interests," in the words of the magistrate in the film. If Baartman is subjected, subject to intimidation and/ or found to not have the capacity to enter into the contract, she is hailed as a subject to be "rescued" from the enslavement system Britain created and then denounced, only to be sent back to indentured servitude in Cape Town, foreclosing imagined desires such as to "have a child and raise it in freedom" (her testimony in the film), to legally, if not de facto, enter into the role of business partner, or to perform—or choose not to perform—as both artist and racial representative.

Contract, then, entails the promise of the good life beyond enslavement, even as it occludes and often forecloses the actual resources, including cultural capital, needed to attain such a fantasy, or what the "fantasy" of freedom, as Baartman lives and feels it, entails. As such, contract is exposed as one of the vectors of "cruel optimism," or the ways that what one desires from the neoliberal state is the very thing acting as an obstacle to attaining freedom (Berlant 2011). As the center of the film, the contract testimony and trial are also fictions: public performances of (semi-)resistance, of the power of the speech act to testify to the very system that has created the legal limbo of slave/legal person and to claim the distinction between the two as the promise of contract. The film stages the public drama of law, its power as cultural form and forum, and the ways that the courtroom scene is no less graphic or explicit a scene of her subjection than the scene of the violent prodding and groping of Baartman's shows. Baartman is still an icon, a symbol—but in the fiction of the filmic courtroom, fully clothed, she is imagined as spokesperson, more than a tragic dupe. The film, which marks its opening and continued force on the repeated filming of Baartman's naked form, both allows for this desire for resistant, respectable speech and undoes any "truth" clinging to said performance by encasing it in the deeply sexualized terrain of compromised, embodied existence that was Baartman's daily state of living. Rather than think of the jarring, insistent redisplay of Baartman's body as reexploiting her, then, one can read the film as imagining embodied exploitation—of labor, of sexuality—as the vulnerable state of being that Baartman exposed as paradigmatic subject of Enlightenment modernity, with its fictions of law, contract, and the order of sociality.

Infamously on the overexposed, nonrealist, and thingness side of the Baartman critical scale, Suzan-Lori Parks's 1996 play *Venus* also makes Baartman's trial the literal temporal center of its drama even as it is not her major plotline. Parks's version of the trial begins not with Baartman's testimony, but with the writ of habeas corpus—false imprisonment—brought by abolitionists against Dunlop and Cesars, her enslavers/employers/business partners. Habeas corpus is an intriguing charge here, as it is usually used to oppose the very state that the court represents—that is, the wrongful imprisonment by the state of a subject, or literally, *a body*. This is the express history of the law, and one of the reasons it is adopted early into, for instance, the constitution of the United States; its legacy in England is as a legal recourse against the royal sovereign. Heeding the law's call to "bring up the body" affirms that Baartman's testimony and subjectivity in Parks's vision are never confused as to their continued marking of Baartman as property, as object—as the body.[7] The question often asked of the play and of Baartman's performative legacy is whose spectacle is it to author, and to behold? Parks infamously costumes the play to include prosthetic buttocks that cite Baartman's racial-sexual significance and purported radical difference—the site of her celebrity, the site of her symbolic value as an anthropological specimen, the supposed exceptional-because-exemplary reason/impetus for her "contract." By synthesizing explicitly contract and body in the temporal center of the play, Parks marks both sites as fictions of freedom-seeking, not just in Baartman's own day as impossibilities to be escaped, but crucially in the contemporary critical moment of hyperconcern over the promise of representation that unsettles the lofty, unlibinal, "bloodless," in Elizabeth Anker's (2012) terms, versions of the human in rights and social justice discourse.

Parks published an essay, "The Rear End Exists," in January 1996, just before the play was produced, that emphatically, as the title suggests, insisted on the materiality of Baartman's body but also those of other black women performers such as Josephine Baker, from whose words the title is taken. On the side of the representational methodology that argues for Patricia Williams's (1991) adapted proliferation and Claudia Tate's (1998) plenitude, stands Parks, but also Nicole R. Fleetwood (2010) and Jennifer C. Nash (2014a), as well as artists such as Renee Cox who "bring up" the excessive "body" of Baartman to stage a refusal to look away or to repair black humanity. Instead of constantly engaging in the understandable critical project of "rehumanizing" Baartman and her body—which risks acquiescing to the narrative that black people must prove their humanness—I delve into the intersection of humanity/bare life (Weheliye 2014; Wynter 2015), where the very tenants of human and posthuman come into focus via Baartman's "trial" and the bringing up of her body over and over again.[8] While Kimberly Juanita Brown (2015) focuses on the repeating body of enslaved corporealities, her attention to the ways that repeating that body with a difference brings meaningful political shifts here are significant to thinking about the work of representations of Baartman and the risks of re-exploitation that critical and creative labor engenders. Baartman, envisioned in the play as a body with overwhelming appetites for sex, love, and chocolate, inhabits her thingness in Parks's narrative, wholly, but that objecthood does not demand a disavowal and stripping of desire and appetites as an answer to the rights/representation "problem."

Instead, Parks squarely refuses interiority as a project of respectability, as something that offers love, integrity, intelligence, and other markers of civilized humanity to confer worthy subject status. The play stages the question of what it means to be a body—a thing that can be violently imprisoned or can consent to enclosure, or any number of anti-"freedom" constraints. Parks digs into, and forces her audience to confront, what it means to be flesh, subject to but also the vehicle for sex, food, alcohol, money. Why do black bodies have to be inhuman in their goodness, she seems to ask, to gain access to "human rights"? Rather than an explanation of the off-putting of social and sexual appetites onto black bodies as a way of negating desire in the social and legal order, Parks stages the way desire's threat can overtake the structural forces that swear desires are aberrant, exempt from post–social contract freedoms. Parks, Darieck Scott (2010), and others who invest in the significance of abjection suggest how corrective histories invest in the neoliberal possibilities of legal/ capital contract as well as that of the autonomous body, as when Venus explains from a jail cell (that she did not historically occupy), "The Venus: (rest) Habeas Corpus. Literally: 'You should have the body' for submitting any of several common-law writs issued to bring the body before the court or the judge" (Parks 1997, 65); or as when the Baron Docteur—Cuvier—is staged as a witness who cannot testify as "I'm speaking on the Venus subject at a conference. You'll have to wait till then" (71). Here, Parks shows, as Soyica Diggs Colbert (2017, 75) compellingly argues, the links between commodified knowledges and the limits of liberal subjectivity—where even the law requires the vulnerable "for submitting" before it dismisses the charges against her managers. "[R]ules/not rules," as the law's construction cannot allow for the enfleshed challenge of the Hottentot's being, and being there, and then, and in that state of embodiment. Baartman exceeds the fiction of the labor contract with her public sexuality and exceeds the fictions of sexuality, desire, and choice in her labor as a contracted body.

Colbert's assertion that Parks's play—along with other cultural representations of black female enfleshment that "summon" and perform complex histories of black women's embodiment—"do[es] not always find recourse in flight but can also embrace the possibilities that webs of affiliation and disaffiliation introduce" (103) is potent here, in that it points to the ways that individual consent and agency become contemporary traps for both historical inquiry and future politics of black feminist thought. To put it another way, "bringing up the body" is, at this point, destined to be a repeated performance of black feminism, albeit a potential "repetition with a difference," in the infamous construction of Judith Butler (2016). Parks's play pushes black feminist methodologies on their attachment to the promise of contract in her insistence on the impossibility of cultural production, the public sphere of distribution, and the receiving audience entering into the picture as anything like equitable partners, and the impossibility of the play acting as a vehicle to freedom for black women beyond or despite, rather than through, "the rear end"—through embodied existence.

In the most traditionally humanist genre—and the most feminized form of the three genres discussed in this section, given its association with the sentimental and with romance—the novel *Hottentot Venus* by Barbara Chase-Riboud (2003) gives us interiority into not (just) the fictional feelings of Baartman herself, but into the complex networks of settler colonialism, indigenous displacement, racialized violence through war and through law, domestic labor, sexual violence, romantic love, marriage, humanitarianism, sexual desire, feminism, sex work, and wage labor that define and overlap with Baartman's legacy. Chase-Riboud has made a career of writing slave narratives that do not and cannot hew to the structure of bondage to freedom in easy, recognizable, or comfortable ways. She brings up different overlaps, coalitions, and alliances than Parks, Lowe, and Weheliye in her own emphasis on the quotidian abjectness of Baartman's daily life under the cover of protection, privilege, and free will. Her novel does, however, recall certain scenes in the narrative film, scenes that align some women in cautious relationships of responsibility to each other. Here, the trial scene also sits at the temporal center of the novel, but not of action—it is told through a series of transcripted affidavits and historical documents. Baartman's character, true to the romance genre, situates love as a contract that precedes the legal where "all I had in the world was my contract with him" (130). But this reliance on promise—romantic or legal—is undermined from the start of the text, where someone references her employment contract as "like a marriage contract" (134), as a false promise of protection not just from an individual but from the culture who constructed it, like wage labor, as a promise to protect power, not vulnerable populations.[9] In fictional encounters with a freed male slave who is part of the African Society, Baartman is imagined to be urged to "Flee! Flee!" even if it means "going home" to South Africa, where Baartman had already lost all family and where options, unlike for this legally freed slave or even Cesars in actual history, were severely limited by her gender and her previously enslaved/indentured status, as well as her ethnic identification within Cape Town culture and Dutch colonization.

Finally, Chase-Riboud's Baartman is urged after the fact to reconsider her marriage to Dunlop by another female performer—a white woman who lays out the minimal rights and protections that Baartman stands to lose in moving from employee/laborer to wife (even as she assumes Baartman and herself would be equally protected under labor laws in practice).[10] In this one act of "consenting" to the marriage contract with Dunlop, Chase-Riboud's Baartman forfeits in future perpetuity her consent, sexually or financially. Under coverture, the temporality of the marriage contract absolves—and, really, dissolves—demands about contract and rights and blurs the line between bondage and contract, a line which is imagined, as Amy Dru Stanley (1998) puts it, as "freedom." A woman consents, through the marriage contract of the day, to give up all claim to her financial freedom and indeed personhood, and yet marriage is virtually compulsory to survival as a "free" woman in the era. Away from any other networks to intervene beyond the law, such as kin,[11] Chase-Riboud's Baartman has only the promise of Holloway's fiction of contract and its gendered, racialized, sexualized, and monetized articulations of possibility in which to form her legal-social connections. The intimately con-tracted body, rather than the seemingly disembodied rational person of legal personhood, sits against the temporality of a singular event of "consent."

Baartman, in these representations, is at the heart of contract's exposure rather than the victim of her own—not as resistant or oppositional force, but as a subject who might imagine, feel, and desire political being and social intimacies that cannot be measured or advocated for in the terms of contract alone. The attention paid to Baartman's impulses, desires, or lack thereof, in each of these creative articulations of the trial does not have to read as just an attempt to bring evidence of humanity, the cycle of "proof" that has faltered in the uncertain legacies of both Wheatley and Hemings earlier in this book. Rather, the attention paid to affect through the close-up, through an atten-tion to libidinal appetites, and through willful interpretations of sexuality and romance as that which contains risk and violence in its attachments are ways of understanding relations that include but do not strictly yield to the promise or the inevitable failure of contracting freedom through law. These represen-tations agree with Christina Sharpe (2010) in the lack of remedy for the vul-nerable body of Baartman and further suggest reading practices that might not end on the failure of contract but on investigating a politics of what is left in its wake (following C. Sharpe 2016)—the living and dying done once we acknowledge contract as a social form, not just a legal one, is bankrupt in its capacity for black women's embodied freedom. The kinds of social relations contract can and does broker let go of the fiction of negotiating permanent equity between consenting persons.

Baartman's Value and International Human Rights as Contract

The above stagings of Baartman's trial rehearse contract's promise as a legal innovation to replace older relations of property and servitude that run along the same routes of relationality with the cunning exception that contract re-quires the coerced to perform consent to their own objectification and then fetishes consent as an achievable, ideal, permanent political goal. This dynamic resonates, too, with the representation and analysis of the drama surround-ing the deployment of Baartman's posthumous body within the more con-temporary, twentieth- and twenty-first-century discourse of international human rights, complete with treaties, international courts, and the public theater of the politics of memorialization. As international human rights law is notoriously unenforceable and aspirational, Baartman's perverse point of struggle within it forces us to think of contract, again, as a fiction—as doing cultural work not just in a strict, legal realm, but also as it is engaged in the management of peoples, resources, and rights that are constantly being negotiated through the cultural realm in the form and vehicle of black women's bodies, here engaged as art and art object itself.

Baartman's human remains were kept in France after her death and autopsy, where they were displayed by the Musée de l'Homme until 1971, but were not returned when the exhibit closed. The nation-state of South Africa, postapartheid, publicly petitioned for and successfully fought for the "return" of her remains, which were interred in 2002. In this way, the afterlife of Baartman in the late twentieth and early twenty-first centuries is both highly representational and symbolic, but also deeply material in that it is about the struggle over her bodily material. International law, human rights, and death-bound subjectivity are cathected around Baartman's body and figure in the twenty-first century in surprising permutations of contract between nations, and including international agreements about postwar and postcolonial laws of ownership, which exceed the temporal and political boundaries of nation-states into the realm of geographic and cultural sovereignty on the international stage. The debates, presentation, and reverberations of Baartman's remains and discourses of belonging are rooted in the complicated history of colonialism, indigeneity, and the promise of the nation-state in South Africa. Baartman's juridically bound movement and juridically identified body speak to the innovative possibilities and political limits of contract in the recasting of the black political sphere.

These moments provide the means to think through, with Hershini Bhana Young (2017) and Meg Samuelson (2007), some of the legal-political dimensions of Baartman's latest performances—ones also overmanaged by masculine declarations of meaning and calls for interpretation that claim her for the nation-state and for political identities and identification through her body. When then president Thabo Mbeki spoke at Baartman's "funeral" in August 2002, he spoke in terms of the political contract that Baartman's remains represent:

> This means that we still have an important task ahead of us—to carry out the historic mission of restoring the human dignity of Sarah Bartmann, of transforming ours into a truly non-racial, non-sexist and prosperous country, providing a better life for all our people. A troubled and painful history has presented us with the challenge and possibility to translate into reality the noble vision that South Africa belongs to all who live in it, black and white. When that is done, then will it be possible for us to say that Sarah Baartman has truly come home. The changing times tell us that she did not suffer and die in vain. Our presence at her

graveside demands that we act to ensure that what happened to her should never be repeated. This means that we must act to restore the dignity and identity of the Khoi and San people as a valued part of our diverse nation. It means that we must act firmly and consistently to eradicate the legacy of apartheid and colonialism in all its manifestations. It means that we must not relent in the struggle to build a truly non-racial society in which black and white shall be brother and sister. Our presence at this grave demands that we join in a determined and sustained effort to ensure respect for the dignity of the women of our country, gender equality and women's emancipation. It demands that we defend our democratic order and our regime of human rights with all necessary means. (2002)

Mbeki weds the enormous contours of the moral and political contract to Baartman's "story" and to those witnessing the burial of her remains in South Africa to the only and acceptable trajectory of human rights. These rights "demand," he suggests, an absolute interpretation of Baartman as "defenceless," "lonely," and on a "voyage of misery and death." In fact, Mbeki takes the mourners/audience through the proper affects of nationalism—where one should feel "joy" at Baartman's return "home" and then "courage" to speak of feelings other than joy surrounding the racist, misogynist, colonialist story of Baartman, and then a swell of national feeling through civic participation. Many able scholars have taken Mbeki and the South African postapartheid constitutional and political discourses to task for their lofty language unmatched by action (for instance, against a growing AIDS crisis or providing for the health, safety, and education of women and LGBTQ citizens). These critics show how Baartman's remains and her figure are deployed for political posturing and gain unmatched by resource commitment (Hoad 2005; Samuelson 2007; Young 2017). Several have noted the lack of agency ascribed to Baartman even in these recovered national-political moments of "healing" and the way she is reanimated as a passive, tragic victim without a recognition of her complex personhood (Young 2017).

This is performance of corrective history as contract, performance asserting a legal and cultural agreement that is always unequal or affectively bound, rather than as an ultimately equalizing act. Baartman's repatriation and the political theater surrounding it have been the focus of commentary from a group of South African and black diaspora scholars in complicated ways that mirror the skepticism of her performative legacies.[12] This scenario plays out, as Christina Sharpe outlines, as a problematic scene of redemption and political hope for critics and activists/citizens, with public coverage from the likes of the BBC, emphasizing the corrective history such repatriation engages. Says one indigenous activist, Matty Cairncross (*BBC News* 2002), "We have a rich history and culture which needs to be revived and shown to the world. We need to hear more stories about forgotten people like the Khoisan in books and theatre to correct the imbalances created by the previous system of apartheid." She continues, "The return of Saartje Baartman to South Africa is a victory for all South Africans and indigenous peoples of the world. It's an historic moment for everyone, especially for women in South Africa. She can be a unifying symbol for us." From the local indigenous peoples to the national to the world stage, Baartman's "return" comes to stand in as a narrative of historical repair, where her return becomes the fulfillment of a type of cultural-political contract, whereby to gain her right of return is, in the words of Mbeki, "to restore to our people and the peoples of Africa their right to be human and to be treated by all as human beings."

Such a tall order in the project of "nation-building," as Wicomb (also the author of the 2002 novel *David's Story*, in which Baartman's history features) puts it (1998), and human rights expansion is destined to produce disappointment and deconstruction. Both Hoad (2005) and Christina Sharpe (2010) attend to the temporality of such a public commemoration and how it focuses on the past in an effort to obscure the contemporary political issues that are born from the very legacy of colonialism, including Victorian mores about sexuality and racist underdevelopment, xenophobia, and full citizenship rights in South Africa itself.[13] The resonant critiques above question how this iconographic political work is done through both the language and the law of contract as the sign and limit of human rights. But the material remains of Baartman—as black object, as the thingness of blackness—become a site to remake political investments in contract though the very bureaucratic and intellectual innovations in international law that colonialism wrought and that define, in part, black political futures. Here, then, the focus on Baartman's bones tells a different set of stories about the construction of black "homes" for black feminist thought and how, critically, if distantly, the field might engage with the fiction of contract to rethink the valuing of black women's bodies in the liberal humanist market.

The tail end of Mbeki's speech is far less inspiring in its rhetoric, seemingly making the rounds of bureaucratic entities that had a hand in Baartman's repatriation. What is astounding, again, is the breadth of those acknowledged—the level of legal, bureaucratic, local, and international organizations dedicated to the fulfillment of the performance of death-bound subjectivity attributed to Baartman by her return—and the ability to "heal" and move on to a future state only after the dead are named and claimed:

> On behalf of the Government, the Parliament and the people of South Africa, I am privileged to convey our heartfelt and profound thanks to the Government, the Parliament and the people of France for agreeing to return our Sarah to us, and for living up to the noble objectives of the French Revolution of liberty, equality and fraternity! On behalf of our Government and people I also extend our gratitude to the Minister of Arts, Culture, Science and Technology, to the delegation that received the remains of Sarah Baartman in Paris, including our Ambassador, the Reference Group, the National Khoi-San Consultative Conference, our National Defence Force and others who have contributed to the success of this occasion. I would also like to thank the Premier of the Eastern Cape, MEC Balindlela, the rest of the government of the province and the Mayor and Council of Hankey for everything they have done for this solemn ceremony to succeed.

The undefined "ancient freedom" that Baartman represents and makes whole in her bones and her burial emerge here as the "gift" of freedom that French diplomacy and liberal humanist ideology are bestowing on her, and on the nation (Nguyen 2012). But the list also functions to highlight the sheer labor of contemporary democracy and its languages of "success." This list is a litany of the neoliberal entities and performances required to prove, assess, and stage Baartman's value as both narrative and material possession. Lisa Marie Cacho (2012, 4) argues in a different context about the criminalization of non-white US populations, that "human value is made intelligible through racialized, sexualized, spatialized, and state-sanctioned violences," that law is frequently the means used to define, assign, and assess said social value, and that no act to restore value to a member of those defined as of little value can do more than validate the existing system. Baartman's bones represent a unique case of advocating for value not just in the forms of the struggle of her habeas corpus case—there arguing the value of her consent to a labor contract—but in finding a way to articulate the value of Baartman's remains through and exceeding international law, and her body's international, national, and political value in the contracts that bind but are also "promises" and fictions between the contemporary world of nation-states.

The promise of contract then becomes not to make equal or fair but to mark, instead, the relations that lead to the act that the contract covers—to make visible, to leave a trace of the uneven relations that define living and life, as well as death and dying. The contract is an archive, then, in all of the messy senses of the term as a colonial invention and resource, but also one that might look not to the promise or the failure of equality but to the invention of new modes of relation. The contract is a technology of producing subjects that is appended to liberal humanist recognition, because it was invented by and through that system, but that does not always have to be employed or centered as such. Instead, reading and interpreting contract can refuse to recenter roots or boundaries of ideal political subjectivity—as the idea of "home," and its "ancient readers," before contact and contamination by the West is so frequently posited to specifically disenfranchise black women and queer peoples in the postcolonial world.

While Folarin Shyllon's (2006) essay on looted sub-Saharan antiquities returns and ultimately trains itself on an argument about the collusion of postcolonial officials and academics in the valuing of the objects beyond return to homelands, it also lays out the incredible bureaucratic systems that lie as obstacles in the process of legally arguing for the return of said objects. These legal gymnastics rely on contracts—official and customary—between nations in a human rights system meant to address racial genocide (largely invented in the wake of the Holocaust, but which also and clearly applied to colonial legacies once human rights frameworks were established after World War II [Weheliye 2014]). As Margaret Clegg and Sarah Long (2015) address in their work, contract is here also an act of interpretation, where "the concept of respect, which is used in the statutes, as well as in the Human Tissue Authority Code of Practice of Display, is undefined but is one of the most important points of interpretations. Respect is difficult to define; how an individual interprets respect will depend on a variety of factors including their personal experiences and sensitivities, community and religious origins as well as their moral and ethical compass" (xv). This "respect" may come up against the "caring for and understanding" (xv) of a given museum's collection in the way that "respect" is configured as "a recognition of our humanity whether we are living or dead. . . . It is about consent, recognizing different concepts of importance and value and being open to understanding those differences" (xvi). To answer one vague, variously interpretable concept of rights ("respect") with another ("consent," which was unpacked in the previous chapter) seems appropriate in this thorny conversation about contract, its duration, its meaning, and its own variable interpretative qualities that offer it up as a promise and practice of rights—a fiction.

Like Anker's (2012) sensitive interrogation of attachment to the terms of human dignity and bodily integrity, I do not seek to set right, repair, or remedy the co-optations of Baartman's material body. *Infamous Bodies* also does not propose the teleology of death-bound subjectivity as origin story and end point in its investigation of the questionable terminologies of rights discourse in relationship to Baartman—nor does it contest the narrative accuracy of said claims. A long legal struggle ensued over Baartman's bones—over their symbolic interpretation and the legal interpretation of human rights law and international law that attempt both to impose a bureaucratic and definitive system of repair and to enforce recognition that will "fix" the problem of Baartman's life, death, and dead body as it inhabits the world. What I mark in thinking about this struggle is how imagining reciprocity through the terms of the law or some inviolable term of rights—respect, dignity, and the like—enforces interpretive norms that are bound to "fail" as universalizing litmus tests due to the very terms of "difference" that Clegg and Long suggest. Such an impossibility marks misunderstanding, or the very risk of interpretation, as the rule and not the exception. This is the political that black feminist thought represents, even as it struggles with the radical instability of representation. Rather than end at misreading as diagnosis, and hence default to an argument that to restore rights is to restore right reading, I suggest leaning into misinterpretation as method. The critical energy surrounding Baartman is one that theorizes not right reading but the ongoing fatigue that accompanies critique when one sees the political not as a realm to be restored, but as an ongoing fiction—a critical fabulation that can cut through not just the most obviously generative of black feminist representations of difficult histories like Baartman's, but through critical work and its critical contract with social justice to produce a better world through better readings, and naming better objects. The critical terrain of black feminism is also inflected by a weariness and wearing down as it survives and lives through institutionality, repetition, and the illusions of choice and performances of consent demanded through the very form of academic critique, no more so that the fictional and yet materially bounded imperatives of legal contract.

The "Cultural Contract" of Critique and the Possibilities of Black Feminist Fatigue

A range of performances of consent to contract both expose and think otherwise about investment in better representation as a "cultural contract" to be enforced. Taking Grace Kyungwon Hong's (2015) warning and description seriously—that we cannot imagine anything we call "politics" outside of social value, or what she calls "the allure of legibility"—I'd like to pivot here to another contract, this one defined as a cultural construct around what Peggy Phelan ([1993] 2003) terms "the lure of visibility" and the dominant focus on representation as both the problem and the solution for antiracist and feminist political agendas—a fallacy that scholars such as Fleetwood have pointedly challenged in their own work. In *The Invention of Women* (1997), as well as in her foundational collection *African Gender Studies* (2005), Oyèrónké Oyěwùmí argues that the West's obsession with the body comes from its preoccupation with sight as *the* sense of knowing. She writes that "the body is the bedrock on which the [Western] social order is founded" (2) and offers an incomplete but suggestive account of alternative dominant ways of perceiving the world (she rests on the tonality/focus on the auditory of Yoruban culture) that might decenter the body as the site of order and of difference. She laments the un-examined reuse of what she deems "body-reasoning" that allows the Western definitions of the body and sight to dominate and naturalize discourses around gender and feminism, while simultaneously lamenting their seeming inescapability, even in the very pages of African feminist theory to come in her own edited collection.

Oyěwùmí's dual articulation of the often unacknowledged Western—and liberal humanist—contours and limits of discussion of gender and the body in contemporary discourse alongside the difficulty of escaping those conceptual parameters in the field as a whole encapsulate the fatigue that many critics face when trying to say something "new" about Baartman and her symbolic legacy. It also confronts, specifically, the fatigue around repeated entanglements with the representational economies—and antiblack scopic regimes—of African and African diaspora women's bodies. This fatigue, as it is theorized by Nash (2019a) as a byproduct of intellectual defensiveness, surrounds the "cultural contract" that adheres to black women's reparative-minded representation and the demands of black feminist response. Baartman's body in many ways stands as a litmus test of these demands for better representation and immediate critique of dominant culture's repeated failures to represent black women's subjectivity differently; her celebrity also marks a growing black feminist critical fatigue around agency and representation.

Fleetwood (2010) astutely describes the critical impulse that seeks both cause and cure in the realm of (visual) representation. And, like Fleetwood, the field might choose, then, not to turn away from representation but to try to make transparent critical desire to find a better or purer version of it so as to fulfill an imagined political contract. Instead we might focus on interpretation that questions critical compulsions to comment on the good or bad of her representations, instead trying to imagine the terrain of Baartman studies that might exist apart from what is in breach of the ethical contract we, as critics, are to conjure.

I say this with grave trepidation, since outside of black feminist discourse, the continued "casually" racist renderings of Baartman and her visual legacy still abound, whether it be in a Swedish corporate cake or the *New York Times* review of Parks's restaged *Venus* (Brantley 2017). As one think piece against the review argued, in the language of correction we have come to know throughout this book's pages regarding black women celebrities: "Baartman is not a Kim Kardashian of another era, nor did her figure afford her the same fortune. She is a significant fixture in our history, and the retelling of her story should be used to acknowledge how the Kardashians of the world are able to make their own fortunes by mining blackness and profiting off of the same aspects which have been cited as reason enough to dehumanize us" (S. Brown 2017). This objection to the review both counters the tone-deaf tweet (since removed based on backlash) that click-baited by aligning the two figures of Baartman and the Armenian American reality star Kardashian and the review text itself, which is worded as a warning to women about how various difficult-to-achieve beauty ideals will both require incredible labor and endurance, but may also lead to precarity and ruin. The critic's cheekiness belies, of course, the responsibility he puts onto women themselves to regulate the consumption and distribution, let alone the formation and interpretation, of their own bodies. But the critical response—one of many—that uses the familiar terms of "should" to denote the prescriptive boundaries of a presumed collective agreement in black feminist thought about the story one "needs" to tell about Baartman also eclipses the play itself, which seeks to expose the racist history of Baartman as well as the critical desires demanded of proper feminist reckonings of her body and her body of work. In the persistent cycle of racist representation and antiracist response, of which this is just one minor but illustrative node, this prescriptiveness and imagined contract between black feminist studies scholars about what constitutes the stories that *should* matter in the field is in and of itself telling. It is a dynamic that, within the field, stands as a critical desire, as an imagined, resistant unified front against white patriarchal supremacy and its own demands for narrative control and prescriptive political value that assume reasonableness and like-mindedness—a liberal humanist performance of critique that is itself a contract, a fiction, a freedom plot that will never be fulfilled or fulfilling.

Baartman's story, along with her infamous body that spurs such calls for corrective histories, not just stages a necropolitics of colonialism but also interrogates what is promised in corrective histories about these lives and deaths. What is it one might seek to "repair" by redeploying Baartman as icon? How

FIGURE 3.2. Hank Willis Thomas, *When Harriet Met Saartje*, woodcut (2009).

are critics and artists trading in and on her for critical desires to be fulfilled, however ethical one may find those political appetites? This is the work that is performed by both Christina Sharpe and Samuelson in thinking about the impossibility of narratives of national redemption or postcolonial triumph. Hank Willis Thomas's *When Harriet Met Sartje* (2009; figure 3.2), the meet-cute title (which is itself a reference to the staple film of white US romantic comedy) of his woodcut that represents Baartman and Harriet Tubman next to each other, might also help navigate this terrain of critical fatigue.

The constant return to, and reproduction of, Baartman's image and the debates about her image represent a site of black feminist critical fatigue around the economies of tragedy and heroism so starkly represented in Thomas's woodcut. What other relations could we imagine across the time, geography, and cultural receptions of Baartman and Tubman, it seems to ask even as it engages the comparative mode?

In *The Frenzy of Renown*, Leo Braudy (1997, 11) suggests that fame is created through "the 'contract' between performer and audience." Turning to the representations of Baartman in the visual realm and the critical scholarly audience that receives, interprets, and reinvests in their images and meanings, I parse out here what this critical cultural contract entails, the very meanings embedded in its obvious and less obvious fragilities. The visual evidence of Baartman is all drawn—literally, figuratively—from the antiblack imaginings of her performative era in Europe. Thomas's laser etching comes from the infamous political cartoon sketch of Baartman being ogled by a variety of British men, for instance, and then there are the likenesses from the pens of Cuvier and his students. In the contemporary moment, debates about reimaging these constructions remain difficult. But if renarrating them remains inevitable in scholarly work on her history, the politics of representation—whether digging into the antiblack enfleshment of these images or attempting to evade corporeal presence[14]—returns again and again as her contracted body's critical, tense domain.

One interpretation of Thomas's juxtaposition imagines the Baartman image and the Tubman representation as oppositional—visions of victim and agent, "excess" and resistance, abundance and agency/control. Following Fleetwood's (2010) and Daphne Brooks's (2006) reading practices of finding not agency but "viability" in the "materiality" of black women's corporeal representation, Thomas's title and the positionings of each figure in three-quarters profile facing each other but looking outward suggest other intimacies, other connections, other (after)lives for his subjects. One could read the piece as staging a genealogy of black women's embodied subjectivity, staging a range of publics that are not in opposition to each other, but in dialogue about what it means to occupy an endlessly comparative mode of critique that emphasizes exclusion, loss, death, and injury and yet seeks visual and public markers of opposition and resistance rather than shared, inevitable misinterpretation, and missed interpretations.

Thomas's piece also attempts to both highlight and dislocate the "scopic regime" (Metz [1975] 1982) of the naked black woman's body as the primary black feminist terrain of injury, critique, and critical fatigue. In Baartman's out-of-historical time "meeting" with Tubman, I question the driven permanence of the cultural contract between performer and audience, recognizing not just its radical reliance on interpretative practice but the ephemeral temporality of the public sphere and its cultural and political desires. Baartman's enfleshed

FIGURE 3.3.
Renee Cox as
Baartman in
Lyle Ashton
Harris's *The
Good Life* series
(1994).

naked body (Levine 2013) becomes the unquestioned sign of her enduring injury and exploitation. But another set of artists have imagined Baartman, such as in Lyle Ashton Harris's (1994) *The Good Life* series (figures 3.3 and 3.4), in conversation with other ordinary, injurious, intimate, and heroic versions and visions of black life, including Toussaint L'Ouverture, the heterosexual black family, and the queer artist. This piece, so often ascribed just to Renee Cox and not to Harris, is the kind of contemporary visual work around Baartman and black women's embodiment that Deborah Willis's groundbreaking volume gathers (2010). Here, I relocate it back to the installation series' context as way of reckoning with alternative political desires, promises, and economies Baartman's legacy might point us toward, in intimate relation with queer, feminine, quotidian, and domestic identities.

Following Erica R. Edwards (2015) here, one might ask what constantly politically inhabiting the nonnormative does for black queer feminist practice,

where the stakes of representation have always already cast black women outside of the normal. In Cox and Harris's infamous portrait, as contextualized in
The Good Life series, "normalizing" Baartman into a genealogy of black life also
means refusing the poles of injury/agency—the visual contract of critique—as
the overarching interpretative frame of black women's sexuality. Instead, the
"spectacular" Baartman and her experience of sexuality is reinscribed into everyday life.

Returning to Oyěwùmí's critique, I think of these visual works, even and
through their emphasis on the body, as ways to dislocate the body's primacy
in negotiations of Baartman's legacy as the primary site of black gendered
self-making. Rather than a turn to representing interiority, then—and akin
to the complex work of Weems's *Jefferson Suite* installation in the previous
chapter—work like Thomas's and Cox and Harris's uses the surface of the
body to articulate different interpretive strategies of black women's skin. Anne

Anlin Cheng (2011) has reread black skin as a complex historical formation that can signal more than the epidermalization of antiblackness. Michelle Ann Stephens (2014), in *Skin Acts*, similarly reinvests in the complexity of black embodiment and its audiences, arguing for the psychoanalytic complexities of subject formation that attend to the formation of black masculinity as a visual, social object. Fleetwood's (2015b) and Tina M. Campt's (2017) work on reading against the grain of seemingly bureaucratically authored photography of black male bodies at the site of the prison and the passport, respectively, also pushes against interpretive frames of self-authorship and agency—that "contract between performer and audience" (Braudy 1997) that assumes a fixed relation rather than multiple points of entry into black embodiment, including that of antiblackness. While none of these critics would argue that the regimes of meaning attached to Baartman are not overdetermined by racist conceptions of the excessive black body, they all suggest alternative methodologies that do not assume fealty to this cultural contract's terms. I read not for and as resistance, per se, but for a moment of stepping back from the very terms of debate to imagine other modes of meaning making within and from the critical fatigue of facing the cultural contract. This pause sets up a reflective acknowledgment of the fictional relations between the black woman's performing body, the critic's writing body, and their audiences, rather than positing them as moments of "choice." It digs into a critical fatigue by representing it, through and with Baartman's body, not in the temporality of moral crisis but in everyday knowing, reading, and interpretation.

The Labor of Representation, the Labor of Sex

To make another slippage visible in the discourse around black women's embodiment, rights discourse, and the ways the field of black feminist studies attempts to manage representation with the implicit tools and in the conceptual terrain of the contract, let me briefly return to the review of the 2017 *Venus* production once more: "But Ms. Jah, who was wonderful as the captive bride of an African warlord in 'Eclipsed,' is just as good as another kind of sex slave here. She makes it clear that Sarah is complicit in her own exploitation, and yet finally feels bewildered and imprisoned by her immense, dubious fame. 'Love me?' she asks, again and again, with infinite hunger" (Brantley 2017). The reviewer blithely references Lynn Nottage's play and the limited range of dramas staged on Broadway by black women playwrights and the few roles for black actresses as he also marks Baartman's body in a continuum with contemporary sex-trafficked women. And, in keeping with his earlier reliance on tropes of personal responsibility for human exploitation, he emphasizes the dilemma of Venus as one of individual reckoning with desire—to be seen is to be known to the modern world, and to possibly be "loved" by it—in terms of capital remuneration as much as interior fulfillment. Such constructions show how icons of black womanhood and the collectively imagined victims of sex trafficking and purveyors of sex work are all grouped into forms of corrective histories that demand particular performances of self—cultural contracts that exchange narrative for political affects of suffering and saviors that rarely imagine the quotidian life, before, during, or after, of those engaged within sexual economies and their mostly illicit contracts.[15] As Uri McMillan (2015) considers in *Embodied Avatars*, turning to a concept of distance—like the distance imagined by Patricia Williams (1991)—provides a key interpretive tool not just for critics, but for how critics assume the frames of meaning that define their subjects and objects of study. Here, I would organize critically fatigued responses to Baartman and embodied representation around Daphne Brooks's (2006) conception of "viability" as a constantly open and surprising question, rather than a narrative or interpretive given, that considers vulnerability as the basis of creating livable histories and embodied lives.

In Robin Coste Lewis's (2015) cataloging of the visual obsession with black women's bodies over centuries of Western art, her long poem "Voyage of the Sable Venus," she also imagines a reinvestment in this black feminist fatigue, in the literal laundry list of antiblack renderings of the black female body. Composed entirely in the titles of works of art that depict black women and organized around historical teleologies of contact that begin long before the Middle Passage and end long after emancipation, Lewis's poem is both exhaustive and exhausting—much as the history of trafficked women and of sexual labor on a continuum of coercion:

Girl Tending a Cow
Black Girl from the Cottingham Suite
Girl Writing a Letter
Girl in Partial Native Dress

And also:

In Front of Chalkboard Girl
Talk Girl
Walking Girl
Jumping

Rope
In Maryland Park Girl (86)

The labor of the "Catalog" betrays both repetition and encyclopedic variety in the already "known" territory of exploited black women's bodies in the visual frame—and even risks boredom, as recently theorized by Aida Levy-Hussen (2019) as one mode of registering critique and intellectual differentiation within black arts and literary study. The labor of representation, like sexual labor, here is less dramatic and more tedious, the kind of work that historically gets written out of public discourse on rights and the public protection of contract. This exclusion is no accident, much as marriage until very recently (and even still, in custom) offers high risk and little recourse when it comes to violence and exploitation of women and their bodies at the same time that it promises some form of responsibility between subjects (Fineman 2015b). The cultural contract, like the marriage contract, both orders everyday life and remains an exhausting site of critical and political practice to demand recognition and renegotiation even as "the treaty" could never, and was never meant to, solidify equity but instead to offer a temporary promise of equity, of consent, of choice under the sovereign to whom one is already bound. The treaty—an agreement created from the base of black women's subjectivity—then offers a performance of vulnerability as politics, not its lack or need.

Humanitarianism around sexually trafficked bodies again marks a discursively similarly terrain as the surface responses to figures such as Hemings and Baartman—and a reminder that the "human rights" framework is about how one tells and imagines the stories of living as well as dying (Hua 2011). This is particularly critical when thinking about vulnerable populations, especially women, as their value and vulnerability are marked through the sexual— through sexual violence, labor, use, and reuse. Against the limit of being marked for death, it becomes hard to wrangle with "choices" that put them in precarious but more "promising" positions. Baartman is defined and disavowed by her repeated erotic presence and the spectacular nature of her contracted sexual, emotional, and cultural labor. But as this chapter has also envisioned, in the "blatant acts of exposure" (Colbert 2017, 103) strategically deployed by various cultural and legal entities in representing Baartman and "her" supposed interests, these spectacles expose the everyday abjections, the invisible contracts, that order lives directly and indirectly, but immersively: marriage, labor contracts, etc. These contracts shape gendered, sexual, raced, and classed identities in nonspectacular ways deep into the postemancipation era (Hunter 2019). Rather than imagine those instances as desecrations of what was once pure or whole, like the white paint splashed on Baartman's grave in 2015, this chapter analyzes them as the ongoing state of political living that cannot be rectified or unmarked—a vulnerability in embodiment, and through representation, that cannot be alleviated, a risk that is unevenly distributed and nonetheless ever present in the act of living.

That Baartman's name now adorns a center for women and children survivors of domestic and sexual violence, then, seems to be a way forward that imagines the practical, material care needed to go on living and sustaining, through institutionality and institution building even while one remains knowing about their impossible purity. Steeped in the direct language of human rights, the center ties her legacy to the ongoing state of vulnerability and the many ways and forms the inequality of the social contract demands that black women and children be coerced into submission. It also imagines their positive rights as material needs for child care, job training, counseling, and other direct and interrelated services. While I make no claims about the practical work of running of such a state-sponsored entity, I do want to recognize that Baartman's cultural legacy lives on in built space beyond imagined irrecoverable trauma and desecration—that her cultural work can imagine how to continue living and building in the wake, beyond political and civil law but not fully released from its grasp, its discourse, its capital. In arrested development lay the plans for a memorial museum near the gravesite, however, years after an international design competition that was met with controversy not least because the only visual remainders of Baartman are racist renderings of her in print and in the drawings of Cuvier. History and ongoing living collide; a fence is built around her gravesite; structures built or not built to stave off, to delay, to mark the difficulty of living as a vulnerable political subject, to mark how political subjectivity is by definition a state of vulnerability, rather than its rescue or repair from a supposed Rosseauian state of nature.

That the texts above re-present Baartman's testimony, sometimes displacing it to a public testimony and/or criminalized capture/seizure, sometimes displacing it onto the voyage of her remains, demonstrates not just the necessity of drama and conflict in art, but the fictions of law and contract needed to sustain a sense of political efficacy and value in opposition to hegemonic violence. Like Baartman's, scholarly performances and representations are "acts" that include critical desires but also spectacularize them and the possibilities of critical interventions in the public body and public discourse. And like the sexual trafficking of women, the cultural traffic in black women's bodies, including critical investment in and repetition of them, is not a scene or scenario that can be avoided—that can be unseen—in the quotidian ways lives are organized around these contracts, these promises and their failures.

I return to Madison Hemings's characterization of his mother's consent as well as to Alexander's poem on Baartman here to consider both the pathos of this longing for a different version of this contract and the overwhelming, fatiguing time of the spectacular as outlined by Lewis in her poem—a quotidian temporality, it turns out, one that can engender list upon list of representative works. In Alexander's haunting declaration of duration and endurance, "That was years ago," a line recalled in Trethewey's poem about the distance between her two visits to Monticello with her father. The reader is asked here to imagine Baartman's own fatigue—the waning of her individual desire for the promised experiences of Enlightenment modernity in the face of a relentless racial-sexual social contract that bars her from its equally fictional security. This chapter posits reading practices that are ready to stay vulnerable to all that we, as readers, viewers, and critics, cannot know or assume about the right ways to live and endure in a black feminist life, to adapt Sara Ahmed's (2017) formulation, or where to mark that life's proper analytical, social, and political ends. It also tentatively imagines innovative and creative ways of being and living inside of institutionality, engaging both bluntly and otherwise with the exhausting fictions of cultural and legal contract. In the following chapter, I pursue these ambivalent yet deeply felt black feminist relationships to institutionality and inclusion more directly, following the trace of Baartman's conjured desires and ambitions into the terms of the picaresque promise and limits of postemancipation citizenship.

Chapter Four

CIVIC DESIRE

MARY SEACOLE'S ADVENTURES IN BLACK CITIZENSHIP

A 2010 segment of the BBC series *Horrible Histories* (Clarke and Connolly 2010) locates itself in the offices of Cliff Whitelie, historical public relations agent. His mission, in this "Vile Victorians" episode, is presented in the form of two figures: Florence Nightingale and Mary Seacole. Their pairing is a modern-day fable of multicultural inclusion in practice, particularly of what I have termed "corrective histories," or those representations of historical figures of blackness meant to recover and repair past racial injury. Seacole ([1857] 2005, 80), as she says in her own words in her 1857 memoir, *Wonderful Adventures of Mrs. Seacole in Many Lands*, becomes again and again "the right woman in the right place" for such cultural labor, where historical desires to reclaim and resituate blackness in the public sphere meet civic desires—modes of engaging and performing citizenship that include memorialization, public service, and curriculum mandates.

Sometimes referred to as "The Yellow Doctress" and "Mother Seacole" by British soldiers and the press during the Crimean War, Seacole was extraordinarily well traveled, an entrepreneur-nurse who worked in the Caribbean, Central America, Eastern Europe, and in the UK, as documented in her memoir. Florence Nightingale was, then and now, her foil: the middle-class, British white woman who institutionalized modern nursing practices. Nightingale became a national and global icon of the profession; Seacole went from British Victorian celebrity to a century of disappearance, resurrected in the contemporary moment as a heroine of multiculturalism as much for her accomplishments as for her racist snubbing by Nightingale, and her eventual "triumph" in becoming a famous nurse and celebrity of the Crimean War. That triumph is rehearsed and replotted in the sketch above as one of publicity, as "winning" over Nightingale's racism in the contemporary moment to earn her rightful place in the historical record—and in the public imagination.

Seacole, in short, wins by becoming a celebrity in the current moment, where celebrity is read as a sign of racial progress and as a correction of the racist silence that omitted her from "history" heretofore, rather than Baartman's trajectory of overexposure. "Correcting" Seacole's historical geography redeploys her in the service of several competing narratives of national, postcolonial, and racial belonging, as well as antiracist political and intellectual discourse. This chapter traces these reanimated histories of Seacole as a citizen in order to suggest the current limits of and the future possibilities for inclusion, access, and resource distribution as goals for black feminist thought. It does so by pressing on the freedom of desire that Toni Morrison ([1987] 2004, 162) so provocatively suggests in *Beloved* to deeply consider *critical* desires surrounding a difficult figure like Seacole, who in many ways stands as the inverse of Baartman's tragic interpretative trajectories. This chapter takes as its starting point Crystal Parikh's (2017, 6) insistence on a turn away from narratives of lack, abuse, and charity and toward desire in rights discourse, "the complex *desires* of these subjects and how such desires—sexual as well as social—mediate the subject's experiences of vulnerability and agency." In other words, and as Parikh cites Ann Cvetkovich, this chapter and this book take seriously "the unpredictability of desire" not just in subjects/objects of analysis but in critical practice. In reading Seacole, I refuse an evaluative mode that seeks to find in our readings of black women's civic desire either freedom or submission. Instead Seacole's "adventures"—pulling not just from her own titular description but also from its reference to imperial Victorian adventure novels that feature boys and men on dangerous quests in "foreign" lands—and their contemporary circulations offer a difficult model of understanding black feminist citizenship at its base as including as well as regulating desires that exceed the formal sphere of politics and more implicit assumptions of home, family, and community, "protocols of comfort and protection" that hem in readings of feminized political subjects (Parikh 2017, 6).

Born in 1805, Mary Jane Grant Seacole was a mixed-race Jamaican nurse and "sutler" (a hotelier/general-store keeper), who served soldiers in the Crimean War as well as in Jamaica, New Grenada, and Panama. *Wonderful Adventures of Mrs. Seacole in Many Lands* repeats this geography as its lure and as the basis for Seacole's inclusion into British history. The text has gone from a popular text in its own time to general obscurity, only to be reprinted and commemorated within national histories of Britain and Jamaica (and in academic circles) in more recent years. Told partially in the genre of a travel narrative, and partially as a celebrity war memoir (of the Crimean War, fought against Russia from 1853 to 1856), the volume sold out its first print run in its day. Upon its 1984, 1988, and 2005 editions (the last of which will be the edition that is cited throughout), critics tend both to marvel at Seacole's position as a well-known, respected colonial subject who was able to write her own version of her life apart from connection to any political movement, and to note the difficult affiliations with the British nation and empire required to achieve this position.[1]

Seacole, as in the above sketch, is tasked with the difficult cultural and political work of the present day, and her symbolic value remains stretched across British, Jamaican, black diasporic, and black feminist geographies. As someone who claims her financial, professional, and geographic mobility through genealogies of black women's sexuality and emerging capitalist enterprises of empire, Seacole, through her innovative expression and deployment of civic desire, challenges existing models of historical, sexual, geographic, gendered, and political agency in black feminist political thought. Seacole's recovery complicates contemporary historical practices of history from below—of recovering the lost lives and significance of black peoples across the routes of the chattel slave trade and beyond—by imagining the continuities between her position as "akin" to a citizen (she lacks, of course, formal enfranchisement, as do all women and almost all of the colonial subjects of the British empire at the time) and the ways that these unofficial continuums of citizenship included (as well as excluded) black diasporic peoples, creating "loopholes" for thriving that couple with national and capitalist structures in uncomfortable ways. In this, Seacole engages with a public notion of citizenry made through media reception and consumption, in the formulation of Lauren Berlant (1997), though Seacole herself is a difficult example of her "diva citizenship" in that she engages the sentimental only in regards to her wistful love of war and adventure, rather than in her appeal to public affect around personal loss or traditional femininity.[2]

Harriet Jacobs ([1861] 1988, 60) famously wrote that there was "something akin to freedom" in carving out alternate arrangements of power and desire within bondage. In the previous chapters, I have considered the paths of desire within what appear to be, on the surface, deeply constrained lives. Here, I consider the operations of desire within a significantly less politically and geographically bounded frame. This chapter traces civic desire, or the individual and collective will to access the basic civil and political rights of personhood, as well as the impulse to recognize that personhood and will to personhood in others. In the concept of freedom as both "a marker of individual choice and as an index of belonging" (F. Cooper, Holt, and Scott 2000, 10), Seacole embodies what since 1948 has been called "human rights."[3] Seacole's expansive legacy connects most particularly to the field's thornier questions of social, cultural, and economic rights. These rights are up for debate in contemporary discussions around international law, development, and the role of nongovernmental organizations as they sometimes call for more than legal recognition but also systemic shifts in the distribution of health and resources that go beyond the recognition of individual political rights.[4] They exceed the frame of bondage/freedom, as Seacole does, even as they are contained within the borders of colonial and imperial histories. Seacole's span included pre- and postemancipation Jamaica, Central America during the building of the transcontinental railway, Crimea (the Russian territory for which the British fought to obtain easier trade access to the East), and Victorian England. This expansive terrain, though, should not code as easily "free" from concerns about the sustainability of economic life in the borderlands of empire; the uneven distribution of social mobility across various designations of race, class, and gender in Seacole's time; or the limited cultural access to institutional support that such identifications marked.

Seacole's assertion that she wishes to be "only the historian of Spring Hill," the Crimean battlefield she served, reveals the tensions of "personal desire and social demand" that critic Claudia Tate (1998, 10) sees as productive of a particular "black textual desire," where desire is "not simply sexual longings but all kinds of wanting, wishing, yearning, longing, and striving—conscious and particularly unconscious," here exhibited by Seacole as an author, by her critics, and by the state itself. Mary Seacole's adventures question critical commitments as they relate to social, economic, cultural, and historical justice. How might one reconcile the intangible affects that colonialism and globalization produce—desire for cosmopolitan travel or capital ambition, for instance—with modes of reading and producing raced and gendered identification that privilege "home," indigeneity, and loyalty to local communities? Through Seacole's circulations, both then and now, there emerges a vision of the complex relationship between Seacole's contemporary status as a multicultural icon and the ways that historic conceptualizations of "race" can remain attached to narratives of resistance and exclusion, despite the complicated history of capitalism, colonialism, and gendered mobility that a figure like Seacole conjures. Though Seacole's exclusion from formal categories of national and empiric citizenship was and is made across both raced and gendered lines, Seacole's own work and her circulation in contemporary Britain and Jamaica mark other routes, and other territories, for understanding the complexity of black women as political subjects.

History, Citizenship, and Civic Desire

Seacole, as a black celebrity of her Victorian era and of contemporary Britain and Jamaica, sits at the front of debates around corrective histories of citizenship. She is recast as a national, cultural, racial, and "global citizen," in the words of Cheryl Fish (2004). I join a generation of scholars seeking to rethink the legacy of Seacole's 1857 narrative—one that critics have located as alternatively subversive of imperial regimes, indulgent of empire's violent economic and military imperatives, and challenging to the terrain of agency in black feminist history and theory.[5] At its heart then, this chapter investigates the thorny representation of agentic subjectivity and its usefulness in articulating—or not—the fullest spectrum of black civic participation and desires to participate in the New World, with black women as the center of this historical and political imagination. Seacole has been cast in this problematic role of agentic subject since her Victorian-era fame, and hence tracing her public circulations offers a unique window into the discourses of agency, inclusion, empire, and race as they attach to black women's subjectivity in the postcolonial era. Seacole's continuity as a presence across transnational poles reveals black women's centrality in fashioning both the limits and the possibilities of civic desire and its diasporic representations. Her adventures emphasize, in Derrick Spires's (2019) recent terms, "the practice of citizenship" for early black authors as a project of "doing." Seacole presents "doing" as a model of wanting, feeling, and desiring, as well—all modes of engaging the public, civic sphere that rest uncomfortably in her claims to what Kavalski (2003) terms "voluntary citizenship" or willed belonging in the British Empire.

As "the historian of Spring Hill" in her own terms (Seacole [1857] 2005), and in W. H. Russell's ([1857] 2005, 5) preface, "a plain truth-speaking woman, who has lived an adventurous life amid scenes which have never yet found a historian among the actors on the stage where they passed," Seacole markets her highly specific experience into a public persona both of and ahead of her Victorian times, extending beyond British boundaries and public sympathy toward sentimentalized cases of racism. Seacole, as "historian" of her time, documents the quotidian experience of empire's others, including Creole women hoteliers; New World transnational laborers; middle-class women seeking mobility through writing, nursing, and the discourse of philanthropy; foreign correspondents; and those serving in the burgeoning industry of modern warfare. Empire was immensely popular and a widely reported on topic of the press of its day. In this, Seacole's Crimean heroine, an avid producer and consumer of empire, embodies a difficult representative for black women that, in Christopher Taylor's (2018, 8) terms, "model[s] postliberal forms of imperial relation" and hence can seem anomalous in its infamy as Seacole is rendered as empire's key example and promise in some contemporary politics.

The opening text is such a didactic example of corrective history, aired on June 8, 2010 (Clarke 2010). It features an imagined public relations director for historical figures (Cliff Whitelie), whom a tall, pale Florence Nightingale and a dark-skinned, anachronistically Jamaican-accented Mary Seacole are consulting to correct the historical record that forgets to properly commemorate Seacole (figure 4.1). After some back and forth, the overly slick, white public relations director agrees to take the case of Seacole, promising to tell her story via a nationally televised episode of the very same television show we are watching. Thus, British history, and its accompanying racism, are literally corrected and Seacole can now take her rightful place next to Nightingale's significant national legacy. The satiric skit does this with a wink and a nod, acknowledging how crass historical recoveries of "multicultural" histories are even as it promises, meta-promises, and performs corrective history. In this way, it asks the audience to both participate in and be critical of their own historical and civic desires to "see" black citizens of the Commonwealth restored to public prominence.

After her Victorian-era fame, Seacole moves from Crimean War historian, of sorts, to the annals of British history. She goes from being reported on in *News of the World of the London Times* in 1856 to more marginal, incidental fame through to her death in 1881 in Britain. Seacole's brand of exemplary empiric celebrity fails to sustain itself for many years in institutional forms in Britain the way that Seacole's main comparative figure, Florence Nightingale, does— for instance, in the form of the Florence Nightingale museum, textbook and curricular presence, and other media devoted to this pioneer of nursing culture and feminized labor. But as Seacole is "rediscovered" in the 1980s and 1990s by both the British public and by academics, Seacole's image and cultural significance shift. Seacole's legacy highlights a national narrative struggling to come to terms with its makeup as a multicultural body of citizenry after the virulent racist politics of the late 1960s and 1970s, bleeding into the neoconservative 1980s. Her redeployment in the contemporary British moment emerges in a familiar multicultural narrative that emphasizes racial injury as the identifying force of black histories and identifies multicultural inclusion and correction as the difficult but necessary cure for said injury.

FIGURE 4.1. Seacole and Nightingale argue for their respective versions of history on the BBC show *Horrible Histories*, series 2, episode 6 (2010).

In tracing Seacole's meteoric rise from a posthumous century of anonymity to the number one "Black Briton" (*BBC News* 2004), I also track a complicated narrative of how citizenship hails black subjects and polices the boundaries of their blackness through the very discourses of agency, freedom, and cultural belonging. In various national, professional, and ethical communities, Seacole's legacy is employed in the service of these corrective histories of race. Seacole's performances of civic desire tell a story about the expectations and limits ascribed to black citizens and their civic desires, particularly those who endure in the public eye. Diverse and divergent paths of historicization and commemoration allow for alternative interpretations of her legacy to the contemporary moment's relationship to citizenship—less a corrective history of an individual in service of a predetermined set of political goals than a continuity of difficult sites that empire sets up for black women subjects, in particular, in their living and modeling of viable lives across and beyond the diaspora.

Representations of Seacole multiply this equation beyond her lifetime by occupying multiple ideological positions just as she did geographic ones. In these nuanced representations, the difficulty of "recruiting" Seacole into "a single canon or national cause," as critic Sara Salih (2005, xlii) notes, is exposed as a labor as well, highlighting some aspects of Seacole's legacy and image at the expense of other, more difficult ones to acknowledge and process. But the struggle over her representation, and the continued insistence on the significance of her image in "multicultural" Britain and in the globalized economies of Jamaica and the Caribbean, suggest the significance of culture itself in shaping and claiming histories of race in the modern world. I term this struggle as one over "civic desire," a will not just to fortify the neoliberal state's "colorblind" racist policies but one also traced to those fraught discussions of representational justice over who represents and how the state marks its most difficult histories.

To study Seacole is to study how black life is and was organized not just through a lack of civil and political rights but via the uneven management of social, economic, and cultural rights for both the free and the enslaved populations in what historians Frederick Cooper, Thomas C. Holt, and Rebecca J. Scott (2000, 16) describe as the "mixture of coercion and consent involved" in upholding state fictions of free will and the voluntary participation of postemancipation citizens of empire. Formal and informal civic participation were and are constructed by complicated sets of privileges and desires, a necessary recognition in researching African diaspora experience. This recognition suggests that the postcitizenship forms that Eva Cherniavsky (2017) so compelling reimagines as political practice in the contemporary moment—forms of unofficial, cultural, informal, and consumptive engagement—are also models for understanding black civic desire in the history of empire.

Seacole's adventures in global citizenship interpret "citizenship" as a marker of public participation that entails and exceeds bare survival or basic recognition of personhood. Seacole stands as an exceptional figure to consider the multiple axes of citizenship, or something "akin" to them in her unusual performances of global citizenship during an era when her "exclusion from the active category of citizen" was made across both raced and gendered lines (Cooper, Holt, and Scott 2000, 17). Formal citizenship was at this moment solidifying "rights" as a resource for citizens alone, reinforced through the discourses of free labor and contract: "In the age of Emancipation, the attributes of free personhood became identified with the rights and privileges of the citizen; and that individual 'freedom' thus became identified with the nation-state, and understood as possible solely through national citizenship" (Phan 2013, 19). As Amy L. Brandzel (2016) argues in her forceful and compelling *Against Citizenship*, echoing Lisa Marie Cacho (2012), an appeal to be included into the fold of official national citizenship, especially to gain access to rights of state protection and security, necessarily excludes others—the incarcerated or refugees, for instance—from access to those rights and privileges. Though I share this critique of the discourse of contemporary citizenship and its calls for inclusion, I do want to think here about a positionality that can hold this impossibility and not think of it as a zero-sum game through Seacole. Seacole is also attendant to dynamic modes of civil participation and cultural representation that are created by those "decommissioned"—or never commissioned from the start—as citizens (Cherniavsky 2017, 10). Cherniavsky's imagining of the contemporary moment as a neoliberal postcitizenship society is prefigured in the radical re-formations of citizenship happening during settler colonialism, modes that Seacole is savvy to in her claims to more traditional forms of empiric pride.

The very discourse engendered by the colonial state to marshal investments in belonging that both is and is not quite citizenship in the imperial era is one that many scholars have argued creates a space where the colonized can imagine themselves as "equivalent" to the official or "real" citizens of the colonizer state (Kazanjian 2003, 19). As Sukanya Banerjee (2010, 3–4) argues about Indian subjects in a slightly later historical period, "In claiming their perceived rights as subjects of the Crown, British Indians simultaneously underwrite themselves as citizens of empire, imperial citizens." Seacole certainly occupies this realm of "flexible citizenship" (Ong 1999) in informal capacities, understanding citizenship as Seyla Benhabib (1996) does, as a "social practice" that, in Berlant's (1997, 20) terms, is "continually produced out of a political, rhetorical, and economic struggle over who will count as 'the people' and how social membership will be measure and valued." Seacole is neither a resistor of citizenship nor its dupe if read in Banerjee's (2010, 5) terms of a "language of citizenship" that exists "not so much in the realm of statutory enactment as in the cultural imaginative and affective fields that both engender it and are constituted by it." This is not at all to suggest that these imaginative formations are transcendent of the material conditions of citizenship, but that inclusion/exclusion is too binary a frame to consider the active category of citizenship and how in-flux it was in the era across the terrain of Enlightenment modernity. It is not so much that as one group "received" citizenship status another was summarily "excluded" from it, but that the shifting dynamics of inclusion were actually shifting definitions and forms of citizenship itself, which is itself a category that is nuanced and stratified by racialized and gendered difference, as argued by comparative racial literary historian Edlie L. Wong (2009) of the period just following Seacole's in the US context. The British Caribbean is an early experiment in the multiracial "languages of citizenship," one still finding its footing, and hence producing a set of discourses and slippages that Seacole inhabits, exploits, and creates in addition to being hailed by in her own and others' uneven civic desires.

This attention to corrective histories and their intersection with forms of citizenship is a complement to what Salamishah Tillet (2012) has termed "civic myths," or "form[s] of collective memory" that serve the aims of, in her formulation, the US state, as well as countermemories that challenge these narratives. Those myths, she argues, are surprisingly adaptable in the service of national narrative. This chapter points to racial myths that cross national lines, with "myths" standing as the specific stories told, retold, and adapted in service of the concept of race—frequently that of white supremacy, but also in the reparative mode of restoring black histories to the public sphere, a mode that is often but not always closely associated with either resisting the neoliberal state or rehabilitating the now repentant racist state. Seacole's narrative and her figuration in academic work, in state-sanctioned commemoration campaigns in Britain and in Jamaica, and in public culture surrounding multiculturalism and diversity are not sites of slavery, per Tillet. Rather, they are postenslavement narratives that register as sites of renegotiation for Tillet's concept of "civic estrangement," the alienation experienced by those black citizens of empire hailed to belong as their (hi)stories are denied or relegated to the margins by the postslavery states that now claim them in and as acts of racial repair. These histories suggest the multiplicity of black lives, experiences, and subjects, as well as the fungibility those lives had and have for the reinforcement of empire's aims through to the present day.

"Empire" here signifies both the historically defined empire as the geographic, military, and capital reach of a sovereign state (i.e., the British Empire) as well as the more modern use of the term as a description of the complex network of global capital (Hardt and Negri 2001) and African diasporic political and patriarchal belonging and/or exclusion (Stephens 2005).[6] Seacole is poised at this intersection as a woman authorized by empire to chase dangerous capital success in its furthest reaches. At the same time, she stands outside of official channels of citizenship that allow her to claim rights as a black or Creole woman, as well as experience exclusion from official rights.[7] In the more contemporary moment, she is also taken up by Jamaica, Britain, and postcolonial and African American studies scholarship as a reworked figure of national pride, multicultural inclusion, and a problematic supporter of empire and its violent and exclusionary exploits. Seacole's enthusiasm for empire confounds, as it finds in the social gaps that capital produces a path toward personal desires and ambitions as a Creole-identified woman in the nineteenth century. Those histories also overlap with exemplary stories—that of the Creole woman hotelkeeper, and that of the imperiled colonial subject toiling in the borderlands of empire's reach, building, in this case, the

Panamanian railroad—that show how these narratives of civic desire intersect with enslavement and the displacement and genocide of indigenous people in the name of development.

In Seacole's own genealogy, one can find the underside of empire's violence and the ways that black lives, and black women's lives in particular, sit at the precarious center of racial history—economic, social, corporeal, sexual—in the innovative ways that some came to engineer available narratives of belonging and exclusion as a means to problematic but no less powerful visions of civic participation and vulnerable articulations of civic desire. These desires are defined partially through a mobility that is often denied to black women in antiracist discourses that might deify women who "stay home"—or "resist" within the recognizable bounds of either masculinized action or feminized spheres of family and community.[8] As wary as cultural and historical scholars of race might be, the British public has embraced her adventures as a kind of multicultural heroism. This chapter now turns to that contemporary reclaiming of Seacole as a celebrity in the service of not racial but national community through public education.

Seacole's Adventures in Multicultural Britishness

Modern-day academic critics remain concerned about the lack of a recognizable racial plot in Seacole's autobiography, rattled by what her biographer Jane Robinson (2005, 167) describes as the necessary "business venture" and branding that Seacole constructs for herself. The *Horrible Histories* clip that opens this chapter dramatizes her circulation as the site of corrective history, as a question of racial injury and repair via the redress of multicultural representation. This video clip is a study in comparative racialization—a dark-skinned Mary Seacole next to the stark white Florence Nightingale—that follows Seacole across her modern image as the illuminated foil to Nightingale's legacy. Arguments for Seacole's representation of and representativeness for contemporary Britain most often ground themselves in the Nightingale comparison, building off of "The Lady with the Lamp's" established credibility and legitimacy as an exemplary citizen to make their case, whether for a stamp (issued in 2006), a statue controversially erected in 2015 after a protracted fight with Nightingale supporters and rightwing protesters, a gravesite (restored), or two official historical plaques (one hung in 2005 and the other in 2007 when the first site was demolished). "Seacolites" even successfully organized a bicentenary exhibition in the Nightingale Museum in 2005 to mark the Crimean heroine's contributions to the field of nursing.[9] Even Salman

FIGURE 4.2. Seacole's main page on the UK learning site My Learning, emphasizing fame, geographic difference, medical knowledge, and philanthropic aid. Accessed 2017, mylearning.org.

Rushdie ([1988] 2008, 292) employs the Seacole/Nightingale comparison as the exemplar of the failures of Western history in *The Satanic Verses*: "Still the motionless figures dance between the shimmying of sisters, the jouncing and bouncing of youth. What are they?—why, waxworks, nothing more—who are they?—History. See, here is Mary Seacole, who did as much in the Crimea as another magic-lamping lady, but, being dark, could scarce be seen for the flame of Florence's candle." Several graphic illustrations of Seacole show her alongside an increasingly perturbed and actively racist Nightingale, imagining Seacole's exasperation with and/or active resistance to Nightingale's individualized racist discourse (here made to stand in for structurally racist history, that which is "fixed" by exposing the bad racist/racism). These corrective feminist histories seem to trace an arc where white feminists learn the error of their ways through Seacole's history—something repeated in, for instance, podcasts about Seacole, or Kate Beaton's (n.d.) popular feminist comic strip *Hark, A Vagrant*'s rendition of Seacole.

Seacole, then, becomes representative of British history as a corrective measure for including too much of Nightingale's "light," and her whiteness, in the

FIGURE 4.3. Mary Seacole's portrait as the primary/only image of black women in British history and imagination at the Black Cultural Archives in London. Photo by Edmund Sumner (2014).

institutionalized versions of the Crimean war, national service, and the history of both nursing and philanthropic medicine. Her celebrity is restored via the politics of liberal multiculturalism, which, as political theorist Will Kymlicka (1996, 20) outlines, "has costs and imposes risks, and these costs vary enormously both within and across societies."[10] This inclusion, as many critics of multiculturalism have pointed out, reveals a commitment to the institutionalization of difference that incorporates and manages it into the dominant structure.[11]

This sense of a zero-sum game on both sides, reading through the recognition of Seacole as a way to "erase" Nightingale's white feminist limelight, is replayed again and again. On April 25, 2011, the *New Yorker* printed a short piece on Seacole that opens with a telling declaration: "Florence Nightingale strongly disapproved of Mary Jane Seacole, but that did not stop either of them" (Frazier 2011). In the contemporary moment, a long-planned statue of Seacole in fact became a lightning rod for debates around multiculturalism in Britain. As Seacole's place in the national curriculum was threatened by some parliamentarians in 2013, a series of Nightingale supporters began to publicly contest the commemoration of Seacole, particularly in any kind of "equivalent" recognition to Nightingale. Their key public argument was that Seacole contributed little to pioneering the profession of nursing. Of course, in doing so, they conveniently leave out the structural racism that didn't allow nonwhite women into newly institutionalized nursing, any question of Nightingale's individual racism aside. Those supporting Seacole's statue and inclusion turned to solidifying her bona fides in science and medicine, as the new curriculum site mylearning.org emphasizes ("Mary Seacole Activities," n.d.; figure 4.2).

Seacole's commissioned sculptor, Martin Jennings, had to argue not just for the validity of UK's first statue in honor of a black woman after a twelve-year campaign, but for its size and its placement after public questions about who should have the taller statue, Nightingale or Seacole, as well as objections to the urban geography of the statue, across the House of Parliament's ground of St. Thomas Hospital, the home base of Nightingale. Seacole's image becomes even more iconic, used to "reimagine black women in Britain" at the Black Cultural Archives exhibit of 2014 (figure 4.3).

Her representation also stoked right-leaning pundits who argue not just that Seacole wasn't "really" black, but that "long after she was dead, zealots used Mrs. Seacole in their bitter campaign to abolish Britain and replace it with a multicultural nothingness" (Hitchens 2013). The efforts to memorialize Seacole, then, are met with objections to her material and ideological taking up of space in and as British history, always in competition with the assumed substance and depth of whiteness that is that history's presumed property (embodied by Nightingale's assumed place and presumed displacement), or vice versa, in Cheryl Harris's (1993) terms, and later George Lipsitz's (1998) terms of "possessive investment."

But if the conservative Right and white feminist Nightingales argue for diminished glory, the "multicultural nothingness" that Seacole signifies in the face of British history, those working toward racial justice have their own ob-

FIGURE 4.4. Seacole's official British portrait by Albert Charles Challen (1869) on a National Gallery stamp.

jections to Seacole as the face of vulnerable and nonwhite populations, given the history of racism in Britain. Here, too, Seacole's blackness is found lacking, as in a 2015 op-ed in *The Voice* (Adebayo 2015), self-identified as London's black newspaper, entitled "What Did Mary Seacole Ever Do for Black People?" As nursing awards, housing associations, nursery schools, and expressive cultural productions are performed in the name of Seacole and under the rubric of racial and social justice across Britain, some antiracist activists see the symbolization of Seacole as the stand-in for race *and racism* as an act of whiteness itself—where "white Britons love her even more than we do" pithily summarizes the assumed audience for Seacole's corrective histories. Those activists see not meaningful black inclusion into British history, nor an acknowledgment of systemic racism, but more a nod to one who "rises to the challenge" of British racism—an ideal and idealized racial subject meant to assuage white colonial guilt without a deep reckoning with the history and present of structural racism.

Her mother was a nurse and treated people with local medicines and herbs.

FIGURE 4.5. Educational website drawing of Seacole's mother teaching her about natural medicine. From Megan Maxwell, "Mary Seacole: Famous Nurse, Born 1805, Died 1881," accessed December 5, 2019, https://slideplayer.com/slide/9966567/.

Seacole's inclusion into the national discourse of Britain is both significant in recognizing the changing ethnic makeup of the UK post the *Windrush*'s landing in 1948, and a move that staves off what sociologist Carl E. James (2008, 108) calls "an education that unsettles the notion of cultural democracy and meritocracy." One can see this in, for example, her British-issued stamp, which is made up of her portrait from the National Gallery in the UK (figure 4.4). The stamp figures her as "Mother Seacole," showcasing her likely mythic war medals. Seacole's portrait hangs in the British National Gallery through these simultaneous narratives of racial injury and devoted service to the empire. Merely including a nonwhite person in the long line of British history, it needs hardly to be said, does not disrupt narratives of Britishness that rest on colonial subjection and exclusion. Seacole's story, especially, with its concentrated effort to convince the reader of her individual industry and selflessness, is particularly and repeatedly written into the template of exceptionalism and the incidental consequences of racial and gendered difference, all the more easily marshaling her into the British national fold through a

FIGURE 4.6. Mary Seacole, carte de visite taken by Maull & Company, c.1873. Courtesy Ian Dagnall Computing, Alamy Stock Photo.

strategic tokenism that erases antiblackness even as it renders black women publicly visible.

After her mandatory if continually contested inclusion into the national curriculum just before the turn of twenty-first century, a veritable cottage industry in Seacole has emerged, with a range of children's books, plays, course guides, documentaries, and a BBC website devoted to the study of Seacole within the British educational system.[12] Almost all allude to her refused offer to serve in the official Nursing Corps in the Crimea, and some, like Marcia Layne's (2007) play, also dramatize the only other instance where Seacole herself speaks of her experience of blatant racism in England—when she traveled there as an adolescent and was heckled by working-class white children for her and (she emphasizes, more so) her companion's dark skin. Several of these texts take liberties with Seacole's own de-emphasis on her Jamaican "roots," as they imagine her into indigenous and Afro-influenced Caribbean identity today, with pages devoted to Seacole's "natural" healing methods (figure 4.5).

Along with the "costs" and "risks" of a multiculturalism that narrowly defines racism to include difference into the national narrative, this nationalist frame reimagines Seacole, like some of her academic critics do, in a genealogy of ideal Jamaican identity and heroism today—identifying with Afro and indigenous roots, sporting "natural" hair and dark skin, and combating overt racism through industry, tenaciousness, and innovation. Combining the hallmarks of race, including stereotypical phenotypic and cultural features and narratives of racial injury and selfless service to those in need as well as of material success, these updated visions of Seacole stand in for an ideal Race Woman even as they point to her anomalous status as the "only" black British woman "worthy" of the history of her time. This is a reminder of the difficulty of teaching legacies of structural racism as the same bodies exploited are employed now to speak to these histories as a (national) corrective—something I have traced in the memorialization of each figure in this book. This figuration aligns with the image of her carte de visite (figure 4.6), a form of celebrity culture, where she mixes medicines while wearing her war medals in her old age. In this photograph, it is her labor that is foregrounded—the work that made her famous—rather than the contemporary racialization offered as celebrity in the images above.

Seacole's status is, of course, not just a corrective to British history's absences. It also marks some of the erasing of Seacole's ambivalent relationship to a racial community or solidarity, especially with fellow Creole or black Jamaicans. Seacole barely mentions her own mixed-race side of the family in her memoir, or local politics around race, class, labor, and rights in her narrative, nor does the press in her time usually take on her race as a significant or defining feature of her fame and service directly. Even *Punch*, the popular Victorian humor magazine, refers to her "berry brown face" just once ("A Stir for Seacole" 1856). But Seacole's contemporary reissues feature her as foremother, in Britain, to the more equitable distribution of both antiracist sentiment and institutional worth. In the BBC curricular site for teaching Seacole, for instance, the instructional video included begins with a visual and verbal affirmation of Seacole's Creole heritage and a declaration, in first person narration, of Seacole's Creole pride (https://www.bbc.com/teach/class-clips-video/history-ks2-mary -seacole-ep1/z72prj6). While this, too, is how her memoir begins—setting up Seacole's story as exceptional in a burgeoning market of Crimean media and memoirs—the short video then spends almost a full four minutes of its five-minute running time visualizing Seacole's encounters with racism and racial injury, erasing her history of colonial and frontier nursing completely in order to emphasize her maternally received education on nursing. Layne's drama for school-age children expands this vision from Seacole's individual experience to imagine her as the start of a long line of Caribbean-descended nurses working to earn respect in the British national health system. This genealogy is realized in the numerous health institutions that have taken Seacole's name for all or part of their commitments to multicultural healthcare; a building of the Home Office, the British government's agency for immigration, crime, and diversity, was named after her in 2005 as an "inspirational tale" (https://jis.gov .jm/uk-home-office-building-named-after-mary-seacole). The contemporary deployment of Seacole as "Black Briton" rests uneasily on limited narratives of racial injury and industry, and their intersections with Seacole's professional and national affiliations. But it also emphasizes her global connections and her recognition by multiple national bodies for her service in the Crimea—a reminder that the war industry itself is a transnational endeavor dependent upon diverse bodies, labor, and geographies. These emplotments then fit into multicultural scripts for an antiracist education that emphasize racism and racist injury as the catalyst to success in the national fold—their plots insist on racial injury as the driving force for the historical actor as well as for the young audience's attention. Adventure and ambition here are then deeply racialized, and rendered in the service of altruistic agency in the past and corrective compulsory consumption in the present in the UK.

Seacole as Caribbean Heroine

As the school curriculum materials on Seacole make clear, Seacole is also being reimagined into postcolonial Caribbean celebrity. Seacole's routes across various New World territories extend far beyond Britain's shores—to Jamaica, New Grenada/Panama, and Crimea.[13] Seacole herself traveled not just to conflict zones, but back and forth between Jamaica and England for the rest of her life post-Crimea, and so too does her genealogy extend and expand to postcolonial Jamaica. Jamaica's relationship to constructing a history has much different stakes than British multiculturalism. If Seacole in the British system is "the right woman in the right place" (Seacole [1857] 2005, 80)—the resurrected singular "black" exception to the white rule of the history of empire—in the Jamaican context, she is never fully disappeared from public vision or imagination, staying in local news, as in her sister's obituary in a Kingston newspaper, the *Daily Gleaner*, which said of Mary Seacole, "She was an old Jamaican character who was quite a notable figure in her day and who was representative of a class of Jamaican women which have almost wholly passed away" ("Seacole" 1905). Seacole's turn-of-the-century reference is nostalgic for the waning privileges of empire for Creole elites, an intimacy foregrounded in the history between Creole women and English men.

This move toward Seacole as Jamaican national heroine despite her mobile racial and geographic identifications in her lifetime reflects postcolonial investment in Afro-Caribbean culture as a unifying national culture in the consolidation of independent national identity. As Deborah A. Thomas (2004, 2, 5) argues about "the emotional resonance of nationality" in Jamaica, "the attempt to consolidate a nationalist state, to inculcate soon-to-be-ex-subjects with a sense of national belonging and loyalty that would naturalize new relations of authority, validated a particular kind of citizen and a specific vision of cultural 'progress' and 'development.'" Seacole is reclaimed into the Afro-Caribbean fold even while narratively distancing herself from enslaved and black-identified Jamaicans in an effort to marshal representations that combat the "development dreams that positioned Africa, Latin America, and the Caribbean as 'backward' but ultimately recuperable" post–Second World War, as Thomas has argued (7).

Seacole's innovative civic desire, then, comes particularly from her status as a Creole colonial subject. Her narrative's hybrid form reflects her understanding of the very visible recognition, legally and culturally, of the great variety of racialized categories and their contingent "plots" available to colonial subjects in the Victorian era.[14] This is especially true of Seacole, of course, who inherits capital opportunity and mobility from her Creole status, which puts her in a privileged position beside those freed black workers who are dangerously laboring on the Panama railroad construction, for instance.[15] Seacole, according to Caribbeanist Rhonda Frederick (2003, 498), "repeatedly asserts her exceptional colour and professional skill" to differentiate her body and her labor in compromised frontier locations where she is, as in Jamaica, among a range of races, classes, and classifications. But like her marriage, she barely mentions Jamaica at all (a point that many of her contemporary critics note), particularly its complex racial and political context.[16]

"Creole," for Seacole, designates a sticky area of race politics, a question of "vanguard or buffer," as Shirley Elizabeth Thompson argues in *Exiles at Home* (2009).[17] Understandings of race and power in this mid-Victorian era were not contained by freedom and bondage alone, nor was there necessarily a sense of racial community or solidarity among those designated non- or not-quite white. Mixed-race Creole citizenship in Jamaica, and for Seacole, was bound up in its "buffer" status between the white planter class and the freed

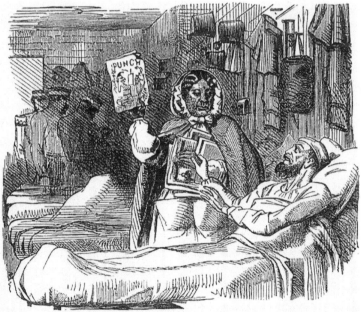

FIGURES 4.7 AND 4.8. Seacole in her recognizable roles of hotelier and doctress: *Mrs Seacole's Hotel in the Crimea*, frontispiece, *Wonderful Adventures of Mrs. Seacole in Many Lands*; and *Our Own Vivandiere* from *Punch* (1857).

black community, in part due to the long history of freeing children born of slaves and masters in Jamaica, as opposed to the custom in the United States; Seacole's mother, in fact, was also a free Creole who kept a hotel and nursed British soldiers.[18] Counter to novelist Anthony Trollope's ([1859] 1968, 195) comments after staying in Seacole's sister's hotel—"There is something of a mystery about hotels in the British West Indies. They are always kept by fat middle-aged colored ladies who have not husbands"—Seacole's own frank admission of her parentage and the genealogy of her trades, that of hotelier and "doctress" (figures 4.7 and 4.8) recalls the open secret of Hemings's relationship to Jefferson and to the mass sexual entanglements of enslavement, colonialism, and its afterlives.

In fact, a "Creole" woman as hotelier was so common that, though women had no official access to politics, the position of playing host to men of power from the colonies had "social effect," as Frederick (2003) attests and as postcolonial critic Jenny Sharpe (2003) has outlined in her work on concubinage in the nineteenth-century Caribbean. There was power and protection in the influence of these unofficial socialities between Creole-identified Caribbean women and white British soldiers, sailors, and businessmen—as well as vulnerabilities in these genealogical links.

Seacole then extraordinarily extends a long line of Creole women's civic participation in hospitality and care, outlined in the work of scholar Sean X. Goudie (2008), laced as it is with the fraught history of forced and coerced sexual relationships. To trace this genealogy of Creole women's subjectivity to Seacole is to understand both the opportunities and the limits that, as Sandra Gunning (2001a, 33) argues, "color, status, region, and gendered experience" introduce into diaspora discourse. Seacole's Creole identification leaves her vulnerable to claims like Nightingale's that she was running "I will not call it a 'bad house' [i.e., a brothel]—but something not very unlike it—in the Crimean War. . . . She was very kind to the men &, what is more, to the Officers—& did some good—& made many drunk" (quoted in Seacole [1857] 2005, 180). It also stands as a recognizable and even safe role, despite or diffusing spectacular tensions in colonial centers around free black and Indian insurrection potential (Rappaport 2007, 4).[19] But Seacole and the civic desires surrounding her narrative are not strictly palliative and palatable colonial citizenships in their ties to the long sexual histories of black women's experience of violence and limited entry into the political sphere (Winters 2016). The genealogical traces of this sexualized history are largely erased in Seacole's corrective histories, except in the service of pointing out Nightingale's racism—thus reproducing respectability politics in antiracist discourse. Rather than fetishize masculinist

FIGURE 4.9. Seacole stamp from Jamaica (2005).

rebellion, then, as the only civic agency and desire that can be appropriately appended to black political thought, the complexity of Seacole's own visibility, reception, and insistence on civic participation makes other histories of the political available in and to black feminist thought.

Mention of Seacole picks up in Jamaica in 1954, when her name is given to the Jamaica Nurses Association headquarters. In 2005, in commemoration of the bicentennial of her birth, Jamaica, too, issues stamps in her honor. Unlike the reproduction of the National Portrait Gallery painting with an elderly Seacole wearing three Crimean war medals in stately three-quarters profile (one among several portraits including Virginia Woolf and Winston Churchill issued in commemoration of the gallery itself), the four Jamaican stamps attempt to contextualize Seacole's historical and institutional significance.[20] In full color, the first engages Seacole's youthful education in "herbal remedies and medicine," connecting her to Jamaican science and innovation, and also to Afro-based notions of Jamaican identity. The second, showing a slightly older Seacole in the same yellow with an image of the residence hall named for her at the University of West Indies, Mona (figure 4.9), claims educational importance beyond her mere insertion into an already existing curriculum as the black Nightingale. The third stamp imagines an even older Seacole in bright dress attending to a soldier wounded in the Crimean War. The fourth and final stamp in the series presents the same national portrait image that is on the British stamp, with the relief image of a closeup of Seacole's purported medals from Turkey, France, and Britain for her service, and that now include a 1990 awarding of the Order of Merit from the Government of Jamaica. Though Seacole is still being adopted and adapted into strategies of nationalism here, her contextualization within institutional and world history is instructive as to the different claims being made on her image here linked to a complex and multifaceted history of skill, service, and continuing education. And though

Seacole does not have a statue in National Heroes Park in Kingston, unlike Nanny of the Maroons, she occupies the space of public memorial as a Jamaican heroine who contributed to the shape of the modern world, something akin to if not fully aligned with decolonized nationalism.

Seacole, in her 1857 narrative, as many contemporary critics note, also refuses to disavow empire. Seacole in fact positions herself as a philanthropic agent to the British themselves. Seacole repeatedly describes both herself and her fellow Creoles administering aid to the British, as in the following passage:

> It was a terrible thing to see young people in the youth and bloom of life suddenly stricken down, not in battle with an enemy that threatened their country, but in vain contest with a climate that refused to adopt them. Indeed, the mother country pays a dear price for the possession of her colonies.
>
> I think all who are familiar with the West Indies will acknowledge that Nature has been favourable to strangers in a few respects, and that one of these has been in instilling into the hearts of the Creoles an affection for English people and an anxiety for their welfare, which shows itself warmest when they are sick and suffering. I can safely appeal on this point to any one who is acquainted with life in Jamaica. Another benefit has been conferred upon them by inclining the Creoles to practise the healing art, and inducing them to seek out the simple remedies which are available for the terrible diseases by which foreigners are attacked, and which are found growing under the same circumstances which produce the illness they minister to. So true is it that beside the nettle ever grows the cure for its sting. (1994, 58–59)

Seacole plays on the dual concepts of contagion theory and racialized climatic constitution discourse here, suggesting that the British are racially different, and hence vulnerable in their colonial endeavors. In doing so, she highlights how colonial civic participation is a necessary part of imperial success, even as it is produced through the pathologizing of native and black bodies.[21]

Seacole's repurposing of the Western discourses of "white men saving brown women from brown men" (Spivak 1999, 287) is clear here: it is, literally, a brown woman saving white male bodies (and a few indigenous peoples in New Grenada and Panama) from their own colonial desires. Her narrative takes pains to characterize her good works, with words like "benevolent" and "service" cropping up in her lengthy appendix multiple times, and with journalist W. H. Russell writing of her "singleness of heart, true charity, and Christian works" in his preface (Seacole 2005, 5). Similar to the white abolitionist introductions

FIGURE 4.10. Mary Seacole represents for all of the widowed Creole nurses in *Horrible Histories* (2012).

to slave narratives, this authenticating maneuver, instead of verifying truth (for Seacole and her story are already well known via newspaper accounts and the like), is an attempt to manage Seacole's story against charges of "opportunism" and toward women's philanthropy, a newly more accepted middle-class Victorian occupation.[22] Seacole's narrative is a story of getting out of Jamaica and on to Crimea by any means necessary; she attempts to go through state channels, trying to join Nightingale's flock of "angel" nurses, and is rebuffed many times by many government-affiliated persons for a complicated mix of age, class, sexual, and racialized reasons intimated earlier in the bad house quote. The nursing profession was attempting to rehab its image as the domain of working-class, hard-drinking, morally loose women, and Seacole, forty-eight years old in 1853, used to run hotels for soldiers that served alcohol and were associated with the long line of mixed-race women who were themselves evidence of sexual, and hence racial, impropriety. She then turned to her hotelier experience to garner capital support for her trip when her British resources were exhausted. Commerce is painted as a means of attaining access to "soft" rights of opportunity, like transnational mobility and the right to work, beyond the basic life needs articulated and limited by contemporary humanitarian enterprises. Capital, for Seacole, opens up adventures that the law never could for a mixed-race woman of the empire, paths opened up through culture that expose her to vulnerability at the same time that they exploit the vulnerabilities of empire.

By relocating Seacole's celebrated adventures and racial subjectivity within the unstable border territories of empire's expansion, I confront how imperialism opened and opens up roles for women, including nonwhite women, roles that enable an expansion of rights outside of colonial and national laws.[23] Seacole constructs herself as a "pioneer" on the frontier of the New World, an entrepreneur in the businesses of war, hospitality, and public health. Of course, Seacole's narrative of entrepreneurship repeatedly plays on what Gunning (2001b, 953) names "the politics of white crisis"—the global catastrophes that are constructed out of manifest destiny and the expansion of empire, such as the capital campaign to build the Panama railroad, the Gold Rush, and the Crimean War over trade routes. Seacole (2005, 132) is open about her policy of charging the officers who could pay and ministering free to those of the lower ranks in the Crimean battlefield. Her alignment of capitalism and humanitarianism mimics the complexity of the industry of war and the nationalist affective rhetorics that undergird its public face even today. It is this relationship to empire and capital to which this chapter now turns, to trace the histories of Seacole pinned to ambition in her own moment, as well as to map black women's performances of civic desire across empire and their difficult inclusion into critiques of empire's racial routes.

The Self-Made Black Woman; or, "Going Down in History / That's My Prize for It"

Building on Seacole's own blatant representation of herself as both savior and entrepreneur of empire comes another mode of imagining Seacole, one that makes a heroine of a different sort through Seacole's adventures. Not needing to be seen as a selfless helpmeet, like Nightingale, whose virtue stands against the perverse moralism of her racism, Seacole emerges as a very modern black subject in contemporary historical modes. A second *Horrible Histories* clip, aired on April 13, 2012, further embodies this difficult balance of recuperating a complex and varied black women's history with the ever-present risk of fetishizing black women via that historical recovery (Cohen and Connolly 2012). Set to a beat that resembles Beyoncé's "Single Ladies," this segment once again features actress Dominique Moore as the heavily accented Mary Seacole. Here, our heroine sings an R&B version of her tale, complete with choreography that features white male dancers costumed as Victorian British soldiers in Crimea (figure 4.10).

FIGURE 4.11. A reproduction of the original cover of Mary Seacole's 1857 narrative.

While the characterization of Seacole as R&B/pop chanteuse points to a dangerously reductive stereotype of black women and their limited performative idioms (much as Seacole's exaggerated and anachronistic accent keys to an essentialist script of Jamaican identity), the complicated staging of history here starts to slip into different forms of historical and civic desire than those already mapped, forms that the flipped script of contagion and cure suggested. The dancing British soldiers who surround Seacole in every scene of the music-video-style clip mirror Seacole's support during her day, not from abolitionist women of the nineteenth century, but from British troops and high-ranking male British royalty themselves (Keller 2011; Figes 2012). This lack of feminized sentimentality in the company of men translates to the tone of Seacole's narrative itself, with its emphasis on her love of war and its narrative of economic innovation and self-reliance.[24]

As Seacole tells her history of being an "Independent Woman" (spliced with medical advice), the genre begins to gel: Seacole becomes the hardscrabble equivalent to the romantically and financially self-sustaining heroines of contemporary R&B, a recognizable version of black womanhood that merges capital success, race, and gender. In this, she is marked as a pioneer for alternative models of black women's history that emphasize financial stability and self-reliance as political acts alongside more traditional models of collective racial politics. Constructing different genealogies makes sense of Seacole's difficult place in historical narratives involving sexuality, capital, and ideals of social justice today that are implicitly haunted by a respectability politics in their reluctance to recognize the sexual and the performative as politically dynamic and viable spheres of civic desire and participation for women. In other words, celebrity and commodity culture don't have to denote only suspicious political reading, and in fact are feminized modes of articulating the political.

In her own time, the 1857 publication of *Wonderful Adventures* capped off a capital campaign for Seacole, who was left bankrupt by the sudden end to the war. Unable to rely on state or other institutional support, Seacole relied on public appeals to try to gain financial sovereignty on her return. Her memoir was written hastily in the months after Crimea and aimed to fit into the growing body of journalistic, travel, and photographic accounts of the conflict.[25] But as critics have also noted, *Adventures* is both of its time and genre and more "idiosyncratic," as Salih (2005, xxxii, xxxiv) notes, commodifying the already circulating reputation of its "unique" author as frank, flamboyant, and unsentimental except for her British patriotism—an image that Seacole plays up on her narrative's original cover (figure 4.11). Dressed in militaristic garb, Seacole directly appeals to her constituency—her market of white British citizens in the colonial metropole, London, who are riding a wave of nationalism after the Crimean campaign. Seacole's performance and then her repeated redeployments expose all citizenship as performance of civic desire, as well as vulnerable to the fungibility of this desire through law and institutionality as political and social means of living.

Seacole's liminal racial, gendered, geographical, and sexualized position then allowed her to perform such anomalous adventures and to have such an expansive enjoyment of empire's constructed privileges. Seacole was not, of course, alone as a "black" celebrity of the time period, from Queen Victoria's "adoption" of Sarah Bonetta Forbes, an African girl given to her as a "gift" in 1850 (Gerzina 2003, 3), to visits from Harriet Jacobs and Frederick Douglass during their own publicity tours that also highlighted the culture of abolition and racial acceptance in Britain at the highest level of royal public relations (Hawthorne 2000, 319–20). At the same time that England was vilifying "savage" colonial subjects in Jamaica and in India in their newspapers after the Morant Bay rebellion and the Indian Mutiny, it was also consuming shows of *Uncle Tom's Cabin* adaptations and other racialized types of entertainment (Salih 2005, xxvii; Brody 1998, 74–82).

Seacole participates in this racialized economy—an economy where, as Elizabeth Fox-Genovese (1987, 172) suggests with refreshing honesty about the claims of black women's autobiographical writing of the period, "Black women write to be read by those who might influence the course of public events, might pay money for their book, or might authenticate them as authors." She stands as a celebrity not fully constructed or originating as an example of racial injury. Her publicity tour is not asking for recognition due to her fame as the named representative of one of a sentimentally rendered mass of those "lacking" rights, but instead as a citizen of empire who desires and lays claim to both private and state protections—to the institutions that can sustain life where it stands.[26] Following Hannah Arendt's ([1951] 2004, 418) provocative claim that "only fame will eventually answer the repeated complaint of refugees of all social strata that nobody here knows who I am; and it is true that the chances of the famous refugee are improved just as a dog with a name has a better chance to survive than a stray dog who is just a dog in general," I argue that Seacole's Victorian reception manages to inhabit contradictory responses to race and gender and to wriggle just outside of them—due to the genealogical intersection of the civic desires surrounding her age, widow status, Creole identification, and the historical rise of mass media. Arendt's pessimistic take on fame and civic inclusion instructs in its diagnosis of the legal limits of cultural representation and attention, but it cannot account for celebrity circulation and reception that exceeds the law and contains the possibility of public recognition for women and minority subjects.

Endorsed by various British societies of men and individual members of the royal family, Seacole nonetheless remains a "free agent" in terms of her own cultural strategies for recognition, if not her financial solvency. Seacole's entry into the public eye—her much reported exploits in the Crimea—are, as she herself names them, "my one and only claim to interest the public" (131). Her express goal to become "a Crimean Heroine!" is indelicate and unvarnished (76). Victorian representations of Seacole are no less direct in their praise; as the *Times* reports on Seacole's 1857 Surrey Gardens fundraiser, of which there were four nights of sold-out performances:

Notwithstanding that the charge for admission was quintupled, there was an immense concourse in the hall, and it need scarcely be said that the audience was of a character more "exclusive" than is customary at the transpontine musical performances. . . . Mrs. Seacole sat in state in front of the centre gallery, supported by Lorde Rokeby on one side, by Lorde George Paget on the other, and surrounded by members of her committee. Few names were more familiar to members of the public during the late war than that of Mrs. Seacole. . . . At the end of both the first and second parts, the name of Mrs. Seacole was shouted by a thousand voices. The genial old lady rose from her place and smiled benignantly on the assembled multitude, amid a tremendous and continued cheering. Never did woman seem happier, and never was hearty and kindly greeting bestowed upon a worthier object. (Seacole [1857] 2005, 32)

Patron and patronized, Seacole's imagined textual community extends beyond her already difficult to categorize autobiography, into the public sphere of newspapers and periodicals in Britain and Jamaica, and in her own memoir's circulation (Salih 2004, 173).[27] Seacole manages her way into history through what Sandra Pouchet Paquet (1992, 67) refers to as "an entirely public account of self" in her memoir. Void of most sentimental investments or "private" concerns such as marriage or motherhood, *Wonderful Adventures* is also part of an extraliterate conversation with the cartoons, portraits, and other circulating accounts of Seacole as British and Jamaican heroine, a campaign of sorts for Seacole's social, cultural, and economic recognition by the national body politic. Indeed, the newly global (thanks to print technology) theater of war made sure that "all the soldiers and sailors knew her," according to illustrator William Simpson; she was also covered by journalist William Russell, the *Times* (which frequently reported on Seacole's fundraisers and the like), and the popular Victorian humor periodical *Punch*, whose poem about Seacole she reproduces nearly in full in her own text (Frederick 2003, 494).

Celebrity itself is the "prize" for Seacole by the *Horrible Histories'* song's end: "Going down in history / that's my prize for it." The "it"—Seacole's hard medical, social, and cultural labor—like the historical rehabilitation campaign imagined in the video this chapter started with, is a question of "Public Relations." By making the question of history literal, *Horrible Histories* and Seacole's own narrative's claim to be "the historian of Spring Hill" nod to the constructed nature of history itself, especially as it rests on the celebrity shoulders of great figures in its most mundane and popular iterations. In this sense, Seacole joins the other figures in this book as they are recruited into a racialized celebrity around various contemporary politics that construct, manage, and discipline difference. And though barely mentioned directly, Seacole's "berry-brown" face is, of course, part of why she is notable in the first place. Her exceptional status as a woman of color in the Crimea, along with her widow and working-class status, allows her innovative adventures in labor and self-representation that few middle-class white women or working-class black women in their respective "home" countries were allowed. That difference is what affords her her exceptional, celebrity status in her own era as much as it is what systemically erases her from institutional memory for so long—and what makes her an uneasy fit into corrective multicultural histories of today.

Nursing Diaspora Desires

In 2019, Jackie Sibblies Drury staged a new play, *Marys Seacole*, at Lincoln Center, that offered an "exploration of what it means to be a woman who is paid to care" (Drury 2019b). Drury had rocketed to literary fame with the disorienting *Fairview* (2019a), which won the Pulitzer Prize for its disquieting, surreal representation of white media literacy and visual bias in viewing black subjectivity. *Marys Seacole* disorients, too, by making visible the feminized labor of care both within the assumptions of family roles and socially within a labor workforce of immigrant women across time periods signified through lighting and costume though often occupying the same stage. The play moves between Seacole's past and the contemporary present filled with "Marys"— nannies and nurses doing intimate care work at low pay—in order to locate the "impossible roles" of both white and nonwhite feminized labor beyond progress narratives that occlude care work as a significant sphere for both feminist and racial justice (https://www.lct.org/explore/blog/marys-seacole -trailer/). "Impossible" here denotes the mix of duty and adventure that care work toggles between for feminized subjects. Following the pioneering work of Darlene Clark Hine (1989a) on early twentieth-century black women and nursing, as well as work on contemporary South Asian diaspora nurses by Sujani K. Reddy (2015), Drury's play and my reading of Seacole and civic desire reflect on the complex figure of the nurse in global networks of gender, race, and empire. The *New Yorker* article (Frazier 2011) mentioned earlier in this chapter also treads on this terrain beyond its Nightingale comparison to give us a glimpse of a more nuanced reading of Caribbean women's particular history with/in nursing; when the women who organized the local event on Seacole that occasioned the "Talk of the Town" piece pronounce her a "model" for Caribbean women in "global society," they also articulate a kinship with

Seacole's intangible ambition. As one organizer claims, "Nothing is more exciting than being a nurse"—a sentiment met, the reader is told, with "nods of approval" from the crowd. Feminized labor and celebrity are the available vehicles to authorize civic and personal desire for black diasporic women, as formal politics excludes and excluded them, as does the unprotected violence of solo travel and migration. Culture and cultural scripts offer viable paths for modern desires rather than certifying respectable desires and disavowing others.

Mirroring Seacole's own overwhelmingly articulated desires to experience the practice of science, the thrill of travel, and the rush of war, *Marys Seacole* and the article in the *New Yorker* begin to expose Seacole as more than the photo-negative of Nightingale, more than a heroic historical recovery project. Instead, the contemporary care workers and Caribbean nurses can claim her exceptional adventures as "educational" at the level of social, economic, and cultural mobility for black women. While Taylor (2018) sees distancing from empire in such affectively inflected economies in Seacole's own era, I read both the historical and present moments as less about reciprocal models of care and more about collective desire and the right to desire. Such ambition—Seacole's and the contemporary nurses'—is difficult to reconcile in much nineteenth- and early twentieth-century historical research on women as more than a narrative strategy, as Kali Gross (2006) theorizes in her study of black women and criminality, *Colored Amazons*. Seacole skirts the boundaries of social appropriateness in her time and beyond, but her *Adventures* are, in Omise'eke Natasha Tinsley's (2010, 184) words, "quite a bit queerer" than either a narrative of Victorian mimic or Race Woman. "Queer," here, is not necessarily subversive in the contemporary progressive political sense, but instead an alternative version of a contemporary immigrant narrative that traces the routes of privilege, difference, and worldly desire through the "historical specificity" of black women as political subjects across two centuries (S. Hall 2014, 308).

Beyond the limits of corrective history that the recasting of Seacole as racialized hero suggests, the reorganization of Seacole's genealogy serves as a reordering of the possibilities of distributive justice in the contemporary global market of labor and capital, especially the collective health and healthcare labor of black diaspora women that Seacole has come to represent. For instance, in an April 2010 article in the *Economist*, "The Caribbean Brain Drain: Nursing a Grievance," Seacole is offered up as the foremother to a long line of Caribbean nurses who "train" at home only to work abroad. Citing a World Bank study on nursing shortages in the region due to low pay, the short piece scoffs at the World Health Organization's initiative to change recruiting practices to "strike a balance between the human right to health, and the right of health-care professionals to make their own career choices." While the *Economist's* historically unmoored conclusion is that the Caribbean needs to pony up more money for nurses to stay, the picture the World Bank study paints resonates with ambivalent reactions to Seacole herself, especially in the academy.

With massive structural inequality stemming from the histories of colonialism and imperialism and their creation of global markets in black labor, "history" hardly provides ideal forms for exemplary black subjects, particularly for black women. Seacole crystallizes the false "balance" that empire offers as professional and class mobility that globalization promises to some and denies others, casting women in two narratives of social pathology. More than the *Economist* could fathom, Seacole stands at the intersection of critical and ethical desires to see the postcolonial world lean toward a justice that seems contradictory at best, and so echoes Roderick A. Ferguson's (2003) own call to attend to how capitalism opens up spaces for the "nonnormative" in its very construction of alienated labor and commodity culture, spaces that are deeply gendered, here feminized even as they are cast in the masculinist mode of historical adventure.

Seacole's nationalist and pro-empire claims are hard for us as contemporary critics to swallow, as her race-related duties seem minimal in the narrative, mostly condemning white US racism and often cast as incidental to the duties to empire. But if her philanthropic claims next to personal gain seem crass to us, it may be because they call out capitalism and philanthropy as coterminous industries built on the imperial expansion of civic myths of race. They also expose the myth or ideal of racial belonging as founded on an assumed collective history of racial injury and vulnerability. Her representation leaves us seeking ways to narrate black women as subjects that account for the difficult affects of empire—ambition, desire for mobility, desire for capital success— that reckon with the patriarchal constructions of women's positionalities as domestic citizens of their "home" communities and discarded political subjects in colonial centers.[28] Seacole's quest, her adventures in search of social, cultural, economic, and historical rights, endures partially because she maps the complicated world made publicly accessible via technologies of print and photography, themselves related to the "study" of racial difference within colonialism. This intersection marks a history of black academic, national, and civic desire with histories that insist on black diaspora citizens as architects and consumers of the public sphere, as well as savvy readers of available models of civic participation. Those routes to political and civil as well as economic, social, and cultural rights are not always models that those of us doing feminist and antiracist work feel politically comfortable with, but they must be explored as we answer their legacy in today's world—especially in how we think of multiple points of access to health, wealth, and rights in discourses of "development" in the Caribbean, Africa, and other sites of settler colonialism.

Seacole embodies a global citizenship that merges the expected routes of historical power exacted from metropole to colony with a reminder that the colonized world critically engaged and transformed the body politic of colonial centers with a range of practices akin to citizenship, practices that left subjects vulnerable to violent dissolution as well as to new and exciting adventures in self-making. These entailed innovative interpretations of a social contract with and for women of the African diaspora. Seacole's histories remind us of the affective and material possibilities, traced in C. Taylor's (2018) reading of her memoir, that empiric modernity created and sustained for black women, in her era and today, as a vanguard of black mobility through global capital that troubles the intersection between race, gender, and rights at a time of uneven global black bondage. What we, as critics, make of Seacole's exception does not have to be corrective histories of individual triumph over individual and structural racisms, or endless feminist competitions with the Florence Nightingales of the world. Instead, Seacole's celebrity offers embedded histories of race and gender that imagine the full complexity of black women's political subjectivity and its innovative engagements with and responses to civic desire, rather than agency, in the face and wake of Enlightenment modernity.

Chapter Five

#DEVELOPMENTGOALS

SOVEREIGNTY, SARAH FORBES BONETTA, AND THE

PRODUCTION OF THE BLACK FEMINIST POLITICAL SUBJECT

Mind is your only ruler, sovereign.
—MARCUS GARVEY

Amid the current controversy of whether and which woman should appear on the exclusively white, male canvas of US currency, there was an all too common identification error on the internet: a picture that purported to photographically represent a young Harriet Tubman was actually a photograph of nineteen-year-old Sarah Forbes Bonetta, an African woman who grew up as the "orphan ward" of Queen Victoria after her kidnapping at age eight. Cultural studies scholar Janell Hobson (2017b) notes this slippage with keen interest, arguing that the misidentification made her think of the seemingly stark differences between the "colonized" Bonetta and the "self-emancipated" Tubman, and led her to a more nuanced consideration of Tubman's own trajectory as a black heroine, feted by Queen Victoria herself. Hobson argues that "such interlocking histories obviously require transnational critiques that interrogate how we construct 'colonized' versus 'liberated' subjects" in her brief post on the occasion of a newly recovered carte de visite of a young Harriet Tubman, this time correctly identified. This slippage, like the incongruence of Hank Willis Thomas's *When Harriet Met Saartje* woodcut, asks one to pit ideals about agentic racial subjects against tropes of life under subjection. That both Hobson and Thomas ask us to do that through the medium of visual recognition is a revealing insight into how these positions, and these politics, have taken embodied presence in circuits of black celebrity and what, following Christian Metz ([1975] 1982) and Lindon Barrett (1998), we might call their scopic economies.

This pairing and slippage ask us, as Hobson does, to think across these celebrity bodies and how they stand as and in for the politics of agency and rights in the modern world. *Infamous Bodies* has traced how public negotiations of the meaning of human rights have been waged by, on, and through the embodied presence of black women celebrities. Their lives and afterlives have shaped the concepts and practices of freedom, consent, contract, and citizenship across the Anglophone African diaspora in the era of Enlightenment modernity. As "star images" or the more capacious "star texts" that Richard Dyer (2013) lays out, they operate at the key junction of presence/absence, ordinary/extraordinary, with all of those tensions laid out over the terrain of blackness in such a way as to render these terms quite material. For Tubman, her image as a comely youth disrupts a celebrity image of matriarchal, desexed heroism, strength, and commitment to racial justice and introduces a window into a deeply gendered, sexualized version of the political subject like that suggested by Treva B. Lindsey and Jessica Marie Johnson (2014) in their "Searching for Climax" article on Tubman's sexual history. But, as Hobson nods toward in her own work on the cultural investment in black beauty, it also makes Tubman into an even more marketable icon, an attractive star text for the current era of "Beyoncé feminism" and its critics.

But the infamous bodies this book has considered in depth—Wheatley, Hemings, Baartman, Seacole, and, in this chapter, Bonetta—instantiate a fame, a celebrity, that is formed both with and against the star system as outlined above, even in the "democratization of fame" in the eighteenth century that both Leo Braudy (1997) and Joseph Roach (2007) write from. As Nicole R. Fleetwood (2015a) notes of the formation and circulation of racial icons, they are unpredictable subjects even when cast in predictable scripts, managed not just by themselves or appointed handlers for glory, but also by a public sphere struggling to manage its cultural, political, and legal narratives of race, gender, and rights in the modern world.

Bonetta, as she comes into the contemporary moment of celebrity, charts a path that is both familiar and made strange: a *bildungs* narrative gone meta, graphing Bonetta's self- and star-development at the same time: What kind of political icon was she, or could she be recovered into? As Joseph R. Slaughter (2007) has noted, the trope of self-development can be and has been harnessed into the project of capital, colonial, and postcolonial development. Such a version of development, one that involves resource extraction rather than building, resonates with the counterdevelopment project of so many corrective histories of black women celebrities: defined through plots of racial injury so as to develop antiracism through negative example. But here the reverse strain of critique, one that moves from black feminist concerns with self-development and self-possession, key offshoots of agency, flowers out to uncomfortably mirror the hypermasculinized terrain of sovereignty—cultural, national, and individual mastery over one's domain. This final chapter, threading through the difficult commodification of black women's celebrity and self-making practices that engage with this celebrity culture, looks for something more than a diagnosis of false consciousness and displaced desire for self-determination through self-care. Tracing Bonetta's recent curatorial and critical reemergence demonstrates the difficulty of recovering a politically recognizable corrective history in her visual legacy. Examining very recent representations of her history and image reveals a genealogy of compromised self-making as the sustainable, enduring, vulnerable political work of black women's celebrity.

Sovereignty, Sensation, Surface

While Wheatley's writing and Seacole's war efforts cast them into the public sphere for their "positive" accomplishments in line with mores of their times and nation-states, the five figures in *Infamous Bodies* decidedly occupy a terrain beyond that of the "respectable" fame Douglass lays out in his exhortation against the "extravagance" of claiming celebrity. Their accomplishments, if one wishes to track their lives in those terms, are very much cast in terms of suspicious reading. Their highly contested political meanings and cultural significances register in their representations like Roach's (2007, 91) "afterimage" that "does not exist as an object but rather as a sensation that persists even after the external stimulation that caused it has disappeared, like the shape of a flame that lingers in the eye after the candle has gone out." Bonetta, the most cosmopolitan but least "famous" figure I study here, exists less in the realm of "icon"—which usually denotes "a celebrity with staying power," as Fleetwood argues (2015a, 56)—and more as a gauzy afterimage, a sensation of the history of blackness in the West that operates on the surface of the public skin of celebrity.

I return to the construction of celebrity via the image here to consider the corrective histories and representations of Sarah (or Sally) Forbes Bonetta, the young Gambian girl who, social legend has it, was "rescued" from ritual sacrifice by an antislavery British sailor and trader who negotiated her release as a gift from the king of Gambia to Queen Victoria in 1850, seventeen years after Britain finally abolished slavery. Bonetta became a part of the extended royal family, with her care paid for by Queen Victoria and landmark events such as her wedding (figure 5.1) finding her featured in the press of the day. But

FIGURE 5.1. Bonetta in her wedding dress (1862). Photograph by Camille Silvy.

her enduring public presence is through her afterimages, the photographic portraits and cartes de visite that provide us with not (just) the lure of knowability or recognition, but the "sensation" of the incongruous pairing of "black" and "Victorian" that has, in recent years, spurred a series of photographic exhibits—all ostensibly meant to normalize the visible presence of blackness into popular conceptions of what Victorian-era history looked like.[1]

This recovery of black history through the visual has in many ways dominated and organized the recovery of Bonetta's life as told through extant letters—with the photographs acting as window into a set of conventional wisdom incongruities. "You'll never guess who this woman's godmother was," reads one clickbait article (A. White 2014), for instance—and indeed, Bonetta's claim to fame is not through her self-authored performances, her entry into entertainment cultures, or her reproductive life. But, like Hemings, it is her presumed incongruous proximity to white power—here in the form of the maternal affections of Queen Victoria, colonial leader—that makes her famous. And, in the media-saturated age of her life, it is in the visual where this fame resides, in the visual representation of her phenotypic blackness as disruptor of limited notions of historical and colonial intimacy. Her blackness acts as the Barthesian "punctum" that pierces the frame of the illusive white sovereign body of Britishness imagined as history today. In Bonetta's own day, as Gretchen Holbrook Gerzina (2003, 5) argues, the eighteenth-century surge in the black population of England "was transformed by the Victorians into a sense that they had defined, had described, and knew black people." This twinned sensation of exoticization and recognition that characterizes Bonetta's representations and recoveries represents, of course, a longer problem of photography's relationship to blackness—one that dovetails with practices of scientific racism that continue to structure ways of seeing racial meaning, belonging, and exclusion (see Campt 2017; K. A. Thompson 2015). The photographs of Bonetta mark her body's occupation of Victorian fashions that denote self-possession and control—a form of self-sovereignty being denied to the black body through the very medium of photography—in which Bonetta's body finds a public audience.

I push on the visual representation of Bonetta's embodied celebrity here to pick up on another strand of rights theory that I connect to the "sensation" that Roach suggests as the affective power or even medium/form of "it" or celebrity. Bonetta's body is subject to struggles over sovereignty during her own life and beyond. Sovereignty holds a dual distinction of being a key site of and for the enforcement of rights. It is also a key node of debate about the bureaucratic, cultural, and ideological perils of claiming "autonomy" as the key virtue of a rights-bearing entity. As a synonym for autonomy and independence, but also power and authority, sovereignty is at the heart of the struggle over discussions of human rights and black freedoms. On the one hand, sovereignty has been attached to the "necropolitics" of marking populations for death in the era of the nation-state, as well as the violent exclusions of the nation-state as marked by the figure of the "refugee" for political theorists such as Hannah Arendt ([1951] 2004) and Giorgio Agamben (1998), and of the enslaved/colonized body in more recent challenges from Achille Mbembe

(2003), Alexander G. Weheliye (2014), and Jasbir K. Puar (2017). Sovereignty for former colonial states and first nations, as well as Pan-African solidarities, has also been the basis for refusing international, Western interference in the decolonial projects of citizenship within "protective" borders, including incursions and demands by international human rights legal institutions.[2] Sovereignty has then acted as contested terrain, agent and alibi, in the history and present of settler colonialism.

This second deployment of the terms and possibilities of sovereignty has also given rise to discourses of self-determination and the inviolability of the sovereign body. As Crystal Parikh (2017, 55–56) explains in *Writing Human Rights*: "Because self-determination found limited legitimized expression in the sovereign state form, domestic repression and abuse executed by authoritarian or one-party regimes led to the well-publicized scandal and 'decisive failure' of postcolonial governance beginning in the 1960s. The principle of state sovereignty . . . rendered the recognition and protection of *all other* rights subject to the dominion of individual nation-states." Parikh's historical reading of the emergence of postcolonial and international human rights' reliance on sovereign state models also deftly diagnoses the ways that self-determination rights are subsumed under national discipline. She shows the imbricated nature, then, of three "types" of freedom that Orlando Patterson ([1991] 1997) lays out: personal, civic, and sovereign. Choice, belonging, and power share uncomfortable intimacies in Parikh's timeline (here extended to include Enlightenment modernity), and in contemporary interpretive practices that seek to account for material embodiment—the fates and the desires of the embodied—in antiracist analysis. Included in these conversations, then, is the way that sovereign body and self-determination discourses of self-care, bodily integrity, and human dignity, as well as those of consent and visibility, hinge on the metaphoric and structural imperatives of sovereignty as a political and personal goal of social justice. Following the work of Alexandra Moore (2015), Elizabeth S. Anker (2012), and Parikh (2017), among others, I consider sovereignty in relief of the base presumption of this book—a commitment to thinking through embodied vulnerability as the central state of political subjectivity with attentiveness not just to how to mitigate that vulnerability but also to how to incorporate its tenets and values, its own central epistemologies, into practices of reading for and imagining the political.

Bonetta's journey from supposed African royalty to sacrificial object to victim to gift to orphan to ward to goddaughter to colonial subject to arranged bride and finally to missionary represents both the pitfalls and promise of sovereignty. Attention to and corrective histories of Bonetta engage her in these debates over its political power and its potential authority on, in, and of embodiment. In this way, Bonetta as celebrity object also becomes the sensational flesh of Amber Musser's (2014) theorization. Musser argues for a reading of race, sexuality, gender, and embodiment as experiences that offer subjection not as an end but as a beginning to understanding the complex dynamics of power and domination that sovereignty suggests. Her terminology, when paired with the concept and ideal of sovereignty and with Roach's (2007) afterimage as sensation rather than just representation, allows us to think of sovereignty as more than either an object of political contestation or a political goal in and of itself, but as an affective, difficult calling—a critical attachment.

Though Musser's work explores the materiality of power and its experiences in terms of sexual masochism, placing her theory of enfleshed subjectivity next to the Victorian images of Bonetta and their frequent hailings into arguments of imagined repression—here racial and colonial—disrupts the search for agency and submission in/as the black political subject. Hortense J. Spillers's (1987) concept of flesh (the base of Musser's concept) argues that the black body as the vehicle and hope for possible human agency is eviscerated by the historical and material act of the Middle Passage. Bonetta's biography challenges existing visions and versions of that formational violence. Bonetta's enfleshment imagines the limits of the sovereign, the persistent surface and material pleasures of power, authority, autonomy, and independence, as well as those of being enfolded into, subjected to, and submitting to another entity or entities. It is, in short, against the repressive hypothesis of political subjectivity that locks us into a critical agent/victim opposition.

Bonetta's "star image" then provides a bookend to Phillis Wheatley's inaugural black celebrity as the site of black freedom debates and their potential unmaking—another diaspora subject, differently subjected and mobile, "captured" in the technologies and discourses of race and gender of their moment that, centuries later, attempt to discipline and recognize them through their sensational objectness. Recaptured and recapitulated as "black women" understood through epistemologies of agency and injury, Wheatley and Bonetta, as well as Hemings, Baartman, and Seacole, nonetheless persist beyond these frames and knowledges—inviting radical uncertainty of interpretation as they embody the bounds of sovereignty and the pleasures of (em)power(ment).

Wheatley and Bonetta share more than this depth and complexity of subject formation; they share the surface echo of being named for the ships that carried each of them, young girls, from Africa to their respective new Western homes, Boston and London. *Phillis* is, cruelly, the name of the slave ship that the kidnapped Wheatley was "brought" to America on; *Bonetta* was the name of the military ship that Captain Forbes captained, bringing the Gambian "gift" of Sarah Forbes Bonetta bearing both his name and that of his own ship. The renaming of the enslaved by whites in the slave trade, including owners, traders, and shipmen was, of course, common practice. This double conflation of girl and ship, theorized in C. Sharpe (2016), echoes and extends Paul Gilroy's (1993) trope of the black Atlantic—where the ship as chronotope is both the ineffable horror of the Middle Passage and the promise of a "free"(r) life of mobility and diaspora exchange through the masculine labor of modernity as sailors and traveling artists, writers, students, and performers. Mary Seacole most closely approximates this progressive vision of Gilroy's trope, where "the ship" offers unique opportunities to someone of Seacole's specific professional, racial, geographic, class, marriage, and gender background as it exceeds the boundaries of national law.

But Wheatley and Bonetta, literally named for their own difficult means of transport, are both ship and (non)agent, a conflation of chronotope and actor that defies the sovereignty of either body. To put it another way, to imagine Wheatley and Bonetta as the center of the "chronotope" is to draw out of Gilroy's existing model a temporality of deep vulnerability around sovereignty, where states of autonomy, freedom, and authority are as fleeting, complex, and compromised as the bodies and lives of these two extraordinary/ordinary young girls on both ends of the Middle Passage and free-subject-on-ship spectrum.[3] Gilroy's articulation of a need for a shape to diaspora subjectivity that emphasizes the nexus of time and space is then also one that could emphasize the pressures of embodiment—girl as ship,[4] girl on ship, royal ward on ship, wife on ship, widow on ship. Bonetta's gendering both before and after her initial journey to England in Forbes's ship demands a complicated account of any collective diaspora experience of "ungendering" as she performs the roles of enslaved flesh and upper-class British womanhood, both denying her even the illusive promise of free labor or sovereign subjectivity even as they allow her a viable, visible life.

These possible interpretive scenarios provide ways to think about all that can or cannot be known of Bonetta's young life—one narrated by the British as "beginning" with intraracial terror and brutality that was then displaced by the positive possibilities of the freedoms of empire, and another narrated through black studies as defined by the inarguably violent limits and erasures of this colonial subjection.[5] Bonetta, more any of the other celebrities this book traces, is also a uniquely "blank" canvas of black agency, as she doesn't "author" any significant text, performance, or presidential progeny, save for her daughter, Victoria, the queen's namesake and surrogate goddaughter after

Bonetta's untimely death. Instead, she persists almost entirely through the images of her carte de visite photographs as well as in some extant letters, histories, and news reports where it is her unlikely proximity to British royalty that marks her as of public interest, as a celebrity. Her history, like Seacole's, has mostly emerged in its corrective forms in more recent incarnations, "forgotten" until the booming multicultural black British historical industry began uncovering and then covering, as in media coverage, black British history—looking for those who got over, not those who were covered, awash.

Bonetta's extraordinary history is deeply related to her visual appearance in these photographs and its lexical relationship with various sovereign bodies: the king of Dahomey and Queen Victoria as literal sovereigns, the sovereignty of the British Empire, and Bonetta's own (un)sovereign body, her sensational flesh as reappeared in the contemporary era and taken up/disciplined in her own Victorian moment. It is the moment of finding these startling photographs of Bonetta that begins her contemporary story—startling in the juxtaposition of Bonetta's West African body in the high Victorian fashion she sports in each photograph. These fashions, and this era, have been so associated with whiteness that their encounter with Bonetta's flesh piques immediate contemporary interest, as if Bonetta's skin and the fashion are so incongruous in their proximity that the image demands explanation—and explication (Stephens 2014; Campt 2017).

Following this reading of surface, Bonetta's connection to the Victorian era turns out to register a similarly racialized visual mismatch: She was the ward/"goddaughter" of Queen Victoria herself—presented to her as both a "gift" from the self-proclaimed king of Benin, and a rescued intra-African-enslaved girl from a trade mission to Benin in 1850. Captain Frederick Forbes, a naval officer stationed off the coast of West Africa to enforce Britain's anti-slave trading laws (enacted in 1807), was the proverbial messenger, but also the officer of state charged with trying to get the king to agree to stop or lessen the slave trade in his territory, while also keeping relations cordial enough to continue with the trade of nonhuman commodities. Britain's "reformed" image as a crusader against enslavement, then, belied the political realities of the trade they fed for so many generations and the deep wealth that the Dahomey kingdom had gained from slave-trading with Britain. In managing the optics and bureaucracy of Britain and Victoria's images as sovereign political entities, Forbes must claim not only the moral high ground but also the beginnings of a cultural-relativist diplomacy that projects stark "natural" differences between the political rituals of the nations as if their shared economic interests were really a set of anthropologically tinged encounters.

When Forbes writes in his ethnographic account of Dahomey and the Dahomians that "in Dahomey all preliminaries are settled by presents and no matter can be arranged unless commended by a gift," he sets up Bonetta as the "gift" between two sovereigns—as the currency that reinforces their individual autonomy and also allows for a space of negotiation between two mutually recognized sovereign bodies (Gerzina 2003, 12). Here Bonetta is both frozen and propelled through history by this play between sovereigns. Bonetta is not given a gift, but is a gift herself—a thing, but not a commodity purchased, like Wheatley. At the same time, she is "given" the gift of life, posited as "freedom" by Queen Victoria and her sovereign extensions. As both gift and indebted, Bonetta's body signals the fraught ground of national, African, and self-sovereignty as discursive ideals of black freedoms. Her representations, subsumed under discourses of recovery, affiliation, and comparison, offer us a critical map of vulnerability as politics, and a politics of vulnerability that centers on the difficult embodied experience of black women across empire.

The age of Enlightenment maintains a paradoxical stance on sovereignty—embracing the figure of the sovereign and that state of absolute sovereignty as the most important aspect of the state at the same time that it insisted upon the constitution of the sovereign as an act of social contract by the people. As such, the sovereign both represents the people, but is also answerable to them and to the law that the people enact as their description of political will. As such, sovereignty has much to do with the social contract and the overreaching promise of contracts—private and publicly defined—to literally make a "better," more equitable world. When looking at the overinvestment in sovereignty of the period, one has to note again, like in conceptualization of consent and contracts, how agreeing to submit is, in fact, the core constitutive rule of state formation. As such, in a Rousseauian manner, one cedes some freedom to become a social body, to live in a social state rather than in the brutality of a state of nature. And yet, at this particular moment, revolution and independence are always already configured through the nonnegotiable presence of a sovereign—and sovereignty *as a state* comes to signal "freedom" as a collective body, even as individual rights, most importantly that of property, were constructed, as well, based on the image of the absolute sovereign, here within the home.

These tensions—between ruler and ruled, between individual and collective, between public and private, between political and personal—define sovereignty, rather than challenge it. As such, when scholars such as Saidiya V.

Hartman (1997) identify the coercion to consent to one's own brutalization and injury, they are identifying black subjects, particularly black women subjects, at the very heart of sovereignty rather than its antithesis. The shift to what political theorists call the Westphalian model of the state, which still reigns, is a shift to governmentality as the means of operation of the sovereign, where laws and votes supposedly take the place of genealogical bloodlines to articulate "will" and "good," as well as how and for whom freedom should operate, collectively—even as race in the United States gets yoked to blood and voting rights.

This shift comes not coincidentally as royal sovereignty wanes in appearance as well as during the rise of the individual state. In fact, governmental sovereignty and state articulation of radical and absolute good for that particular state comes into vogue at the moment of political consolidation of imperial interests—the articulation of empire, where more and other territories and people are absorbed in the boundaries of the Western sense of the state. It is laws and government that travel as sovereign formations of the West. This is prologue to the work of sovereignty in Bonetta's 1850 moment, as Captain Forbes put it, her role as a gift from "the King of the Blacks to the Queen of the Whites" (Gerzina 2003, 12). Before "the scramble for Africa" in 1881, just a year after Bonetta's death, Britain is expanding its sovereignty, as well, not just through the economic market, or even the land grab that makes the alibi of sovereignty laughable in its transfer of violence to the idiom of governmentality. Victorian England in 1850 is asserting its moral sovereignty—its supposed independence from its previous role in the slave trade and its ability to act with absolute power and authority in the name of its articulated morals. This shift, like the one that requires consent to be ruled and imagines that subjection as the very basis of freedom, marks the turn not just to rhetorics of nationalism, but to what Mimi Thi Nguyen (2012) has deemed the "gift of freedom," or the moral imperialism, or imperialism-as-moralism (to put it crassly), that has defined the project of the Westphalian sovereign state formed in the crucible of the Enlightenment. Through this shift to a gift economy of rights and freedoms, black women, not white men, can be taken as the paradigmatic subjects of, and not just subject to, sovereignty. These formations of black women as, in, and through concepts of sovereignty reveal resistance tactics that rely on the language of sovereignty and autonomy (state and self) to imagine black freedoms. These might be stretched to think of black women not as excluded from sovereignty but as the builders of alternative models and networks of sustained and sustainable vulnerability. Black women as paradigmatic political subjects mark a politics of the durable, of what was and must be endured, to trouble a politics that emphasizes and perhaps fetishizes more eruptive, singular, spectacular temporalities. It is, paradoxically, in these spectacular figures that we glean these more quotidian modes of the political as defined through the everyday lives of black women in Enlightenment modernity.

When thinking of these alternate political economies of vulnerability, I return to Baartman's exchange as art object to think through the exchange of Bonetta as a "gift" between sovereign states (an exchange that recalls Gayle Rubin's [1975] "The Traffic in Women"), a gift that makes explicit an implicit model of negotiations between those imagined and presented as absolute powers—as well as stages the limits of resistance when it is imagined as a fight between sovereign subjects. That Queen Victoria and the king of Dahomey are staged as gendered and raced opposites is both a deft rhetorical move and one that emphasizes the less than incidental nature of visual embodiment in figuring the sovereign. Queen Victoria, who takes reign just as slavery is abolished in the colonies, is marked by her gender both as a very young monarch (initially) and then as a mother. King Gezo, on the other hand, can be seen as an early representation in a line of continuity of constructions of black African (male) leaders as brutal, barbaric, and corrupt that continues into the decolonial present (Anim-Addo in Gerzina 2003). Both stand as figureheads of the enormous market conditions of chattel slavery and resource extractions, violent structures of empire that, for Enlightenment modernity, imagine white rule and its deployment of both state violence and structures of governmentality as extensions of a benevolent, moral sovereignty. In doing so, they imagine African and native resistance, and collusion, as instances of barbarity and shows of brute force and death-dealing. As Michel Foucault (2008) argues, and Mbembe (2003) extends, in marshaling the life-dealing rhetoric and structures of the sovereign state, Enlightenment statecraft imagines that which is outside the sovereign—namely, black and brown peoples—as constant and persistent threats, as the specters of other modes of sovereignty that deal in indiscriminate death.

Sarah Forbes Bonetta, as she would come to be known after her rescue by/gifting to Captain Forbes, is the currency exchanged between these imagined poles of sovereignty. For Forbes, the exchange solidifies black African governmental difference by claiming such a horrific "gifting" of a small human, already kidnapped and brutalized within Africa, as part of a naturalized, native system of diplomacy. It is Gezo, then, who emphasizes the racial and gendered embodied differences between sovereigns as the surface that needs to be traversed, in Forbes's telling, while Forbes, as representative of the queen, is enlightened into a view of humanity that refuses such violence in the name of morality. Of course, this construction of Sarah-as-sign denies the "gift" of African cooperation and collusion with the British Empire in the chattel slave trade, denies their membership in the sovereign rule that established British wealth, denies the violent coercive force of Enlightenment capitalism in the making of Gezo as sovereign. And, of course, it erases the context of the diplomatic presence of Forbes-as-sovereign-representative on the west coast of Africa itself, and his visit to Dahomey in particular: Forbes is there specifically to manage the transition from chattel slave trade to resource and commodities trade that Britain has newly emphasized and is now enforcing via militaristic presence—like Silicon Valley, they disrupt the economy with the "innovation" of horrific trade in human beings, plundering until they have their market full, and then refuse responsibility for the social conditions that ensue from either disruption.

British sovereignty is imagined through and as a series of laws that govern not just its economy but also others in global capital, compelling foreign bodies into participation and enforcing those legal sovereignties not just through corporeal violence but also through cultural narrative. Here, Sarah is the "gift" that might not signal Gezo's behind-the-curve understanding of current British relations to race (which after all had only just shifted from the ostentatious violence of slave-owning in their own colonies and was the diplomatic reason for Forbes's visit and his policing of Dahomey waters), but instead his deep critique of Britain's narrative of moral sovereignty and his refusal to cede the fragile and brutal sovereignty he himself had carved out under their very terms of engagement. "Giving" another human, a small girl, to the queen is an act that acknowledges what Nguyen, via Derrida and Lowe, argues is the foundation of "freedom" as conceived by the Western model of rights, nationhood, and sovereignty, where

> *possessive ownership* is perceived as a historical necessity for human freedom. As Lisa Lowe succinctly observes, drawing on Hegel's original formulations: "Through property the condition of possibility of human self-possession—of one's body, interiority, and life direction—is established." But in this and other accounts, liberal theories measure and manufacture freedom for the human person and society in terms that also presuppose the alienability of the self—or dispossession. Thus, we might grasp the abstraction of human freedom as a property—both as capacity and capital—as the necessary ground for ethical interactions with others and its profound consequences. (Nguyen 2012, 11)

That the king of Dahomey potentially points to this contradiction as the founding tension of British sovereignty through the body and exchange of Bonetta is not to applaud participation in the economies of empire by the African ruler, nor to claim his action as "resistance" or pure coercion. It is, though, to imagine a deeply gendered body—a girl, an African girl, a black girl—as the central paradigm of and currency at stake in such negotiations of sovereignty and African freedoms. It is to focus on the failure of traditional notions of critique, where the act of exposure of contradictions is one that can bring about the fall of sovereignty, or bring us to a better or truer version of freedoms. "The gift of freedom," Nguyen argues, "also discloses for us liberalism's innovations of empire, the frisson of freedom and violence that decisively collude for same purposes—not just because the gift of freedom opens with war and death, but also because it may obscure those other powers that, through its giving, conceive and shape life" (2). Further, "These powers constellate allocations and appropriations of violence with a view toward injury and death, but also with a horizon for the preservation of life—with dispositions and structures of feeling, to invoke Raymond Williams, within and between empire's subjects that rouse and animate love and gratitude, guilt and forgiveness, and other obligations of care levied on the human heart; with political and also phenomenological forms of graduated sovereignty and differential humanity that endure beyond the formal exercise of military operations or occupation" (4).

Bonetta, then, as the narrative and material gift between these two sovereigns, operates in public culture as a liaison not between African and British notions of sovereignty and governmentality (the supposedly anthropological distinction Forbes draws), but between "capital and capacity," between the sovereignty of law and the sovereignty of self that calls attention to the impossibility of separating the two, discursively, politically, culturally, or materially. The exchange of this young African girl, a material enactment of the title and spirit of *All the Women Are White, All the Blacks Are Men, but Some of Us Are Brave* (Hull, Bell-Scott, and Smith 1992) doesn't just give us the necessary pause to consider the intense and all-encompassing refusal of sovereignty to Sarah Forbes Bonetta's body and person, but how her body and black girls' bodies are the very foundation of sovereignty, in all of its contradiction, itself. Through Bonetta's engagements with sovereignty, this chapter and this book imagine other viable political relationships to self and state constituted with and through this vulnerable body, rather than the white male body, as modernity's central political subject.

#Blackvictorianprincessmagic

Forbes's description of Bonetta then relies on establishing both her vulnerability and her exceptionalism. He emphasizes, as do contemporary recoveries of Bonetta's genealogy, that she was likely born into African royalty, largely attributable to markings on her face that were usually reserved for elite families. A "princess," she was targeted by a raid from Gezo's Dahomey and, as the story goes, watched her family slaughtered before being kidnapped and held for a least two years as a captive in the Kingdom of Dahomey. The dual materiality of her trauma and her survival compels Forbes and the contemporary public, as does her seemingly conflicted status as African princess and colonial subject, which mimics the Tubman/Bonetta poles that introduced this chapter. All of these structures of political feeling around her proximity to and refused access to sovereignty are channeled, largely, through her cartes de visite from her late teenage years and from her marriage (figures 5.2 and 5.3).

The carte de visite, as Braudy (1997, 494) traces, is a key technology in the development of modern celebrity in the nineteenth century: "a paper calling card with photograph and signature that could be ordered in whatever quantity the client wanted was introduced in France in 1854. . . . The carte de visite not only added a visual image to the social habit of leaving one's calling card, but, almost from its introduction, it also became a prime means for public figures to strengthen their political or military campaigns with a shower of personalized, pocket-sized portraits." Bonetta's carte de visite establishes her as a celebrity—a person with a public following and social visiting schedule—and serves as the vehicle to celebrity itself. The carte de visite seems to offer an intimate visibility that defines modern celebrity, as an early "star text" meant to conjure availability even when distant, creating an "emotional intimacy . . . between the famous and their audience" (494). Like the ineffable and untouchable sovereign that gave way to the sovereign-by-selection-and-submission model, the distance of heroic fame gave way to a form of quotidian celebrity in the late eighteenth and early nineteenth centuries that demanded both ordinariness and extraordinariness, in Dyer's (2013) terms, in the same body. In the carte de visite, the image remained close enough to be a part of everyday life, even as access to photographic technologies and social visiting schedules signaled the significance of the body "captured" in the photograph.

The simultaneous shift to and rise of Westphalian sovereignty and "democratic fame" (Roach 2007) also marks the historical moment of discursive shift to the "gift of freedom," or the biopolitical orientation toward life-affirming state and empiric power in rhetorical forms that at the same time requires

FIGURE 5.2. One of Bonetta's cartes de visite from her teenage years (1856). Photograph by William Bambridge.

violence, death, and exclusion, largely articulated through the apparatus of the body and its supposed somatic racial differences. This racial difference was, itself, increasingly wrought by proximity and not distance—formed and maintained through the intimacy of contact rather than the anthropologically distanced account.

These cartes de visite were on display in the 2005 gallery show in Manchester, *Black Victorians: Black People in British Art 1800–1900*, alongside both a bust and a carte de visite of Mary Seacole herself, produced sometime in the 1870s (though it may be a reissue of an earlier print), her only known photograph. The gallery catalog's introduction opens with an octet of albumen prints by photographer Camille Silvy, six of which (besides the first and last) are the photographs of Bonetta and her husband on the occasion of their marriage. In the photographs (two of the pair together, two of Bonetta alone, and two of her husband, James P. Labulo Davies, alone), Bonetta wears a light-colored

FIGURE 5.3. One of Bonetta's cartes de visite from her marriage (1862). Photograph by Camille Silvy.

dress and looks directly into the camera for all but one of the shots, where she poses reading a large book. What is remarkable here, for the curator at least, is the unremarkable remarkableness of black Victorians—the exhibit itself meant to "show a diversity of representation hitherto largely unknown" in British culture to stake a claim for "black presence" versus the black absence in the Victorian historical imagination (Marsh 2005, 12).

Seacole's "celebrity portrait," in the caption of the catalog, has her "at work" in front of a war backdrop, medicinal bottles at hand, head down—a collector's item for a specific figure. Bonetta's marriage portraits, however, are clearly one strip of known social poses for the royal photographer—her blackness registering as the hook for the curators of this show because of its extraordinary ordinariness—a star image, to use Dyer's term, overlaid with what Fleetwood (2015a, 10) names the tension in black iconicity, "pulled between the intertwined forces of denigration and veneration" in critical reception. The bulk of the visual material from the show depicts blackness in various faux-"native" performances, with portraits of "modern" black life dotting the pre-ethnographic landscape. As the introduction to the catalog and the exhibition reminds us, "In itself, a display of black figures in visual culture is not a history of the black presence in Britain from 1800 to 1900. Still less is it a history of black experience. It is even difficult to say what relation the visual record bears to historical actuality in dimorphic or social terms" (Marsh 2005, 14). Blackness itself, then, is the celebrity read in the glow of these afterimages—rather than these representations acting as proof, as evidence of black presence.

Caroline Bressey's (2005, 77) essay in the collection helpfully maps the range of black figures in Victorian photography as a way of getting at both the range of black subjects and their relationships to autonomy—a study in extremes from compulsory photographs taken of prisoners and asylum patients to celebrity calling cards like Seacole's. Bonetta's portraits, Bressey reasons, mark her and her husband as "portray[ing] a sense of wealth and spatial mastery" in their customization of their photographic surroundings. A marker of social status and not fame as such, these portraits, then, do not stand in the middle of the poles of archival black Victorian visual life—"the ordinary folk," in Bressey's terms, whose everyday use of photography is largely lost to the official archives of fame, wealth, and power or to its inverses of criminality, illness, and pathology. Instead, they emphasize a private sovereignty, an authority over one's space and image that the images Bressey juxtaposes with reading of Bonetta's do not—Joseph Denny, a black prisoner, in the middle of a contact sheet of nine photographs of inmates in the identical clothes, pose, and angle.

Bonetta's cartes de visite with her husband tell another story of her extraordinary ordinariness: the way her "privilege" was, in adulthood/"freedom," yoked to marriage, and not to work (figure 5.4). Like Wheatley, the self-sovereignty granted by "freedom" enforces the inheritance of personal unsustainability. Unsuited for and excluded from domestic labor by health and by class, Bonetta must marry the suitor chosen by her sovereign or lose her sustenance allowance from the queen (in Bonetta's extant letters)—as any upper-class woman would be expected to do. She marries a Nigerian merchant who is fifteen years her senior, and the coupling is covered through both the carte de visite photographs and in local print cultures. Like Wheatley with a sovereign safety net, and as Forbes takes pains to describe her genius in his letters about "convincing" Gezo to relinquish her to him, Bonetta's personhood is bound up in her adherence to Victorian womanhood and hence in the giving over of one sovereign attachment to another, even more intimate one (recall Wheatley's and Baartman's marriages here). From an extant letter, we know that Bonetta, who was nineteen, did not desire this marriage, but was compelled to do so or else lose her means of livelihood—her allowance from the queen. To marry Davies means not just to shift households but to return to the African continent, this time to Nigeria, to be a part of her husband's missionary aid work, work that would contribute to the colonization of Africa. While there, she bore children and fell into ill health—like Wheatley, she passed at a young age. Unlike Wheatley, she left behind a living daughter named Victoria who also took her place as the goddaughter of the queen—a new black "royal" bloodline, a new proximity to sovereignty.

Bonetta did, though, have previous carte de visite photographs taken—there are at least two others that have surfaced, including another one in this particular show, each taken before Bonetta's marriage, as well as a painting. These predate her marriage but postdate the watercolor portrait of Bonetta also found in this show, which in part mimicked the specificity of scene of Seacole's portrait—only it is not Bonetta's vocation but her Africanness that is emphasized, in keeping with most of the black figurations in the show. Dated 1851, Octavius Oakley's painted portrait of Bonetta has her facing front in "native" dress and with a vague backdrop of the continent involving mostly palm leaves and other African natural resources—though also including the sharp-lined white wall of a built structure (figure 5.5). This painting shows the slow drag of high-art conceptual frames for racial difference, which remain vivid in their flat racializations even as photography ushers in a new scopic economy of blackness within the metropole quotidian. The empty decorative basket imagined next to Sarah at approximately age seven or eight in 1851 morphs into a basket containing ladies' sewing in an 1856 photograph, at age twelve or thirteen; the long earrings marking her African difference in the 1851 watercolor shrink to the delicate hoops barely discernable in the black and white photograph of 1856. And the exposed breast of the girl in 1851 is transposed to the high-necked, full frock of the Victorian era, Bonetta's transition to Victorian girlhood complete even in the bright-eyed vision of Bonetta at "home,"

FIGURE 5.4. One of Bonetta's cartes de visite with her husband (1862). Photograph by Camille Silvy.

and the serious but no less frank expression given in the William Bambridge photograph of 1856 (see figure 5.2).

Both portraits are fantasies of citizenship, of belonging; the ability to trace the genealogy of these representations of Bonetta even within the span of a short few years since her "arrival" mark not just her celebrity, but the way her "brand," her star image, morphed from one of radical racial difference to one of adaptation and integration—for her, but more compellingly for the visual

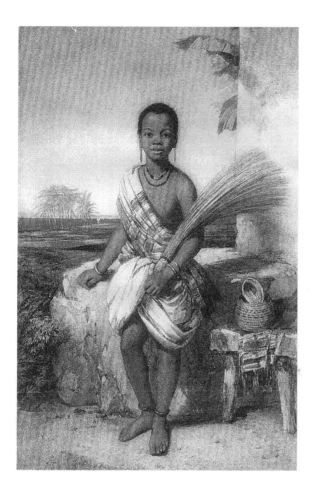

structures of meaning of blackness in Victorian England. Bonetta's proximity to the sovereign gave her access to the emerging mass media technologies that appended royalty and also gave her and us access to her image via the royal archive. That this 1856 image is "in an album at Windsor Castle" (Bressey 2005, 86) allows us a glimpse into the intimacy of Victorian England and Africa not just through the starkly drawn sovereign bodies of "the King of the Blacks" and "the Queen of the Whites," but by the enduring life and image of their exchange—their gift, who is not a temporally fixed object but one who carves out a version and a vision of her body in the public eye again and again. This is reiterated in coverage of her 1862 wedding to Davies, a royal affair that was reported as involving sixteen horse-drawn carriages and a racially mixed bridal party in London.

Bonetta's status fluctuations between African princess and enslaved captive, from the transnational adoptee of the queen to arranged bride, and from political refugee to human rights/aid worker are all able to be seen, to be co-opted, through the images of her cartes de visite. Her representations then claim these sovereign and subjected-by-sovereign positions in the very same visual interpretative practices whereby recent documentaries stage her rediscovery as a project of both inclusion and opposition, a story of subjection to colonial racial-sexual norms and a full-throated embodiment-with-a-difference whose very presence challenges the visual sovereign power of whiteness.

#developmentgoals

What "gift," then, is the discovery of Bonetta to contemporary critics? Her role as an object of diplomacy between sovereigns gives way to a host of ways to legislate racial intimacy (Eng 2010) that include "all the good and beautiful things the gift claims as its consequence—the right to have rights, the choice of life direction, the improvement of body and mind, the opportunity to prosper—against a spectral future of their nonexistence . . . under terror" (Nguyen 2012, 2). This terror is defined both as being rescued from the terms of African sovereignty built on the British slave trade as well as her rescue by contemporary critics and curators to give the "gift" of black visibility—the gift of representation—to present-day populations of black Britons and the high-art audiences of the African diaspora. Recovering Bonetta's African origins in a way that Wheatley's have been lost, readers can get, comparatively, a wealth of information on her life trajectories and capacities both before and after her status as gift, and her being given the "gift" of Victorian-era freedoms. This illusion of bodily sovereignty in the afterimage visibility of Bonetta—one that imagines that through a reassertion of visibility one might claim a more sovereign vision of blackness across centuries—animates her as the aforementioned sensational flesh on which we might pause. This pause, offered by two contemporary artists who engage with Bonetta's history, considers what such reconfigurations and representations offer that disrupts rather than reasserts liberal humanist paradigms of self-determination and collective sovereignty in the public sphere.

In the 2016 photography series *Too Many Blackamoors*, Ghanaian London artist Heather Agyepong takes a series of self-portraits that reference historical relations between Britain and the African continent through reenactments of Bonetta's cartes de visite. Here, instead of Bonetta's distance-proximity, or extraordinary ordinariness, Agyepong restages Bonetta's history, and fictions of sovereignty, through contemporary discourses of self-fulfillment and self-care, exposing and developing (in the photographic sense of bringing into the material visible frame) in her photographic process the iconography of self-reliant African and African diaspora femininity—and feminism—in the face of trauma, violence, and upheaval. In doing so, she develops both representational and political discourses that implicitly rely on the links between sovereignty, autonomy, and freedom, but also practices of representing and reading vulnerability that deny the temporal fixity of concepts such as self, national, or racial progress. Posed in high Victorian fashion, she appears in various photographic stills with a black drape over her head, in mid-scream, with eyes closed, or anachronistically holding a copy of a 1984 history of black Britons (figures 5.6 and 5.7).

Agyepong herself identifies the series not as recovering Bonetta or making claims to her historical heroism but instead as questioning the corrective histories that emphasize her. Her work then engages in but also queries the lingo of celebratory and self-care memes such as #Blackgirlmagic—the commodification of black women's constant resilience and strength in the face of trauma, of their self-sovereignty in the face of exclusion. In the series, she imagines a breakdown of the ideal of black feminine self-possession, and appears to question the effort for its recovery in the articulation of a contemporary black feminist practice. Here the supposed resistant dissonance between black skin and upper-class Victorian fashion is exposed as one also of feminized self-sovereignty. Agyepong breaks the frame with her introduction not just of modern props—a contemporary book, for instance—but what we think of as modern, private, and destabilizing affects.

Picking up on the thread of Bonetta's deeply compromised set of "capacities" within her extraordinary history and revitalized sensational flesh, which included missionary work with Davies in Nigeria, Agyepong's work is a call: to *not* or not only care for the black body but also to question the discourse of self-development as a route to freedom for black women in and under the structures of Enlightenment modernity. Development discourse, based as it is on the assumed inevitability and often the superiority of capitalism and its attendant cultures, structures, and values, has been roundly and soundly critiqued within human rights studies.[6] In antidevelopment discourse, though, there has frequently been too stark and too easy a contrast drawn between capital development as modernity and a romanticization of local culture as a transparent and temporally fixed tradition. Not only was this timeline of unchanging cultural meanings frequently based on historical misunderstanding and inaccuracy, it often hinged on the bodies of black women

FIGURE 5.6. Heather Agyepong, *Too Many Blackamoors #4* (2015).

FIGURE 5.7. Heather Agyepong, from *Too Many Blackamoors* (2015).

themselves—claiming dominion over them, their desires, their bodies, and their life capacities in a supposed utopia.

This, of course, has been aided by Western discourses of development that have been using the status of native women and their supposed barbaric subjection to wage imperial and colonial campaigns for freedom and expanded sovereign territories (Burton 1994). Like Bonetta, black women have been made to serve as currency between warring notions of sovereignty and social justice. Staging her body in the place of Bonetta's in the visual structure and language of the carte de visite, Agyepong instead imagines a politics rooted in self-indeterminacy, one that troubles discourses of both externalized injury and internalized agency as political narratives that serve black women's embodied history.

Marcus Garvey's (1938, 9) directive that "mind is your only ruler, sovereign," adjacent to the very line that begets Bob Marley's anthem to black freedom to "free yourself from mental slavery," is exposed here as an explicit but also subcutaneous current of black politics, one that rests on personal responsibility, a mind/body split, and self-sovereignty as both truth effect and political goal. Agyepong's work presses us to consider the impossibility of black women's embodiment ever "succeeding" in this battle of will, this way of letting internal order bring a political reordering of the body. As such, these photographs offer not just a version of the failure of bodily integrity to cohere for black women's embodied subjectivity, but a questioning of whether bodily integrity might be the "right" to seek in the face of colonial sexual subjection (Anker 2012). Agyepong illustrates not the externalized internal pain of an imagined Bonetta, but the competing desires for wholeness as a commodity of liberal humanism—"wellness" and "self-care" being some of its disseminations—and the very pleasures of commodification and commodities that are denied when insisting that black women's injury be read as resistance to white rule. To be "lured" by the fashioning of self that is business as usual in the West is not, for Agyepong, a betrayal, but an act of black quiet, what Kevin Quashie (2009, 329) refers to as an interiority that is not representative of some whole real protected self but a space of one's "desires, ambitions, hungers, vulnerabilities, and fears. . . . [Q]uiet, as the expressiveness of inner life, can encompass and represent wild motion."

Agyepong is not alone in turning to Bonetta; she also warrants brief mention in Zadie Smith's *Swing Time*, a 2016 novel about race, gender, and sociality between black British girls as they enter into adult subjectivity. Here, Bonetta is both contextualized as a site of forgotten black history and repositioned within a continuum of self- and racial development that Smith's larger text challenges.

Just as Seacole contests the arc of black Atlantic citizenship through her very movement between and across the borderlands of empire (rather than geographies of "home" and "colonial metropole" alone), Bonetta's crisscrossing of Atlantic space denies development and development critique, involving movement to and from various African and European locales across her very brief lifetime: Dahomey, Sierra Leone for school, Nigeria for missionary work/married life, and repeated "returns" to London as well as her death in Portugal, where she sought refuge from her failing health in Lagos.

For Smith, the evocation of Bonetta is an illustration of a kind of literal "education of desire" (Stoler 1995)—her story one of several that the main character is "schooled" in by her politically radicalized, biracial boyfriend in college in order to distance her from any perceived overidentification with white British culture. The narrator meditates on Bonetta's newfound, archive-driven celebrity: "Now I can find out myself in a moment the name of that captian and can learn in the same click what he though of the girl he gifted to a queen" (293). Bonetta is present for Rakim, her ex-boyfriend, in a brief moment to discipline the narrator's self into racial knowledge that is supposed to serve as self-knowledge, and hence spur on political discipline. The text pillories such recoveries, renarrating the carte de visite to gain not depth but its inverse and its escape: surface and movement:

> I know now that her Yoruba name was Aina, meaning "difficult birth," a name you give to a child who is born with her umbilical cord tied round her neck. I can see a photo of Aina in her high-necked Victorian corsetry, with her face closed, her body perfectly still. I remember that Rakim had a refrain, always proudly declaimed, with his overbite pulled back over his teeth: "We have our own kings! We have our own queens!" I would nod along for the sake of peace but in truth some part of me always rebelled. . . . I did not want to rely on each European fact having its African shadow, as if without the scaffolding of the European fact everything African might turn to dust in my hands. It gave me no pleasure to see that sweet-faced girl dressed like one of Victoria's own children, frozen in a formal photograph, with a new kind of cord round her neck. I always wanted life—movement.

But lest we read this as a predictable postcolonial critique issued from Smith herself, the narrator is of course deep into the morass of Africa as Western celebrity, the partner to celebrity activism in the form of white pop star Amy and her attempt to build a school, marry, and adopt from the African continent, à la Madonna. But in centering on the complex experience of the narrator, who is the one left to supervise much of the bureaucratic work of the school and its aftermath, Smith suggests other intimacies between Bonetta and contemporary black women's subjectivity that include but are not contained in the spectacle of Bonetta—or the difficult ambition of the Caribbean nurses on display in the previous chapter. Here, proximity to power is posed against not a loss of but a lack of ambition to find oneself—either in the narrator's mother's intense political discourses of race and feminism that still find her subordinate in private relationships, or in the celebrity version of political culture that seeks fame as its raison d'être.

The narration of the image Smith conjures describes the consumption, production, and inhabitation of black celebrity as a stifling stillness, an act of capture mirrored in the lure of choreographed movement in the book, acting not a savior but as equally bound to the refusal of progress narratives or progressive politics. The narrator's mediocrity, her will to absorb self from that which surrounds her, from other women, is the key conflict of the book, one that various entities try to "instruct" her out of with corrective histories of black women's exceptionalism, even as Tracey's extraordinary talent and embodiment cannot "save" her from her ordinary life of working-class maternal and quotidian labor. *Swing Time*, instead, focuses on the ambivalent experience of embodiment, and also of watching black and women's embodiment as a modern spectacle. Tracey, the narrator's best friend in youth, is an extraordinary dancer leveled to an ordinary life—multiple kids at a young age, no career to speak of, living in the same public housing estates. The narrator is largely ordinary—teetering on the brink of failure, never more than a figuration of mediocrity until her proximity to her megastar boss publicly goes sour, and she is suddenly a scandalous public figure. Like Agyepong, then, Smith's reckoning with Bonetta is also a way into exploring the failure to cohere in a politically coherent way and, hence, the need to engage different practices of reading black politics that do not rely on encoding heroism or tragedy—practices that allow for recognition, yes, but also misrecognition, failure, distance, and ordinariness. Smith's narrator writes of viewing Fred Astaire's blackface performance again in *Swing Time*, in the book's opening pages but many years after her experience watching it as a youth with Tracey:

I felt I was losing track of my physical location, rising above my body, viewing my life from a very distant point, hovering over it. It reminded me of the way people describe hallucinogenic drug experiences. I saw all my years at once, but they were not piled up on each other, experience after experience, building into something of substance—the opposite. A truth was being revealed to me: that I had always tried to attach myself to the light of other people, that I never had any light of my own. I experienced myself as a kind of shadow. (Z. Smith 2016, 4)

Intimacy, attachment, kinship, embodiment—all here are not to be trusted, and not to be trusted to be repaired as if they were actual property, including one's body that, of course, changes and shifts over time and geography. Instead, Smith focuses her critique on the fantasy of a history that will add up if one puts in the work of correcting it. What she lands on instead is the fiction of history as anything other than a temporary custody of the body and that to which the self attaches. The narrative arc of the novel calls not for more self-development or better representation, but for a meditation on the constant vulnerability of critical, cultural, and historical attachments, even to one's own body, to one's own personhood.

Through Bonetta's representation, Smith and Agyepong make transparent the long, layered assemblage of human rights discourses—including progress, development, and economic, social, and cultural rights—that articulate and disarticulate the limits of black women's political subjectivity. As subjects in need of rescue and/or those who are consistently admired for seemingly inhuman perseverance, African diaspora women cannot seem to occupy complex spaces of care, vulnerability, or sociality without pathology. *Too Many Blackamoors* and *Swing Time* imagine, visually and narratively, other feminist relations for and between black women in the contemporary moment, as well as in genealogical relation to the colonial past.

Both the photographic series and the novel also problematize the commodification and consumption of media—including the production of critique—in the service of black feminism. In doing so, they remind us to remain skeptical of how even seemingly empowering calls to self-development under the sign of black feminist thought can inhabit the liberal humanist forms of individualism and mastery. Instead, they offer glimpses into Saidiya Hartman's (2019, 349) recent description/call/parting shot: "So everything depends on them and not the hero occupying center stage, preening and sovereign. Inside the circle it is clear that every song is really the same song, but crooned in infinite variety, every story altered and unchanging: *How can I live? I want to be free. Hold on.*" These parting lines centralize the impossible desires of politics and political subjects while at the same time they do not celebrate the expression of those desires as solely "a refusal to be governed," or acts of resistance (Hartman 2019, xv). These texts offer a reading practice of sustained and sustainable vulnerability that one might bring to Bonetta's "case," even to the gallery and catalog space of envisioning black Victorians that the earlier part of this chapter rested upon. Agyepong and Smith defetishize black women's self-sovereignty by rendering agony, uncertainty, and ambivalence over the rhetorics of personal choice that reaffirm a sovereign and autonomous self. In occupying the embodied territory of Bonetta, an almost but not quite infamous body, they throw into relief the impossibility of debates about the "problem" of black women's representation that plagued the Baartman/Beyoncé controversy on which this book started. The competing desires to represent and to critique the representation of black women's difficult embodied histories are present in Agyepong and Smith's work. But instead of imagining these as resolvable, the artists lays bare the critical desires themselves—their tense, felt irresolvability and the toll that this set of "choices" puts on the body as it cannot retreat to either the promise of abstraction or the disciplinary motions of clear, categorically "good" representation.

The cross-generational intimacy Bonetta engenders in these contemporary works does not imagine the gift of freedom through the body made sovereign, made whole. Instead, it asks us to question the disciplining of black women's historical bodies in the service of contemporary politics. Like Wheatley, Bonetta asks us to look to the infamous body as a way of tracing a genealogy of black feminist political thought that compassionately acknowledges both the lure and the trap of agency, leaning into the vulnerability of the body—of its sensations and its desires. Early black women's celebrity makes plain, and puts center, this vulnerable body not as a Du Boisian problem but as a politics of possibility based on black women's needs, experiences, and endurance in the era of modernity.

CONCLUSION

BLACK FEMINIST CELEBRITY AND THE
POLITICAL LIFE OF VULNERABILITY

In the heat, less
is everything: respect, power, mouths, sex.
All of it is taken from me. I step into a volcano
& melt like the witch I am. I want to be flawed

all the way to bed. Wake up, flawless.
Subjected, flawless.
—MORGAN PARKER, *There Are More Beautiful*
Things Than Beyoncé, 2017

Morgan Parker's (2017) collection of poetry *There Are More Beautiful Things Than Beyoncé*, like Agyepong's photographs, troubles the line between political desires for self-possession and the will to show the self as radically, relentlessly undone. She imagines both a constantly failing self against the sleek visualization of "Beyoncé feminism"—packaged, commodified, "flawless"—and one in tune with Beyoncé's image in its wild, impossible desires for pleasure, coherence, and the interiority of a luxurious bedroom (in one poem), rather than a put-together political soul: "Boss / you all night long. & of course I mean sex / but I mean teaching, too. Black girl rage, flawless" (Parker 2017, 62).

Parker's poetry was reviewed in *Time* magazine for its proximity to Beyoncé even as its title suggests a disavowal, a going "deeper" than celebrity surface, evidenced by Parker's publication in the high literary powerhouse *Paris Review*. I turn to her work as I cast back to the "problem" of Baartman, the problem of representation that makes it hard to reproduce her body but also hard not to, as a black feminist writer or cultural producer is practically required to create one's statement on Baartman's legacy: taboo and yet public, famous and infamous, scientific object and sexually objectified. Baartman's body offers a sign of capture and a sign of vulnerability for Parker (as I read her poem "Hottentot Venus" in this book's introduction) signaling how a desire to represent and to read differently haunts the field of black feminist study—to be seen and known, in the full throes of violence and injury, but also to confound, to exceed, to rebel, to resist; to be subjected and flawless, both, simultaneously; to be captured not just by others' desires but by one's own. This is where Parker, and this book, locate the center of the political—in the contours of the "bedroom," one of the "disavowed geograph[ies] of the world" in a long list offered by Saidiya Hartman in *Wayward Lives* (2019, 347), a space of desire, retreat, violence, intimacy, consumption, fandom, and fantasy.

Watching the debates unfold about whether one is a "Beyoncé kind of feminist" or not resonates with and pushes against the kind of difficult debates over her recent more overtly political turn—a turn that occupies the aesthetics of black nationalism that we've come to associate with the known political world. Beyoncé's "entirely public account of self" (Paquet 2002, 67), to echo a statement made about Seacole's autobiography, is of course, a fantasy, a romance, a fiction, an adventure, a coming-of-age tale that offers strategic exposure, disclosure, and privacies, as well as strategic performances of interiority and feeling, of strength and weakness, of resistance and submission. Beyoncé can be read through this frame to be antifeminist, too reliant on and forgiving of heteropatriarchal structures of meaning, doing too much to appeal to white audiences. Or she's not real enough, she's superficial, she's just giving us a surface, a stage, a production that is not really "her," and hence she is only commodified, capitalized, the opiate of the masses.

Beyoncé is both too public and not public enough, representing the problem of representation as a strategy for black feminine performance—the problem of vulnerability, of black women's sexual, embodied visibility as always politically suspect, a potential liability, a surface to be read *against* to locate the political. When we cannot identify Beyoncé's exterior with a supposedly interior politics that comport with the corrective histories we already have lined up—her on top of a cop car in New Orleans floodwaters, citing Big Freedia but not enough, citing Julie Dash—where can black feminist thought go?

Like Parker's poetic vulnerabilities—simultaneously venerating and denigrating her poetic self, and the poetry's version of Beyoncé—this book has traced the difficult attachments and desires that append to the reception, repetition, and consumption of early black women's celebrity. How might we reckon with our own critical desires and those represented by and through these celebrity embodiments that are formed and transformed through the specific heat of Enlightenment modernity and its afterlives? In "Partition," Beyoncé sings, "I just wanna be the girl you like / the kind of girl you like / is right here with me." She holds the space of desire, and a yearning to be desired. She articulates what has been identified with black women's performance for so long, a space of loss and attachment to what hurts, to what hurt you. Subjected, flawless. Rather than read this as metaphor or allegory for the losses of history—though, surely, one can and critics have, ably—this book, like Parker, reads desire itself as the scene of the political, of political becoming that is neither negative nor positive, but irresolvable (impossible, to return to Hartman), the conditions of black feminist living that are the very conditions of, I argue throughout, political thought and subjectivity.

In *Infamous Bodies*, I have traced the representations of early black women's celebrity as genealogies of a politics of vulnerability, an interpretive strategy that recognizes desire and attachment as capture and pleasure at once, and as the tense base of political subjectivity, not its negative diagnosis. Parker recognizes "of course I mean sex / but I mean teaching, too": Baartman's body and Beyoncé's "body of life" (Alexander 1996) objects of fascination but also of undetermined desire, black feminist theory forged through heat, "the volcano" that is cultural representation and reception. Baartman is the volcano and its witness, making a viable black feminist life through the heat and the ash of culture, in her image and her afterimages. To pivot back to the case that begins the book—Beyoncé both disavowing and affirming the re-performance of Baartman—Parker's collection comes at a moment when black women's celebrity has resurged as a powerful site of political debate in the post-Obama era, while recent black feminist historiography has exploded existing narratives of masculinist political movements. The cultural but also political labor of mainstream black women celebrities—from Beyoncé to Oprah to Michelle Obama to Meghan Markle—pressures one anew to rethink the split between culture and politics, and which black women are narrated as serious political subjects while others remain suspect. *Infamous Bodies*, even as it pivots toward the seeming individualism of celebrity, argues that the act of making, and making public, can be more radically formative for broader visions of political economy and possibility. The political, for this book, is a mode of analysis for social organization that centrally lies in the realms of feminized culture, reception, and embodiment, rather than a designation of a formal space of governance that has never and could never contain the historical and embodied experiences of black women.

As Beyoncé and Parker repeat, update, and navigate vulnerable yet enduring and durable histories that begin rather than end with a diagnosis of subjection, how might we suture that to the fact of, the living through, the afterlives of rights? This book, like Parker's verse above, emphasizes strategies of black women's *living*, even and especially uncomfortable ones that are inarguably intimate with capitalism, whiteness, and sexual and gendered subjection, as central cases of political being and thinking. Reading the long tail of black women's celebrity gives us a hermeneutic inclusive of but not exclusive of plots of subjection and resistance. Instead, like Parker, one might read in these early black women's public presences and more intimate circulations a practice of taking subjection *and* desire as given, as the vulnerable conditions of political subjectivity. The infamous body of Sarah Baartman can never get over or around the difficulty, the incongruity, and the suspicion of being and being made public. As critics and students of black feminist thought, with Beyoncé and Parker, we continue to inherit and inhabit the political world early black women celebrities created; they have given us a map not only for contesting the creation and haunt of liberal humanist political desire, but of alternate ways to conceive of and read for politics itself.

Introduction

1 "Venus in Two Acts" refers not to Baartman but to an enslaved woman whose death is the centerpiece of a legal case.

2 See the debates in critical legal studies and the left (including Wendy Brown 2000) around rights and Patricia Williams's (1991) "defense" of her insistence on our ability to proliferate rights and hence shift their meaning.

3 As previously mentioned, these generative critiques include those of critical legal studies' relationship to rights, critiques of the "human" from black studies, and the near universal consensus of critical human rights studies of the paradox/failure of a human rights paradigm—poisoned both at the origin and in implementation by its attachments to universalism, individualism, capital, and property.

4 Anker (2012) argues for the implicit denial but use of embodied experience in human rights discourse and in human rights critique.

5 I should also note here the significance of scholars like Carby (1986); A. Y. Davis (1999); and Griffin (2001) taking up blueswomen and other cultural producers outside of respectability politics in the early to mid-twentieth century to my own project. Because of their pioneering work, considering the difficult legacies of black women's embodied celebrity and its interface with commodity culture in an earlier period is possible.

6 A brief bibliography of recent work beyond that cited previously would include J. Brown 2008; K. J. Brown 2015; Cheng 2011; Fleetwood 2015a; Paredez 2014; Royster 2003; Stephens 2014; Streeter 2012; Vogel 2009.

7 See also Marcus (2019), who locates modern celebrity in the nineteenth century, deeply considering its active reception, especially by female fans; Berenson and Giloi (2010), also located in the nineteenth century with the rise of mass media technologies; and the work of Latinx celebrity theorists Beltran (2009) and Paredez (2014) on the construction of twentieth-century celebrity cultures around race and gender.

8 Jaji (2014) does this brilliantly in her chapter on black women and the consumption of music culture through magazines. Fleetwood's (2015a) work on racial icons also takes this feminized audience for celebrity culture seriously. Jaji and Fleetwood's work dovetails with the work of Radway (1984) and Sterne (1997) on the market for romance or sentimentalism, as just two genres associated with the readership/audience of women, or Andrade's (2011) work on African women's novels in the era immediately postindependence.

9 This object-oriented relation to black subjectivity has been explored by critics such as D. A. Brooks (2006); C. Cooper (1995); Fleetwood (2010); McMillan (2015); Musser (2014); Nash (2014b); Darieck Scott (2010); Stephens (2014); and others.

10 Black studies has seen an explosion of work reconsidering appeals to "humanity": see Jackson 2015; Weheliye 2014; Wynter 2015. Anker (2012) also comments on not just the critical history of human rights usage of the imperiled body to garner rights but the ways that these critiques of the performance of suffering often find it difficult to represent the body or account for embodied experience at all.

11 These practices are critically tackled by historian Walter Johnson (2003) as well as by Hartman (1997) and J. Sharpe (2003), both of whom engage the theory of Certeau ([1984] 2011) on theories of bounded redress.

12 This necessarily partial list of historians working through black women's experience beyond those listed above include the work of Berry (2017); Feimster (2009); Finch (2015); Fuentes (2016); Gross (2006); Haley (2016); Hine (1989b); J. Jones (2009); M. Jones (2009); McGuire (2011); Mitchell (1999); Morgan (2004); Owens (2015); Painter (1996); Rosen (2009); Sommerville (2004); Stoler (1995, 2001, 2010).

13 For a fuller investigation of the relationship between literary and cultural production and human rights discourse (and critique), see Anker 2012; Hunt 2007; Parikh 2017; Slaughter 2007.

14 Likewise, the turn to investigate "the human" has just recently begun to think through the implications of black feminist thought. A progress narrative of rights that goes alongside a progress narrative of humanity is, not surprisingly, also the narrative, linguistic, and legal bind in which the "humanity" of enslaved peoples is articulated. Eighteenth-century studies scholar F. A. Nussbaum (2003) argues for representations of somatic difference as the locus of what defines "the normal" in this period, while Hartman (1997) argues that enslaved peoples in the United States are actually constructed as human through criminal culpability and responsibility even as they are excluded from so-called positive liberties. Weheliye (2014) ties this yoking of the black body, particularly the enslaved body, to the limits of the human rather than to the site of the camp or the figure of refugee. Weheliye does this to think through how eighteenth- and nineteenth-century racial exclusions could be used as the definitional pressure point of the failures of human rights as surely as the Holocaust atrocity of the twentieth century represented the failures of national protection and the ways that the nation-state itself was used to biopolitically demark different "genres of the human," which Caribbean theorist Wynter (2015) marks as the future of political discourse. Wynter's (2015) own construction of this capacious understanding of "the human" not as a monolithic category but as one that has been culturally constructed with a difference/differences and cannot be fully known is crucial here, both to think about the construction of blackness under the rubric of "rights" and to imagine black political possibilities and limits in and of the human. To imagine a denaturalized human is, for Wynter, a set of practices that require multiple historical, geographic, and cosmological narratives to converge—a recognition of the ways that the world as we know it is also a descriptor of the limit of what is known. Bogues (2010), like Wynter (2015), David Scott (2004), and Stuart Hall (2014), is a Caribbean theorist who sees in Afro-diasporic

thought the possibilities of the human imagination in the world made by the violence of Western modernity. Bogues links the human to the imagination and imagination to freedom, arguing for emancipation and liberation as rights-based but reserving freedom for possibilities beyond the organizations of the body politic and politics as we currently know them.

15 This call to "sensation" both echoes Roach's (2007) language around the afterimage of celebrity that comes to stand in for the celebrity herself and invokes Musser's (2014) work on sensation as embodied, material ways to think about corporeal experience that doesn't give over to binary thinking around good and bad political feeling/action. K. J. Brown (2015) reworks the afterimage in the conceptual frame of Audre Lorde's poem of the same name ("Afterimages") to think through subject formation beyond "narrow containment of black women's visibility" (6).

16 For more on the politics of vulnerability, see Dufourmantelle 2018; Fretwell 2011; Moore 2015; Muñoz 2006; Oliviero 2018; Schuller 2018.

17 As Oliviero (2018) argues, for one, vulnerability is a stance and affect ripe for cooptation by the right. But instead of insisting on the real or particular definition of vulnerability here, instead of arguing that it is perfect but for misuse by some, I suggest black vulnerability as a version of the universal political subject. Instead of negating or collapsing black particularity into the universal, then, and following Nash (2019b) on black maternal aesthetics, I claim blackness here—particularly the experience of black women's embodied vulnerability—as a model for the universal political subject. The peril of this capital of/as vulnerability is also interrogated by K. J. Brown (2015) (who considers the possibilities of/for vulnerability); Nyong'o (2009); C. Sharpe (2010).

18 Holloway (2011) cites this as a deep and direct jumping off from Butler's (2016) turn to a politics of vulnerability through the act of speaking.

19 On abjection in black politics and literature, see Darieck Scott (2010).

20 See the February 2018 forum on rights spearheaded by Walter Johnson in the *Boston Review* for a longer discussion among black studies scholars on the question of investing in or abandoning freedom and agency.

21 Iton (2008) powerfully lays this out as emerging through the post-Reconstruction and civil rights failures of black inclusion in US politics, and I extend that to think about a range of post–Middle Passage and postcolonial organizations of black cultural production.

22 As Cherniavsky (2017, 4) so succinctly puts it in her reevaluation of the contemporary, postcitizenship landscape of critique, "It is difficult to read the present as anything but a degraded version of the past, and we tend to miss the difference of the contemporary moment, even as we also assert its novelty, often in increasingly anxious and overwrought terms." To "miss the difference" between past and present (and future) forms of the political is part of the liberal humanist framework itself, but it also forecloses other patterns and continuities one might locate in the cultures and histories of political thought beyond "better" and "worse," or complicit and resistant. To hope that better representations of black humanity—a better Baartman, a Beyoncé doing better by Baartman—will lead to the recognition and bestowal of rights and personhood might be cruel optimism, but one does not and should not throw out the cumulative power

of culture and cultural representation with the realization that even if blackness, and black pain and suffering, could be seen more and better and differently, antiblackness would still not disappear. For two sensitive sides of reworking depictions of black suffering and pain in sentimental modes, see Foreman 2009 (on reading against the grain of black-woman-authored sentimentalism only as sensationalized depictions of black suffering for white audiences under racist codes and norms) and Wanzo 2015 (which deconstructs the depiction of black suffering as always already mitigated by lingering narrative norms of sentimentalism in politics and media).

1. Fantasies of Freedom

1 J. Brooks (2010), Jordan (2002), and Walker (1983) also resite Wheatley from such a trial to think about her in other economies of vulnerability—the difficult miracle, the public mourner for white women's losses, etc. Bernstein (2011) makes a thorough and compelling argument about the construction of black childhood and children against innocence in the nineteenth century, though we might consider some of those later strains of protest against these figurations in twentieth- and twenty-first-century criticism, even as Wheatley wrote in the eighteenth century.

2 And yet, what if Wheatley, named after the very slave ship that ferried her enslavement (the *Phillis*), was Gilroy's model for the chronotope he constructs? What a different black Atlantic subject, what a different diaspora! I discuss this retroping further in the final chapter.

3 For more on theories of black freedom, see V. Brown 2020; Finch 2015; on liberty, see D. Roberts 1998; on black liberation, see Ferrer 2014; K.-Y. Taylor 2016; on freedom, see McWhorter 2013; Wynter 2003.

4 It's beyond the scope of this project, but one might think about the generation of Wheatley's freedom in terms of sonic blackness here, and a sonic gendering of what that "cry" could or should look like. See Stoever 2016.

5 This is a relationship that scores of feminist critics have mapped and nuanced in literary criticism. See Avilez 2016; Crawford 2017; Dubey 1994; Iton 2008; Jarrett 2007; Murray 2009, 2015.

6 Slauter's archival work documents the convergence of the end of neoclassicism (giving way to romanticism) and its relationship to the distance asserted by many invested in metaphors of political slavery from rhetorical and material overlap with chattel slavery. Reception of Wheatley's work, he argues, finds itself at the center of both emergent discourses of rights and writing.

7 Darieck Scott, in recently published articles and his second book (2010), articulates the genre of fantasy itself as a site of black erotic possibility.

8 Shaw (2006) and Slauter (2006) both research and understand the identification to have no grounds, though even the *Norton Anthology of African American Literature* makes the claim for Moorhead's artistic authorship.

9 From the black feminist and multicultural recoveries, repairs, and wonderment of/at Wheatley's trial, the contemporary critical moment has also turned to Wheatley as a historical figure—enacting a literal corrective history by uncovering her public and

private timeline, influence, African identity, and religious identity. Such a commitment comes out of the incredible work of archival scholars of early African American print culture and Africanist presence in the West in the eighteenth century. Much of this work has helped to illuminate different aspects of Wheatley's literary work, as well, generating readings that place her poetry and letters in public life and US revolutionary and nascent antiracist politics, including the work of Bennett (1998, 2003), J. Brooks (2010), McBride (2001), Rezek (2012. 2015), Shields (2010), and others. This body of scholarship brings depth and nuance to Wheatley studies, complicating earlier narratives of her relationship to white readership by filling out her presence within an emerging black religious speaking and print culture, her strategic appeals within revolutionary US political culture, and her relationship to Africa in terms of geographic origin but also in terms of religion, writing, and culture, just to name a few of these key sites of historical intervention.

10 For more on black girlhood studies, see Chatelain 2015; Simmons 2015; Wright 2016; see also anthropological work by Cox (2015).

11 One of the most creative of these is Waldstreicher 2011, which engages Wheatley as a savvy political agent in the moment of British emancipation. This historical confluence emphasizes what others have argued about her biographical history—that, like Sally Hemings, Wheatley likely negotiated freedom in exchange for returning to the United States with her enslaver after her book tour in England.

12 Bernstein (2011) thinks through the earlier production of race and through children and children's entertainment.

13 To invoke persona here is to evoke the compelling work of McMillan (2015) on nineteenth-century black women celebrities and to dig into the critical distance he imagines their personae to bring to the author and to their performances. Here, I am not suggesting of course that there was a "real" Wheatley or that she sought distance from her performance as a poet; instead, I think of her publicness, her fame, and her recognition of its power and her desire for it as telling scripts for how we might address black women creative producers as subjects who desire the gaze and who seek celebrity, rather than as noble or ignoble charges.

14 For documentation of this grant proposal, see https://securegrants.neh.gov/publicquery /main.aspx?f=1&gn=EH-10446-73.

15 This reading of John Peters is controversial, both for the Ed Bullins representation that follows and for the recent essay recovering Peters (Jeffers in Ward 2016), where the critical speculation that renders Wheatley's husband a poor provider is critiqued as racist.

16 Barker-Benfield (2018) investigates evidence that Wheatley refused an "arranged marriage" to a repatriating African church member and recalls Wheatley's letter that also serves as an epigraph to Shockley's first volume of poetry (2006), where she imagines, after a lifetime of acquiring languages, arriving silent to an African shore, where she is once again rendered illiterate.

17 That grief work is discussed in detail in J. Brooks 2010, which not only decisively lays out the ways that Wheatley could not have been authenticated in a live trial, but also movingly imagines the other scenes of racialized labor we could analyze if we give up that optic, if we include the occluded place of Wheatley's commissioned elegies for

white mothers grieving lost children in the ways that Wheatley is critically taken up and anthologized.

18 Watt's *Phillis: A Musical Drama in Three Acts* (1967) also stages Bertha as "serving" Phillis as she gains education and fame as a poet and includes in its freedom plot a cheery "test" that ends in an upbeat song, "Forgive Me If I Leave," sung by one of the signatories, whose refrain is "So we the undersign'd do solemnly pledge and swear / The poems specified were written fair and square." Newell's *Phillis: A Life of Phillis Wheatley* (1981), another play geared toward young adults, decenters the trial into a series of contentious meetings with individual white men and an increasingly agitated Wheatley speaking back to the burden of proof placed on her authorship. This play also features an extended Middle Passage scene and ends on an ambivalent question of the value of Wheatley's verse outliving her very young body. R. Wheatley's (performed 2002; self-published in 2013; no proven relation) *The Trial of Phillis Wheatley* provides a fictional "transcript" of the fictional trial of authentication in dramatic form. All three of these playwrights appear to identify as white.

2. The Romance of Consent

1 For more on agency as it relates to sexual and gender identity in black historical and cultural study, see Fuentes 2016; Hartman 1997; W. Johnson 2003; Owens 2015; J. Sharpe 2003; Stevenson 2013; Winters 2016.

2 This is also argued/suggested by Kaplan 2009; Winters 2016.

3 There are various historical arguments about the language we use to describe both the roles and the actions of sexuality under enslavement, including Araujo 2014; Berry and Harris 2018; M. Jones 2015; Owens 2015.

4 Gordon-Reed speaks about this in many venues, in print and for the press. Her works that take on the subject of the language used to talk about Jefferson and Hemings include *Thomas Jefferson and Sally Hemings* (1998); *The Hemingses of Monticello* (2009); and most recently in the *New York Times*, "Sally Hemings, Thomas Jefferson, and the Ways We Talk about Our Past" (2017).

5 "Concubine" is also the term employed by Jefferson and Hemings's son, Madison Hemings, in his 1873 narrative given to an Ohio journalist.

6 We might think, then, of Patterson (1982) himself identifying, for instance, that women and children are also always already property under the initial tenets of democratic law in the Americas, which is why he finds that the legal concept of property alone cannot be the limit of examining the bonds of slavery. While coverture and the sexualized violence of enslaved women as property are in no way analogous, we might think of enslaved women's subjectivity (as property, as sexual property, as sexual laborers) as the blueprint for the subjectivity coverture conjures, one that is inherently and inevitably vulnerable—rather than nonnormative in its precarity. In other words, we might think of white womanhood not as a class closer to (white male) freedom but as degrees separated from the fundamental vulnerability of personhood that black women's historical experience bears out.

7 In this, I follow the work of black feminist historians and cultural critics such as Camp (2004); Feimster (2009); Haley (2016); Hartman (1997); Hine (1994); Mitchell (1999);

Morgan (2004); Rosen (2009); J. Sharpe (2003); Sommerville (2004); and Stevenson (1996). I also follow Berry (2017); Finch (2015); Fuentes (2016); Gross (2016); McGuire (2011); and Owens (2015) in their deep and powerful negotiations with enslaved, nineteenth-century, Reconstruction, Jim Crow, and civil rights–era black women's sexuality—in particular their cogent redefinitions of agency within the bonds of slavery and in the registers of freedom. See also Stoler 2001.

8 Among the many scholars who have productively used Taylor's powerful construction of the archive and the scenario, Edwards (2012) deploys a charismatic scenario that resonates across cultural performances of race that include more traditionally defined performances but also the way history itself is written toward and within these scripts. This chapter also engages across forms, genres, and disciplines to include various modes of representation of Hemings.

9 We might return to a term from queer studies here to think through the Hemings/Jefferson entanglement. I use this term not to deny agency or structural inequity, but to make clear the complexity of "relations" in thinking about the attachments between these two figures and their enduring representative functions in its own era and beyond: the open secret (McCune 2014; Sedgwick 2008; Snorton 2014). In speaking of Hemings/Jefferson, the term serves as a euphemism for something that is not at all a secret, predicated on civil agreements to not acknowledge the existence of black bodies and subjects except in terms of their own criminality/culpability and/or property value, following Hartman (1997). Lest we forget, a series of laws enacted in the United States both laid bare the fact of miscegenation and enforced paternal secrecy, partus sequitur ventrem, following the condition of the mother (a legal construct of inheritance that flew in the face of generations of Western/European patriarchy). To claim that we lack enough evidence to confirm sexual relationships is also to fly in the face of a historical methodology that consistently requires leaps of reasonable interpretation from the archive to the narrative of history it spins. To construct enslaved sexual relationships with whites as "open secrets" is also to recognize the oral transmission and particular knowledge—and acknowledgments—of the enslaved and free black persons and communities that possessed and trafficked in said knowledges. To put it in other terms, though there is no direct evidence in the form of photographs or personal confessions that directly say that Jefferson engaged in intercourse with his legal wife, Martha Wayles, historians do not seem to doubt their reasonable inference that the two did, indeed, have sex or that Jefferson's children are his own.

10 Which is also, of course, an imagined transcendence of racism through the proliferation of racial hybridity. For a critique of this mythology in the US context, and a range of work on race in Brazil for a diasporic critique of miscegenation as antiracist futurism, see Nyong'o 2009.

11 It pains but bears noting, as Gordon-Reed (2008) does, that the age of consent was in fact ten at the time of their coupling and that Hemings's age, let alone their age difference would not have been illegal or even very out of the ordinary for the time. Again, we might think of these issues as a continuum of vulnerable women's bodies and sexualities based on the changing needs and demands of a white supremacist patriarchal culture.

12 Ralph Ellison's *Invisible Man* memorably includes an African American character from an insane asylum of sorts misrecognizing an unconscious white man as "his grand-father," Thomas Jefferson—another in a line of literary referents publicly acknowledging Jefferson's African American genealogical line.

13 K. J. Brown (2015) does take the novel up, but skeptically, as she sees it through the genre of romance as commodification—in fact suggesting that Chase-Riboud herself was writing to exploit the story of Hemings for her own financial gain. For more on readings of romance that challenge commodity culture as a necessarily politically bankrupt venue, see Radway 1984. For more on the skeptical use of the romance of blackness—casting it as of the past, in white texts—see "Romancing the Shadow" in Morrison 1992.

14 I read this work by Weems alongside and in acknowledgment of K. J. Brown's work on the *Suite* that sees it more wholly as an overwhelming critique of white supremacy and denial of black authorship and subjecthood. I find in Weems's interest in the aesthetic and scientifically generative a way to shift our conversations about authorship, not away from issues of access but away from the fetishizing of white modes of production and reproduction.

15 See also McCauley's (n.d.) performance piece *Sally's Rape*, which doesn't directly speak to Sally Hemings but, as it is a piece on enslaved women's sexuality, implicitly calls up the reference.

16 See three *New York Times* stories/reviews stemming from the exhibit: one a review by Gordon-Reed (2017), another op-ed review (Stockman 2018), and one claiming that Hemings's history can now no longer be denied (Stockman and Demczuk 2018). See also the "Slavery at Monticello" app (https://www.monticello.org/exhibits-events /online-exhibits/download-the-free-slavery-at-monticello-app/), which offers an interactive tour and historical evidence on the privacy of your phone.

17 I would be remiss to not mention Lott ([1998] 2013) here, as well—another book that posits love as a relation between black and white in the United States not as redemptive or corrective but as a way of starting at the point of cultural appropriation, rather than ending at calling it out. Morrison's *Sula* ([1973] 2004) contains an infamous exchange on this topic when Jude comes home from work with a complaint about quotidian racist experience in the United States. Sula challenges Jude to think about white fascination with black men, and all that that love inspires in the intensity of white response to black masculinity, as a paradigm for interrogating whiteness rather than using white violence to define blackness. Morrison, of course, also infamously has the narration critique the unimaginability of black women's pleasure apart from black men through the black political imagining of all black women/white male relations as rape. In this scenario, Sula's social untouchability within her black community is sealed by the rumors of her sleeping with white men, and it is this casting off of Sula as the nonnormative that allows others to imagine and compel themselves into normative sociality.

18 Such is the dissonance as well when Olivia Pope leaves the president and her on-again, off-again affair in the hallway in a late 2012 episode of *Scandal* with this barb: "I'm feeling a little Sally Hemings Thomas Jefferson about all of this." Instead of comedy

here, we get an interruptive moment of comeuppance—a black woman asserting control over her sexual life with the most powerful man in the world—and yet it also encapsulates the way we imagine power, consent, and desire as complex, pleasurable, and difficult sites beyond the easy bounds of interpreting Hemings/Jefferson that is immediately suggested by such a kiss-off.

19 This, of course, calls to a long history of debates around sexuality in feminist studies, particular the porn wars of the 1980s: Dworkin's (2006) work on the links between rape and marriage in legal history, A. Y. Davis's (1981) early work on rape and black women, as well as Hine's (1989b) work and MacKinnon's (1983) infamous claim that all heterosexual sex is rape. Rather than take up these theories in opposition due to their limited claims of completion in their antisex stances, we might embrace these claims as starting points that acknowledge black women's sexuality as the base of feminist subjectivity—a sexuality that is always in proximity to violence—but to then go on and explore sexuality in relationship to this vulnerability, rather than to imagine sexuality as only a space that could exist outside of these conditions. This is, of course, what scholars of black erotics cited earlier are attempting to do, in various ways.

20 We might also think about Stallings's (2015) compelling articulation of antiwork theorization in black sexual cultures here, building off Weeks's (2011) work.

21 On vulnerability theory in law and politics, respectively, see Butler 2016; Fineman 2010a, 2017.

22 On rape and the language of seduction, see Hartman 1997. On sexual terror as racialized political tactic of white supremacy, see Haley 2016; McGuire 2011; Rosen 2009. On this conflation, see Lowe 2015; Stanley 1998.

3. Venus at Work

1 Hasday's (2000) history of marital rape is also of interest here in negotiating the sexual contract of marriage.

2 Fausto-Sterling (1995), Gilman (1985), Nash (2014a), Sharpley-Whiting (1999), Willis (2010), and Hobson (2005) are some of the major interlocutors with Baartman's legacy, while newer work by Coly (2019) references many of her Francophone afterlives.

3 By deploying fiction, I don't mean uncovering a lie masquerading as a truth but instead why, once a fiction is named as such, we might harness the knowledge that relations are fictional—are scripts, are performed, are misremembered—as a way to catalog our experience of lived reality. Fiction describes our quotidian truths. It is constructed; it is artful; it allows for aesthetics; it allows for critique. It allows for "distance and respect" for and from difference, to cite P. Williams (1991)—again. In doing so, we might also imagine the material privileges of freedom as such or as fictions created around the vulnerability of embodied existence and the violence that a collective can only temporarily escape through the uneven distribution of what Chase-Riboud's Sally Hemings calls the "demands of public and of power" (1979, 209).

4 There are two distinct forms of corrective history here: a reinvestment in the interiority of Baartman in the face of the exploitation of her body and her visual iconography, or a refusal of interiority in favor of an uncomfortable representation of Baartman's

body and history as surface. Both methods act in an attempt to critique the violent, dehumanizing frame of Western modernity; both entail critical appeals to our political desires to create richer modes of black women's subjectivity within modernity's paradigms and beyond the impossibility presented by these racist models of representation. But neither model is as simple or as complete in their inhabitation of these modes of critique as they might seem on the surface. Debates around the reuse of Baartman's body-as-surface tend to focus on the weight of repeating and recirculating racist images and hence renewing their power to deny humanity to black subjects. But recent critics of this "feminist resurrection" of Baartman (Crais and Scully 2009) have also taken up the implicit call to respectability made in seeking to give interiority to a nearly silent historical subject, and how that, too, positions the critic as the rescuer of Baartman, and the one who "argues" for black humanity on the very terms that exclude black women from the category in the first place, and in its formation. Scholars have also focused on the way her body has been commodified and coded into discourses of somatic sexual and racial difference to this day, articulated via biopower—by some of the critics mentioned earlier. See also K. J. Brown 2015; Hobson (2005); C. Sharpe (2010).

5 See R. A. Ferguson's (2003) fantastic read of Marx and the figure of the prostitute in *Aberrations in Black* and Mitropoulos's (2012) stunning trace of the intimacies of contract, capital, and the "household" in *Contract and Contagion*.

6 For more on coercion and the political, see Arendt [1951] 2004; J. James 1996.

7 For more on Baartman's legacy in envisioning black women's performances of testimony to trauma, see Griffiths 2010.

8 Again, Wynter (2015), too, argues for more genres of the human than we can possibly know—a reading strategy that assumes plenitude.

9 This echoes Stanley's (1998) twinned history of free labor and the marriage contract in the nineteenth century, as well as Munshi's (2014) work on their continued, deeply racialized intertwining in antitrafficking laws geared toward punishing interracial couplings and marriage in the early twentieth century.

10 This recalls both the trajectory of Baartman in the film above, where she and the former white female partner of the French animal trainer support each other in their move to sex work, which is itself a reference to the 1983 Claude Mulot film *Black Venus*, set in the nineteenth century and involving the sexual abjection of both a white and a black woman who then leave this "protection"/violence to become sex workers in Paris.

11 Not that kin works out so well for women, either. See Rubin 1975.

12 On the repatriation as the other key meaning-making site of her cultural significance besides her performative scenario, see Henderson 2014; Hoad 2005; Hobson 2005, 2017a; Moudileno 2009; Qureshi 2004; Samuelson 2007; C. Sharpe 2010; Wicomb 1998; Young 2017.

13 Several critics take up more contemporary fictional representations of Baartman as sites of political critique: C. Sharpe (2010) offers Bessie Head's novel *Maru* (2013) as way of yoking Baartman's past with a Southern African feminist crisis in Head's present; Moudileno (2009) offers up Bessora's 1999 francophone novel *53 cm* as one that can reckon both with the transnational promise of Baartman's iconography and

with the "postcolonial present" of African diaspora peoples in colonial metropoles by "stag[ing] a transfer from the European museum to a diasporic space that transcends national affiliations," or in her words, "a story of migration" (Moudileno 2009, 206). If Moudileno's reading is more optimistic in its casting of both Bessora's comic novel and Baartman's teleology of racial redemption, she does suggest, along with Hoad (2005) and C. Sharpe (2010), the complicated intra- and transnational dynamics of claiming Baartman's body, in life and in death.

14 Although, following my reading of Hemings in the previous chapter, I can find value in these disembodied strategies of representation, as well. For Baartman, though, there is the haunt of leaving the scene of the crime, so to speak, of Baartman's body's overexposure—to believe that to refuse its visuality is to repair. I think this is a powerful and complicated pull—one that I hang on to even as I want to mark it, too, as a "promise" in its ephemeral investments and assumptions about what invisibility can do.

15 Mireille Miller-Young (2014) explores the flip side of this in black women pornography performers in what she terms the "illicit eroticisms" undertaken even in the most exploitative and racist set of representative structures.

4. Civic Desire

1 The 1994 Schomburg Library of Nineteenth-Century Black Women Writers reprint is the most recognizable edition for US audiences, while the 1984 release from a very small publisher, Falling Wall Press, brought Seacole's story back to attention in the UK. Penguin now has an edition as well, from 2005. Critical literary readings of Seacole's work include Fish 2004; Forbes 2005; Goudie 2008; Kavalski 2003 (on "voluntary" citizenship); McGarrity 2006; McMahon 2008; Mercer 2005; Nwankwo 2002; O'Callaghan 1994; Paquet 1992; Paravisini-Gebert 2003; Poon 2007; A. Robinson 1994; Simpson 2001; Tchaprazov 2008; and others.

2 Winters (2016) thinks through this knot of commerce and sexuality in her work on signares in coastal colonial Africa.

3 In 1948, in the wake of the Second World War, the United Nations officially adopted the Universal Declaration of Human Rights.

4 The UN technically splits "rights" up into two covenants, the International Covenant on Civil and Political Rights and the International Covenant on Economic, Social and Cultural (ESC) Rights. There has been tension since the adoption of the Universal Declaration about the promise of ESC rights—namely, whether the document promises enough in that area or whether ESC rights are "rights," properly understood, at all, especially as they impede states' right to govern by placing an undue burden on their resources. Most human rights discourse of the contemporary era, including the UN Committee on Economic, Social, and Cultural Rights, sees the split between the two as one of unequal ideological power and enforcement. According to a 1993 statement of the committee, "States and the international community as a whole continue to tolerate all too often breaches of economic, social and cultural rights which, if they occurred in relation to civil and political rights, would provoke expressions of horror and outrage and would lead to concerted calls for immediate remedial action. In effect, despite the

rhetoric, violations of civil and political rights continue to be treated as though they were far more serious, and more patently intolerable, than massive and direct denials of economic, social and cultural rights" ("UN Doc. E/1993/22" 1993).

5 Work on black women during enslavement has particularly taken up this question, including Finch 2015; Fuentes 2016; Owens 2015; building on the work of Camp 2004; Hine 1989b; W. Johnson 2003; and D. G. White 1999.

6 See also C. Taylor 2018, which mentions Seacole and her narrative in an argument about the place of the Caribbean "Americas" as a site of postliberal humanist remaking of personhood (in the wake of a campaign of divestment and "neglect" by the Empire).

7 This is not to conflate the two, but to note how they are conflated in contemporary scholarship on and invocations of Seacole—how "Creole," as a distinct racial-regional identity in Jamaica and in New Orleans, as well as other Americas locales, and as one linked to certain rights and discriminations, is collapsed into "black" for Seacole in the postscript of racial identity in postcolonial postmodernity. It is too hard to hold onto hybridity not just for antiblack purposes of "one-drop" but also for antiracist politics that demand racial solidarity.

8 Scholarship on black women's travel narratives further complicates these binary distinctions and is the base of my argument here about narratives and histories of black women in empire that do not "fit" with corrective histories of "good" antiracist political subjects. See Blain and Gill 2019; M. Ferguson 1998; Fish 2004.

9 In a fascinating public memo found on international development organization RAFFA's website, a detailed 2005 interview with the director of the Florence Nightingale Museum outlines the neoliberal possibilities and pitfalls of including Seacole on the museum's agenda in an effort to promote modern diversity (Atwell and Page 2005).

10 Though Kymlicka (1996), of course, is supportive of taking those risks for the endeavor of a multicultural state.

11 R. A. Ferguson (2012) thinks through this phenomenon in a post–civil rights US context.

12 These texts include but are not limited to BBC 2014; Castor 1999; Layne 2007; Lynch 2005; Moorcroft and Magnusson 1998; B. Williams 2009.

13 The fantastic history of Crimea by Figes (2012) tells the formative story of the key critical territory in the imperial age, but we would also be remiss in not thinking about its renewed significance in the twenty-first century, as Russia attempts to wrest control of the territory from the Ukraine.

14 See Frederick 2003 for a discussion of racial distinction as related to Seacole directly, especially in Jamaica. For more on the creation of racial classifications and the distinct construction of Creole society, see Brathwaite 1971. See S. E. Thompson 2009 on Creole subjectivity in particular, though based in New Orleans in the nineteenth century, and Goudie 2006. For more on British relationships to race, see J. Brody 1998; C. Hall 2010; Levine 2003.

15 This is mentioned by Holt (Cooper, Holt, and Scott 2000) in his work on postemancipation Jamaica, but there are very few studies of nineteenth-century black labor in Panama (such as the L. S. Lewis 1980). There are, however, several studies of early twentieth-century free labor in Panama.

16 Her marriage to a white British officer and possible illegitimate son of Lord Nelson occupies no more than a page of the narrative, with the proposal, marriage, and widowhood following swiftly on one another. Likewise, free black unrest is never mentioned within Jamaica itself in the narrative, nor is the presence of free black labor in Panama mentioned except for the presence and relative power of both freed and enslaved African American men, who receive praise and sympathy accordingly, sentiments that would likely be difficult to extend to those freed blacks in Jamaica who were resisting the system of indentured labor and lack of rights as British subjects at the time (culminating in the Morant Bay rebellion in 1865).

17 Thompson is speaking of Creole racial and social identity in nineteenth-century New Orleans, but her theorization of the racial category is still useful to thinking about circum-Caribbean racial identities.

18 For biographical information on Seacole's mother, see Andrews 1988; Gunning 2001b; J. Robinson 2005; Salih 2010; J. Sharpe 2003. For the long history of Creole and black women as hotel keepers in Jamaica and the Caribbean, and the sexual connotations of those roles, see in particular Fluhr 2006; Frederick 2003; Gunning 2001b; J. Sharpe 2003. See also Brody 1998.

19 This is in the lead up to the Morant Bay rebellion in 1865 and the Indian Mutiny, which happens the same year that *Wonderful Adventures* is published. See C. Hall 2010 for more on the context of empire in the Victorian era.

20 Her biographer Jane Robinson (2005, 167) refutes the assumption that Seacole was an official recipient of these national medals, claiming that they appear to be miniatures and that there are no records of her being awarded.

21 On how empire produced racial distinctions and white racial pride even as the boundaries of British "subjects" expanded, see Howell 2014; Levine 2013; Salih 2010; see also C. Hall. 2010; C. Hall, McClelland, and Rendall 2000.

22 Melman (1995) makes this point, as does Levine (1987), who is careful to distinguish the work of philanthropy from feminist occupations and activity of the Victorian era.

23 One might also view Seacole's characterization of border law as it relates to race and economic standing. In a truly remarkable section of her "adventures" she talks at length about her encounter with white Americans on the frontier and their virulent racism. In one interlude, she writes about a formerly enslaved person of African descent who becomes a magistrate and is, at one point, able to pass the judgment of border law on these white US citizens. Like her own narrative's emphasis on civic desire and opportunity, empire's expansionist moments offer unprecedented violences, including the disruption of typical racial orders.

24 Seacole early and repeatedly mentions her love of war, which she attributes to her "Scottish blood." There is even a lengthy mournful passage about the end of the Crimean conflict where Seacole openly and without shame confesses that she is sorry that the war is over.

25 The Crimean War is often described as the first modern war, particularly in its use of media technologies—photojournalism, front reporting, and war memoirs (by soldiers, nurses, cooks, officers' wives, etc.). For two thorough accounts of the conflict's multimedia significance, see Figes 2012; Keller 2001. See also Fletcher 2004.

26 Regarding the role of publicity and claims to rights, I argue that the tension/balance between rights (what one is owed by the state/world) and duties (what one owes to the state/world, and to other citizens in the upholding of rights) is one taken up frequently in human rights discourse, both in terms of the obligations of the state and of individuals.

27 Andrews (1988, xxvii) begins his introduction to the Schomburg reprint of Seacole with the declaration that "no autobiography by an Afro-American woman of the nineteenth century defies classification more that *Wonderful Adventures of Mrs. Seacole in Many Lands* (1857)." As much as it differs from either the spiritual and/or slave narratives of the nineteenth-century Americas, it also breaks from conventions of Crimean War memoirs, as it is part autobiography (beyond Crimea) and largely avoids battleground scenes that characterize the realism of most accounts. As critics have also noted, it also defines Victorian travel narrative conventions by refusing the copious description of exoticized landscapes. Nonetheless, or perhaps in response to these various popular genres of the time, Seacole potentially engages the wide readership of all three generic forms.

28 As Levine (2013, 95) emphasizes in *The British Empire*, "though the theme of reluctance has been so frequently favoured by interpreters of nineteenth-century colonialism, the speed and scope of growth, the public interest in colonial conquest evinced by storybooks and exhibitions and by the formation of pro-imperial bodies such as the British Empire League and the Imperial Federation League, and the constant attentiveness of the press to colonial affairs, hint further at a nation whose very identity was bound up with possessing, ruling, and keeping hold of an empire of epic proportion."

5. #developmentgoals

1 Campt (2017) reframes some of the most bureaucratic of photographs from a slightly later period to think through how we might read dissonance as an attempt not to restore respectability politics, but to proliferate the visual languages and economies of black life.

2 Theories of sovereignty abound in contemporary postcolonial and ethnic studies, trying to grapple with irresolvable questions of individual sovereignty and ideals of postcolonial self-determination: Anker 2012; Byrd 2011; Getachew 2019; Hardt and Negri 2004; Hensley 2018; Hoad 2005; Mbembe 2003; Quashie 2012; Rifkin 2017.

3 We see this pushing at the boundaries of black girlhood studies once more, in the ways that black girls are stuck between a disarticulation of themselves as hyperdeveloped and the projection of injury to innocence (Bernstein 2011; Chatelain 2015; Simmons 2015).

4 This is C. Sharpe's (2016) gorgeous and grounding articulation of a haunting photograph in the aftermath of the Haitian earthquake.

5 There have been brief biographical chapters or slim volumes on Bonetta's history, including in Lindfors 2014; Myers 1999.

6 Sen (2001) argues for the mutability of the term "equality" in arguments about rights and the structures that surround them.

Abdur-Rahman, Aliyyah. 2012. *Against the Closet: Black Political Longing and the Erotics of Race*. Durham, NC: Duke University Press.

Adams, Abigail. 1776. Letter to John Adams, August 29. Boston. https://www.masshist.org/digitaladams/archive/doc?id=L17760829aa&bc=%2Fdigitaladams%2Farchive%2Fbrowse%2Fletters_1774_1777.php.

Adebayo, Dotun. 2015. "What Did Mary Seacole Ever Do for Us as Black People?" *The Voice*, May 7. http://www.voice-online.co.uk/article/what-did-mary-seacole-ever-do-us-black-people.

Agamben, Giorgio. 1998. *Homo Sacer: Sovereign Power and Bare Life*. Translated by Daniel Heller-Roazen. Stanford, CA: Stanford University Press.

Agyepong, Heather. 2016. "Too Many Blackamoors." http://www.heatheragyepong.com/toomanyblackamoors.

Ahmed, Sara. 2017. *Living a Feminist Life*. Durham, NC: Duke University Press.

Alexander, Elizabeth. 1990. "The Venus Hottentot (1825)." In *The Venus Hottentot: Poems*, 3–7. Charlottesville: University Press of Virginia.

Alexander, Elizabeth. 1996. *Body of Life*. Sylmar, CA: Tia Chucha.

Andrade, Susan Z. 2011. *The Nation Writ Small: African Fictions and Feminisms, 1958–1988*. Durham, NC: Duke University Press.

Andrews, William L. 1988. Introduction to Mary Seacole, *Wonderful Adventures of Mrs. Seacole in Many Lands*, xxvii–xxxiv. New York: Oxford University Press.

Anker, Elizabeth S. 2012. *Fictions of Dignity: Embodying Human Rights in World Literature*. Ithaca, NY: Cornell University Press.

Araujo, Ana Lucia. 2014. "Gender, Sex, and Power: Images of Enslaved Women's Bodies." In *Sex, Power, and Slavery*, edited by Gwyn Campbell and Elizabeth Elbourne, 469–99. Athens: Ohio University Press.

Arendt, Hannah. (1951) 2004. *The Origins of Totalitarianism*. New York: Schocken.

Atwell, Alex, and Rudi Page. 2005. "Mary Seacole Bicentenary London 2005: Case Study." http://www.raffa.org.uk/wp-content/uploads/Mary-Seacole-Bicentenary-London-2005-ALM-Case-Study12.pdf.

Avilez, GerShun. 2016. *Radical Aesthetics and Modern Black Nationalism*. Urbana: University of Illinois Press.

Banerjee, Sukanya. 2010. *Becoming Imperial Citizens: Indians in the Late-Victorian Empire*. Durham, NC: Duke University Press.

Baraka, Amiri [LeRoi Jones]. 2009. "The Myth of a 'Negro Literature.'" In *Home: Social Essays*, 124–36. New York: Akashi.

Barker-Benfield, Graham J. 2018. *Phillis Wheatley Chooses Freedom: History, Poetry, and the Ideals of the American Revolution*. New York: New York University Press.

Barrett, Lindon. 1998. *Blackness and Value: Seeing Double*. Cambridge, UK : Cambridge University Press.

BBC. 2014. "Mary Seacole, 1805–1881." *BBC History—Historic Figures*. http://www.bbc.co.uk /history/historic_figures/seacole_mary.shtml.

BBC News. 2002. "Return of 'Hottentot Venus' Unites Bushmen." May 6. http://news.bbc .co.uk/2/hi/africa/1971103.stm.

BBC News. 2004. "Nurse Named Greatest Black Briton." February 10. http://news.bbc.co.uk /2/hi/uk_news/3475445.stm.

Beaton, Kate. n.d. "Mary Seacole." *Hark, A Vagrant!* Accessed August 9, 2018. http://www .harkavagrant.com/index.php?id=174.

Beltran, Mary C. 2009. *Latina/o Stars in U.S. Eyes: The Making and Meanings of Film and TV Stardom*. Urbana: University of Illinois Press.

Benhabib, Seyla, ed. 1996. *Democracy and Difference: Contesting the Boundaries of the Political*. Princeton, NJ: Princeton University Press.

Bennett, Paula. 1998. "Phillis Wheatley's Vocation and the Paradox of the 'Afric Muse.'" *PMLA* 113 (1): 64–76.

Bennett, Paula. 2003. *Poets in the Public Sphere: The Emancipatory Project of American Women's Poetry, 1800–1900*. Princeton, NJ: Princeton University Press.

Berenson, Edward, and Eva Giloi. 2010. *Constructing Charisma: Celebrity, Fame, and Power in Nineteenth-Century Europe*. New York: Berghahn.

Berlant, Lauren. 1997. *The Queen of America Goes to Washington City: Essays on Sex and Citizenship*. Durham, NC: Duke University Press.

Berlant, Lauren. 2011. *Cruel Optimism*. Durham, NC: Duke University Press.

Bernier, Celeste-Marie. 2012. *Characters of Blood: Black Heroism in the Transatlantic Imagination*. Charlottesville: University of Virginia Press.

Bernstein, Robin. 2011. *Racial Innocence: Performing American Childhood from Slavery to Civil Rights*. New York: New York University Press.

Berry, Daina Ramey. 2017. *The Price for Their Pound of Flesh: The Value of the Enslaved, from Womb to Grave, in the Building of a Nation*. Boston: Beacon.

Berry, Daina Ramey, and Leslie M. Harris, eds. 2018. *Sexuality and Slavery: Reclaiming Intimate Histories in the Americas*. Athens: University of Georgia Press.

Bessora. 1999. *53 cm: Roman*. Paris: Serpent à plumes.

Blades, Lincoln Anthony. 2017. "Why You Can't Ever Call an Enslaved Woman a 'Mistress.'" *Teen Vogue*, February 27. https://www.teenvogue.com/story/the-washington-post -thomas-jefferson-sally-hemings-slavery-mistress.

Blain, Keisha, and Tiffany Gill, eds. 2019. *To Turn the Whole World Over: Black Women and Internationalism*. Urbana: University of Illinois Press.

Bogues, Anthony. 2010. *Empire of Liberty: Power, Desire, and Freedom*. Hanover, NH: Dartmouth College Press.

Bost, Darius, La Marr Jurelle Bruce, and Brandon J. Manning. 2019. "Introduction." *Black Scholar* 49 (2): 1–10.

Brandzel, Amy L. 2016. *Against Citizenship: The Violence of the Normative*. Champaign: University of Illinois Press.

Brantley, Ben. 2017. "'Venus' Recalls a Woman's Fortune, and Her Ruin." Review of *Venus*, by Suzan-Lori Parks. *New York Times*, May 15.

Brathwaithe, Kamau. 1971. *The Development of Creole Society in Jamaica, 1770–1820*. Oxford: Clarendon.

Braudy, Leo. 1997. *The Frenzy of Renown: Fame and Its History*. New York: Vintage.

Bressey, Caroline. 2005. "Victorian Photography and the Mapping of the Black Presence." In *Black Victorians: Black People in British Art, 1800–1900*, edited by Jan Marsh, 57–67. London: Lund Humphries.

Brodie, Fawn M. 1974. *Thomas Jefferson: An Intimate History*. New York: Norton.

Brody, Jennifer DeVere. 1998. *Impossible Purities: Blackness, Femininity, and Victorian Culture*. Durham, NC: Duke University Press.

Brooks, Daphne A. 2006. *Bodies in Dissent: Spectacular Performances of Race and Freedom, 1850–1910*. Durham, NC: Duke University Press.

Brooks, Joanna. 2010. "Our Phillis, Ourselves." *American Literature* 82 (1): 1–28.

brown, drea. n.d. "flesh memory: an invocation in cento." Georgetown University, Lannan Center for Poetics and Social Practice. Accessed August 1, 2018. https://lannan .georgetown.edu/drea-brown.

brown, drea. 2015. *dear girl: a reckoning*. Los Angeles: Gold Line.

Brown, Jayna. 2008. *Babylon Girls: Black Women Performers and the Shaping of the Modern*. Durham, NC: Duke University Press.

Brown, Kimberly Juanita. 2015. *The Repeating Body: Slavery's Visual Resonance in the Contemporary*. Durham, NC: Duke University Press.

Brown, Sherronda. 2017. "The NYT Review of 'Venus' Is a Reminder That Black Women and Our Suffering Are Often Invisible to Others." *Racebaitr*, May 22, 2017. http:// racebaitr.com/2017/05/22/the-nyt-review-of-venus-is-a-reminder-that-black-women -and-our-suffering-are-often-invisible-to-others/.

Brown, Vincent. 2020. *Tacky's Revolt: The Story of an Atlantic Slave War*. Cambridge, MA: Harvard University Press.

Brown, Wendy. 2000. "Suffering Rights as Paradoxes." *Constellations* 7 (2): 208–29.

Brown, William Wells. (1853) 2009. *Clotel; or, The President's Daughter*. New York: Modern Library.

Bullins, Ed. (1976) 2004. *The Mystery of Phillis Wheatley*. Alexandria, VA: Alexander Street.

Burg, B. R. 1986. "The Rhetoric of Miscegenation: Thomas Jefferson, Sally Hemings, and Their Historians." *Phylon* 47 (2): 128–38.

Burton, Antoinette. 1994. *Burdens of History: British Feminists, Indian Women, and Imperial Culture, 1865–1915*. Chapel Hill: University of North Carolina Press.

Butler, Judith. 2016. "Rethinking Vulnerability and Resistance." In *Vulnerability in Resistance*, edited by Judith Butler, Zeynep Gambetti. and Leticia Sabsay, 12–27. Durham, NC: Duke University Press.

Bynum, Tara. 2014. "Phillis Wheatley on Friendship." *Legacy* 31 (4): 42–51.

Byrd, Jodi A. 2011. *The Transit of Empire: Indigenous Critiques of Colonialism*. Minneapolis: University of Minnesota Press.

Cacho, Lisa Marie. 2012. *Social Death: Racialized Rightlessness and the Criminalization of the Unprotected*. New York: New York University Press.

Camp, Stephanie M. H. 2004. *Closer to Freedom: Enslaved Women and Everyday Resistance in the Plantation South*. Chapel Hill: University of North Carolina Press.

Campt, Tina M. 2017. *Listening to Images*. Durham, NC: Duke University Press.

Carby, Hazel V. 1986. "It Jus Be's Dat Way Sometime: The Sexual Politics of Women's Blues." *Radical America* 20 (4): 238–49.

Carby, Hazel V. 1987. *Reconstructing Womanhood: The Emergence of the Afro-American Woman Novelist.* New York: Oxford University Press.

"The Caribbean Brain Drain: Nursing a Grievance." 2010. *Economist*, April 8.

Castor, Harriet. 1999. *Famous People, Famous Lives: Mary Seacole.* New York: Orchard/Watts.

Certeau, Michel de. (1984) 2011. *The Practice of Everyday Life.* 3rd ed. Translated by Steven Rendall. Berkeley: University of California Press.

Cervenak, Sarah Jane. 2014. *Wandering: Philosophical Performances of Racial and Sexual Freedom.* Durham, NC: Duke University Press.

Chase-Riboud, Barbara. 1979. *Sally Hemings: A Novel.* New York: Viking.

Chase-Riboud, Barbara. 1994. *The President's Daughter: A Novel.* New York: Crown.

Chase-Riboud, Barbara. 2003. *Hottentot Venus: A Novel.* New York: Anchor.

Chatelain, Marcia. 2015. *South Side Girls.* Durham, NC: Duke University Press.

Cheng, Anne Anlin. 2011. *Second Skin: Josephine Baker and the Modern Surface.* New York: Oxford University Press.

Cherniavsky, Eva. 2017. *Neocitizenship: Political Culture after Democracy.* New York: New York University Press.

Cima, Gay Gibson. 2000. "Black and Unmarked: Phillis Wheatley, Mercy Otis Warren, and the Limits of Strategic Anonymity." *Theatre Journal* 52 (4): 465–95.

Cima, Gay Gibson. 2006. *Early American Women Critics: Performance, Religion, Race.* Cambridge: Cambridge University Press.

Clarke, Lucy D., writer, and Steve Connelly, director. 2010. *Horrible Histories.* Series 2, episode 6. Aired on BBC TV. UK: Lion Television.

Clegg, Margaret, and Sarah Long. 2015. "The Natural History Museum and Human Remains." In *Heritage, Ancestry and Law: Principles, Policies and Practices in Dealing with Historical Human Remains,* edited by Ruth Redmond-Cooper, 100–103. Builth Wells, UK: Institute of Art and Law.

Clifton, Lucille. 2014. "Monticello." In *Good Woman: Poems and a Memoir, 1969–1980,* 126. Rochester, NY: BOA Editions.

Cohen, Dave G., writer, and Steve Connelly, director. 2012. *Horrible Histories.* Series 4, episode 5. Aired on BBC TV. UK: Lion Television.

Colbert, Soyica Diggs. 2017. *Black Movements: Performance and Cultural Politics.* New Brunswick, NJ: Rutgers University Press.

Collins, Patricia Hill. 2000. *Black Feminist Thought: Knowledge, Consciousness, and the Politics of Empowerment.* 2nd ed. New York: Routledge.

Coly, Ayo A. 2019. *Postcolonial Hauntologies: African Women's Discourses of the Female Body.* Lincoln: University of Nebraska Press.

Combahee River Collective. 1980. "The Combahee River Collective Statement." Accessed September 23, 2017. www.circuitous.org/scraps/combahee.html.

Cooper, Afua. 2009. *My Name Is Phillis Wheatley: A Story of Slavery and Freedom.* Toronto: Kids Can.

Cooper, Carolyn. 1995. *Noises in the Blood: Orality, Gender, and the "Vulgar" Body of Jamaican Popular Culture.* Durham, NC: Duke University Press.

Cooper, Frederick, Thomas C. Holt, and Rebecca J. Scott. 2000. *Beyond Slavery: Explorations of Race, Labor, and Citizenship in Postemancipation Societies.* Chapel Hill: University of North Carolina Press.

Cox, Aimee Meredith. 2015. *Shapeshifters: Black Girls and the Choreography of Citizenship.* Durham, NC: Duke University Press.

Crais, Clifton, and Pamela Scully. 2009. *Sara Baartman and the Hottentot Venus: A Ghost Story and a Biography.* Princeton, NJ: Princeton University Press.

Crawford, Margo Natalie. 2017. *Black Post-Blackness: The Black Arts Movement and Twenty-First-Century Aesthetics.* Urbana: University of Illinois Press.

Danielle, Britni. 2017. "Sally Hemings Wasn't Thomas Jefferson's Mistress. She Was His Property." *Washington Post,* July 7.

Davis, Adrienne D. 2002. "'Don't Let Nobody Bother Yo' Principle': The Sexual Economy of American Slavery." In *Sister Circle: Black Women and Work,* edited by Sharon Harley and the Black Women and Work Collective, 103–27. New Brunswick, NJ: Rutgers University Press.

Davis, Adrienne D. 2011. "Bad Girls of Art and Law: Abjection, Power, and Sexuality Exceptionalism in (Kara Walker's) Art and (Janet Halley's) Law." *Yale Journal of Law and Feminism* 23 (1): 1–56.

Davis, Adrienne D., and BSE Collective, eds. 2019. *Black Sexual Economies: Race and Sex in a Culture of Capital.* Urbana: University of Illinois Press.

Davis, Angela Y. 1981. "Rape, Racism and the Capitalist Setting." *Black Scholar* 12 (6): 39–45.

Davis, Angela Y. 1999. *Blues Legacies and Black Feminism: Gertrude "Ma" Rainey, Bessie Smith, and Billie Holiday.* New York: Vintage.

Davis, Angela Y. 2016. *Freedom Is a Constant Struggle: Ferguson, Palestine, and the Foundations of a Movement.* Edited by Frank Barat. Chicago: Haymarket.

Dean, Carolyn J. 2000. *The Frail Social Body: Pornography, Homosexuality, and Other Fantasies in Interwar France.* Berkeley: University of California Press.

Deutsch, Helen. 1996. *Resemblance and Disgrace: Alexander Pope and the Deformation of Culture.* Cambridge, MA: Harvard University Press.

Deutsch, Helen, and Felicity Nussbaum, eds. 2000. *"Defects": Engendering the Modern Body.* Ann Arbor: University of Michigan Press.

Doak, Robin. 2006. *Phillis Wheatley: Slave and Poet.* Minneapolis: Compass Point.

Douglass, Frederick. 1845. *Narrative of the Life of Frederick Douglass, an American Slave, Written by Himself.* Boston: Anti-Slavery Office.

Doyle, Jennifer. 2015. *Campus Sex, Campus Security.* Los Angeles: Semiotext(e).

Drury, Jackie Sibblies. 2019a. *Fairview.* New York: Theatre Communications Group.

Drury, Jackie Sibblies. 2019b. *Marys Seacole.* New York: Dramatists Play Service.

Dubey, Madhu. 1994. *Black Women Novelists and the Nationalist Aesthetic.* Bloomington: Indiana University Press.

duCille, Ann. 1994. "The Occult of True Black Womanhood: Critical Demeanor and Black Feminist Studies." *Signs: Journal of Women in Culture and Society* 19 (3): 591–621.

duCille, Ann. 2000. "Where in the World Is William Wells Brown? Thomas Jefferson, Sally Hemings, and the DNA of African-American Literary History." *American Literary History* 12 (3): 443–62.

Dueben, Alex. 2016. "You Are on Display: An Interview with Morgan Parker." *Paris Review,* July 22.

Dufourmantelle, Anne. 2018. *Power of Gentleness: Meditations on the Risk of Living*. New York: Fordham University Press.

Dworkin, Andrea. 2006. *Intercourse*. Anniversary ed. New York: Basic Books.

Dyer, Richard. (1986) 2013. *Heavenly Bodies: Film Stars and Society*. 2nd ed. New York: Routledge. e-book.

Edwards, Erica R. 2012. *Charisma and the Fictions of Black Leadership*. Minneapolis: University of Minnesota Press.

Edwards, Erica R. 2015. "Sex after the Black Normal." *Differences* 26 (1): 141–67.

Ellis, Joseph J. 1997. *American Sphinx: The Character of Thomas Jefferson*. New York: Knopf.

Ellison, Ralph. 1952. *Invisible Man*. New York: Random House.

Eng, David L. 2010. *The Feeling of Kinship: Queer Liberalism and the Racialization of Intimacy*. Durham NC: Duke University Press.

Erickson, Steve. 1996. *Arc d'X*. New York: Holt.

Fanon, Frantz. (1961) 2004. *The Wretched of the Earth*. Translated by Richard Philcox. New York: Grove.

Fausto-Sterling, Anne. 1995. "Gender, Race, and Nation: The Comparative Anatomy of 'Hottentot' Women in Europe, 1815–1817." In *Deviant Bodies: Critical Perspectives on Difference in Science and Popular Culture*, edited by Jennifer Terry and Jacqueline Urla, 19–48. Bloomington: Indiana University Press.

Feimster, Crystal N. 2009. *Southern Horrors: Women and the Politics of Rape and Lynching*. Cambridge, MA: Harvard University Press.

Felker, Christopher. 1997. "'The Tongues of the Learned Are Insufficient': Phillis Wheatley, Publishing Objectives, and Personal Liberty." In *Texts and Textuality: Textual Instability, Theory, and Interpretation*, edited by Philip Cohen. 81–121. New York: Garland.

Ferguson, Moira. 1998. *Nine Black Women: An Anthology of Nineteenth-Century Writers from the United States, Canada, Bermuda, and the Caribbean*. London: Psychology Press.

Ferguson, Roderick A. 2003. *Aberrations in Black: Toward a Queer of Color Critique*. Minneapolis: University of Minnesota Press.

Ferguson, Roderick A. 2012. *The Reorder of Things: The University and Its Pedagogies of Minority Difference*. Minneapolis: University of Minnesota Press.

Ferrer, Ada. 2014. *Freedom's Mirror: Cuba and Haiti in the Age of Revolution*. New York: Cambridge University Press, 2014.

Figes, Orlando. 2012. *The Crimean War: A History*. New York: Metropolitian.

Finch, Aisha K. 2015. *Rethinking Slave Rebellion in Cuba: La Escalera and the Insurgencies of 1841–1844*. Chapel Hill: University of North Carolina Press.

Fineman, Martha Albertson. 2010a. "Vulnerability and Social Justice." *Valparaiso University Law Review* 53:341–70.

Fineman, Martha Albertson. 2010b. "The Vulnerable Subject and the Responsive State." *Emory Law Journal* 60:251–76.

Fineman, Martha Albertson. 2011. "The Vulnerable Subject: Anchoring Equality in the Human Condition." In *Transcending the Boundaries of Law: Generations of Feminism and Legal Theory*, edited by Martha Albertson Fineman, 161–75. New York: Routledge.

Fineman, Martha Albertson. 2013. "Vulnerability, Resilience, and LGBT Youth." *Temple Political and Civil Rights Law Review* 23:307–30.

Fineman, Martha Albertson. 2014. "Equality and Difference—The Restrained State." *Alabama Law Review* 66:609–26.

Fineman, Martha Albertson. 2015a. "Fineman on Vulnerability and Law." New Legal Realism, November 30. http://newlegalrealism.org/2015/11/30/fineman-on-vulnerability-and-law/.

Fineman, Martha Albertson. 2015b. "Vulnerability and the Institution of Marriage: The Evolution of Plural Parentage: Afterword." *Emory Law Journal* 64 (6): 2089–91.

Fineman, Martha Albertson. 2017. "Vulnerability and Inevitable Inequality." *Oslo Law Review* 4:133–49.

Fischel, Joseph J. 2016. *Sex and Harm in the Age of Consent.* Minneapolis: University of Minnesota Press.

Fish, Cheryl J. 2004. *Black and White Women's Travel Narratives: Antebellum Explorations.* Gainesville: University Press of Florida.

Fleetwood, Nicole R. 2010. *Troubling Vision: Performance, Visuality, and Blackness.* Chicago: University of Chicago Press.

Fleetwood, Nicole R. 2015a. *On Racial Icons: Blackness and the Public Imagination.* New Brunswick, NJ: Rutgers University Press.

Fleetwood, Nicole R. 2015b. "Posing in Prison: Family Photographs, Emotional Labor, and Carceral Intimacy." *Public Culture* 27 (3): 487–511.

Fletcher, Ian. 2004. *Crimean War: A Clash of Empires.* Staplehurst, UK: Spellmount.

Fluhr, Nicole. 2006. "Their Calling Me 'Mother' Was Not, I Think, Altogether Unmeaning": Mary Seacole's Maternal Personae." *Victorian Literature and Culture* 34 (1): 95–113.

Forbes, Curdella. 2005. "Selling That Caribbean Woman down the River: Diasporic Travel Narratives and the Global Economy." *Journal of West Indian Literature* 13 (1–2): 1–27.

Foreman, Pier Gabrielle. 2009. *Activist Sentiments: Reading Black Women in the Nineteenth Century.* Urbana: University of Illinois Press.

Foucault, Michel. 1967. "The Lives of Infamous Men." In *Power*, edited by James D. Faubion, 3:157–75. New York: New Press.

Foucault, Michel. 2008. *The Birth of Biopolitics: Lectures at the Collège de France, 1978–79.* Translated by Graham Burchell. New York: Palgrave Macmillan.

Fox, R. M. 2017. *Resistance Reimagined: Black Women's Critical Thought as Survival.* Gainesville: University Press of Florida.

Fox-Genovese, Elizabeth. 1987. "To Write My Self: The Autobiographies of Afro-American Women." In *Feminist Issues in Literary Scholarship*, edited by Shari Benstock, 161–80. Bloomington: Indiana University Press.

Frazier, Ian. 2011. "Bedside Manner: Two Nurses." *New Yorker*, April 25.

Frederick, Rhonda. 2003. "Creole Performance in *Wonderful Adventures of Mrs. Seacole in Many Lands*." *Gender and History* 15 (3): 487–506.

Fretwell, Erica. 2011. "Senses of Belonging: The Synaesthetics of Citizenship in American Literature, 1862–1903." PhD diss., Duke University.

Friedman, Jonathan, ed. 2004. *Globalization, the State, and Violence.* Walnut Creek, CA: AltaMira.

Fuentes, Marisa J. 2016. *Dispossessed Lives: Enslaved Women, Violence, and the Archive.* Philadelphia: University of Pennsylvania Press.

Garland-Thomson, Rosemarie. 1997. *Extraordinary Bodies: Figuring Physical Disability in American Culture and Literature*. New York: Columbia University Press.

Garvey, Marcus. 1938. "The Work That Has Been Done." *Black Man* 3 (10): 7–11.

Gates, Henry Louis, Jr. 2003. *The Trials of Phillis Wheatley: America's First Black Poet and Her Encounters with the Founding Fathers*. New York: Basic Books.

Gerzina, Gretchen Holbrook, ed. 2003. *Black Victorians/Black Victoriana*. New Brunswick, NJ: Rutgers University Press.

Getachew, Adom. 2019. *Worldmaking after Empire: The Rise and Fall of Self-Determination*. Princeton, NJ: Princeton University Press.

Gilman, Sander L. 1985. *Difference and Pathology: Stereotypes of Sexuality, Race, and Madness*. Ithaca, NY: Cornell University Press.

Gilroy, Paul. 1993. *The Black Atlantic: Modernity and Double-Consciousness*. Cambridge, MA: Harvard University Press.

Gordon-Reed, Annette. 1998. *Thomas Jefferson and Sally Hemings: An American Controversy*. Charlottesville: University of Virginia Press.

Gordon-Reed, Annette. 2008. *The Hemingses of Monticello: An American Family*. New York: Norton.

Gordon-Reed, Annette. 2017. "Sally Hemings, Thomas Jefferson, and the Ways We Talk about Our Past." *New York Times*, August 24.

Goudie, Sean X. 2006. *Creole America: The West Indies and the Formation of Literature and Culture in the New Republic*. Philadelphia: University of Pennsylvania Press.

Goudie, Sean X. 2008. "Toward a Definition of Caribbean American Regionalism: Contesting Anglo-America's Caribbean Designs in Mary Seacole and Sui Sin Far." *American Literature* 80 (2): 293–322.

Goyal, Yogita. 2010. *Romance, Diaspora, and Black Atlantic Literature*. Cambridge: Cambridge University Press.

Graham, Shirley. 1949. *The Story of Phillis Wheatley, Poetess of the American Revolution*. New York: Messner.

Griffin, Farah Jasmine. 2001. *If You Can't Be Free, Be a Mystery: In Search of Billie Holiday*. New York: Simon and Schuster.

Griffiths, Jennifer L. 2010. *Traumatic Possessions: The Body and Memory in African American Women's Writing and Performance*. Charlottesville: University of Virginia Press.

Gross, Kali N. 2006. *Colored Amazons: Crime, Violence, and Black Women in the City of Brotherly Love, 1880–1910*. Durham, NC: Duke University Press.

Gross, Kali N. 2016. *Hannah Mary Tabbs and the Disembodied Torso: A Tale of Race, Sex, and Violence in America*. New York: Oxford University Press.

Grosz, Elizabeth A. 1994. *Volatile Bodies: Toward a Corporeal Feminism*. Indiana University Press.

Gunning, Sandra. 2001a. "Nancy Prince and the Politics of Mobility, Home, and Diasporic (Mis)Identification." *American Quarterly* 53 (1): 32–69.

Gunning, Sandra. 2001b. "Traveling with Her Mother's Tastes: The Negotiation of Gender, Race, and Location in *Wonderful Adventures of Mrs. Seacole in Many Lands*." *Signs: Journal of Women in Culture and Society* 26 (4): 949–81.

Gussow, Mel. 1976. "Stage: 'Phyllis Wheatley.'" Review of *The Mystery of Phillis Wheatley*, by Ed Bullins. *New York Times*, February 4.

Haid, Charles, dir. 2000. *Sally Hemings: An American Scandal.* New York: CBS Productions.

Haley, Sarah. 2016. *No Mercy Here: Gender, Punishment, and the Making of Jim Crow Modernity.* Chapel Hill: University of North Carolina Press.

Hall, Catherine. 2010. *Race, Nation and Empire: Making Histories, 1750 to the Present.* Manchester, UK: Manchester University Press.

Hall, Catherine, Keith McClelland, and Jane Rendall. 2000. *Defining the Victorian Nation: Class, Race, Gender and the British Reform Act of 1867.* Cambridge, UK: Cambridge University Press.

Hall, Stuart. 2014. "Cultural Identity and Diaspora." In *Diaspora and Visual Culture: Representing Africans and Jews,* edited by Nicholas Mirzoeff, 35–47. London: Routledge.

Halley, Janet. 2016. "The Move to Affirmative Consent." *Signs* 42 (1): 257–79.

Hambly, Barbara. 2007. *Patriot Hearts: A Novel of the Founding Mothers.* New York: Random House.

Hardt, Michael, and Antonio Negri. 2001. *Empire.* Cambridge, MA: Harvard University Press.

Hardt, Michael, and Antonio Negri. 2004. *Multitude: War and Democracy in the Age of Empire.* New York: Penguin.

Harris, Cheryl I. 1993. "Whiteness as Property." *Harvard Law Review* 106 (8): 1707–91.

Harris, Lyle Ashton. 1994. *The Good Life* (photographic series). Jack Tilton Gallery, New York.

Hartman, Saidiya V. 1997. *Scenes of Subjection: Terror, Slavery, and Self-Making in Nineteenth-Century America.* New York: Oxford University Press.

Hartman, Saidiya V. 2008. "Venus in Two Acts." *Small Axe* 12 (2): 1–14.

Hartman, Saidiya V. 2019. *Wayward Lives, Beautiful Experiments: Intimate Histories of Social Upheaval.* New York: Norton.

Hasday, Jill Elaine. 2000. "Contest and Consent: A Legal History of Marital Rape." *California Law Review* 88 (5).

Hawthorne, Evelyn J. 2000. "Self-Writing, Literary Traditions, and Post-Emancipation Identity: The Case of Mary Seacole." *Biography* 23 (2): 309–31.

Head, Bessie. 2013. *Maru.* Long Grove, IL: Waveland.

Hemings, Madison. 1873. "Life among the Lowly, No. 1." *Pike County Republican,* March 13, 1873.

Hemmings, Clare. 2011. *Why Stories Matter: The Political Grammar of Feminist Theory.* Durham, NC: Duke University Press.

Henderson, Carol E. 2014. "AKA: Sarah Baartman, the Hottentot Venus, and Black Women's Identity." *Women's Studies* 43 (7): 946–59.

Hensley, Nathan K. 2018. *Forms of Empire: The Poetics of Victorian Sovereignty.* Oxford: Oxford University Press.

Hesford, Wendy S., and Rachel A. Lewis. 2016. "Mobilizing Vulnerability: New Directions in Transnational Feminist Studies and Human Rights." *Feminist Formations* 28 (1): vii–xviii.

Hine, Darlene Clark. 1989a. *Black Women in White: Racial Conflict and Cooperation in the Nursing Profession, 1890–1950.* Bloomington: Indiana University Press.

Hine, Darlene Clark. 1989b. "Rape and the Inner Lives of Black Women in the Middle West: Preliminary Thoughts on the Culture of Dissemblance." *Signs* 14 (4): 912–20.

Hine, Darlene Clark. 1994. *Hine Sight: Black Women and the Re-Construction of American History.* Bloomington: Indiana University Press.

Hirschmann, Nancy J. 2003. *The Subject of Liberty: Toward a Feminist Theory of Freedom*. Princeton, NJ: Princeton University Press.

Hitchens, Peter. 2013. "How 'Multiculture' Fanatics Took Mary Seacole Hostage." *Daily Mail Online*, January 6. http://www.dailymail.co.uk/debate/article-2257668/PETER -HITCHENS-How-multiculture-fanatics-took-Mary-Seacole-hostage.html.

Hoad, Neville. 2005. "Thabo Mbeki's AIDS Blues: The Intellectual, the Archive, and the Pandemic." *Public Culture* 17 (1): 101–28.

Hobson, Janell. 2005. *Venus in the Dark: Blackness and Beauty in Popular Culture*. New York: Routledge.

Hobson, Janell. 2017a. "Celebrity Feminism: More Than a Gateway." *Signs: Journal of Women in Society and Culture* 42 (4): 999–1007.

Hobson, Janell. 2017b. "Pictoral Manifestations: On a Younger Harriet Tubman." *Black Perspectives*, February 15, 2017. https://www.aaihs.org/pictorial-manifestations-on-a -younger-harriet-tubman/.

Holloway, Karla FC. 1995. *Codes of Conduct: Race, Ethics, and the Color of Our Character*. New Brunswick, NJ: Rutgers University Press.

Holloway, Karla FC. 2011. *Private Bodies, Public Texts: Race, Gender, and a Cultural Bioethics*. Durham, NC: Duke University Press.

Holloway, Karla FC. 2014. *Legal Fictions: Constituting Race, Composing Literature*. Durham, NC: Duke University Press.

Hong, Grace Kyungwon. 2015. *Death beyond Disavowal: The Impossible Politics of Difference*. Minneapolis: University of Minnesota Press.

Howell, Jessica. 2014. *Exploring Victorian Travel Literature: Disease, Race and Climate*. Edinburgh: Edinburgh University Press.

Hua, Julietta. 2011. *Trafficking Women's Human Rights*. Minneapolis: University of Minnesota Press.

Hughes, Langston. (1966) 1997. "200 Years of American Negro Poetry." *Transition* 75/76: 90–96.

Hull, Akasha, Patricia Bell-Scott, and Barbara Smith, eds. 1992. *All the Women Are White, All the Blacks Are Men, but Some of Us Are Brave: Black Women's Studies*. Old Westbury, NY Feminist Press.

Hunt, Lynn. 2007. *Inventing Human Rights: A History*. New York: Norton.

Hunter, Tera W. 2019. *Bound in Wedlock: Slave and Free Black Marriage in the Nineteenth Century*. Cambridge, MA: Harvard University Press.

Isani, Mukhtar Ali. 2000. "The Contemporaneous Reception of Phillis Wheatley: Newspaper and Magazine Notices during the Years of Fame, 1765–1774." *Journal of Negro History* 85 (4): 260–73.

Iton, Richard. 2008. *In Search of the Black Fantastic: Politics and Popular Culture in the Post–Civil Rights Era*. New York: Oxford University Press.

Ivory, James, dir. 1995. *Jefferson in Paris*. Burbank, CA: Buena Vista Pictures.

Jackson, Zakiyyah Iman. 2015. "Outer Worlds: The Persistence of Race in Movement 'beyond the Human.'" *GLQ: A Journal of Lesbian and Gay Studies* 21 (2–3): 215–18.

Jacobs, Harriet A. (1861) 1988. *Incidents in the Life of a Slave Girl*. Introduction by Valerie Smith. New York: Oxford University Press.

Jaji, Tsitsi Ella. 2014. *Africa in Stereo: Modernism, Music, and Pan-African Solidarity.* New York: Oxford University Press.

James, Carl E. 2008. "Re/presentation of Race and Racism in the Multicultural Discourse of Canada." In *Educating for Human Rights and Global Citizenship*, edited by Ali A. Abdi and Lynette Schultz, 97–112. Albany: State University of New York Press.

James, Joy. 1996. *Resisting State Violence: Radicalism, Gender, and Race in U.S. Culture.* Minneapolis: University of Minnesota Press.

Jarrett, Gene Andrew. 2007. *Deans and Truants: Race and Realism in African American Literature.* Philadelphia: University of Pennsylvania Press.

Jefferson, Thomas. (1785) 1999. *Notes on the State of Virginia.* Introduction and notes by Frank Shuffelton. New York: Penguin.

Jenkins, Candice M. 2007. *Private Lives, Proper Relations: Regulating Black Intimacy.* Minneapolis: University of Minnesota Press.

Johnson, James Weldon, ed. 1922. *The Book of American Negro Poetry.* New York: Harcourt, Brace.

Johnson, Walter. 2003. "On Agency." *Journal of Social History* 37 (1): 113–24.

Johnson, Walter. 2018. "To Remake the World: Slavery, Racial Capitalism, and Justice." *Boston Review*, February 20.

Jones, Jacqueline. 2009. *Labor of Love, Labor of Sorrow: Black Women, Work, and the Family, from Slavery to the Present.* New York: Basic Books.

Jones, Martha S. 2009. *All Bound Up Together: The Woman Question in African American Public Culture, 1830–1900.* Chapel Hill: University of North Carolina Press.

Jones, Martha S. 2015. "Julian Bond's Great-Grandmother a 'Slave Mistress?' How the New York Times Got It Wrong." History News Network, August 26. https://historynewsnetwork.org/article/160451.

Jordan, June. 2002. *Some of Us Did Not Die: New and Selected Essays.* New York: Basic Books.

Jordan, June. (2002) 2006. "The Difficult Miracle of Black Poetry in America: Something Like a Sonnet for Phillis Wheatley." Poetry Foundation, August 15. https://www.poetryfoundation.org/articles/68628/the-difficult-miracle-of-black-poetry-in-america.

Kaplan, Sara Clarke. 2009. "Our Founding (M)Other: Erotic Love and Social Death in *Sally Hemings* and *The President's Daughter.*" *Callaloo* 32 (2): 773–91.

Kavalski, Emilian. 2003. "Notions of Voluntary Identity and Citizenship in Wonderful Adventures of Mrs. Seacole in Many Lands." *Jouvert: A Journal of Postcolonial Studies* 7 (2): 1–12.

Kazanjian, David. 2003. *The Colonizing Trick: National Culture and Imperial Citizenship in Early America.* Minneapolis: University of Minnesota Press.

Kechiche, Abdellatif, dir. 2010. *Vénus noire.* France: MK2.

Keller, Ulrich. 2001. *The Ultimate Spectacle: A Visual History of the Crimean War.* Philadelphia: Gordon and Breach.

Kelley, Robin D. G. 2002. *Freedom Dreams: The Black Radical Imagination.* Boston: Beacon.

Kerber, Linda K. 1988. "Separate Spheres, Female Worlds, Woman's Place: The Rhetoric of Women's History." *Journal of American History* 75 (1): 9–39.

Kipnis, Laura. 2017. *Unwanted Advances: Sexual Paranoia Comes to Campus.* New York: HarperCollins.

Kymlicka, Will. 1996. *Multicultural Citizenship: A Liberal Theory of Minority Rights.* Oxford: Oxford University Press.

Layne, Marcia. 2007. *The Yellow Doctress* (play). England: West Yorkshire Playhouse.

Levine, Philippa. 1990. *Feminist Lives in Victorian England: Private Roles and Public Commitment.* Oxford: Blackwell.

Levine, Philippa. 2003. *Prostitution, Race, and Politics: Policing Venereal Disease in the British Empire.* New York: Routledge.

Levine, Philippa. 2013. *The British Empire: Sunrise to Sunset.* 2nd ed. New York: Routledge.

Levy-Hussen, Aida. 2016. *How to Read African American Literature: Post–Civil Rights Fiction and the Task of Interpretation.* New York: New York University Press.

Levy-Hussen, Aida. 2019. "Boredom in Contemporary African American Literature." Post45, April 28. http://post45.research.yale.edu/2019/04/boredom-in-contemporary-african-american-literature/.

Lewis, Lancelot S. 1980. *The West Indian in Panama: Black Labor in Panama, 1850–1914.* Washington, DC: University Press of America.

Lewis, Robin Coste. 2015. *Voyage of the Sable Venus and Other Poems.* New York: Knopf.

Lightfoot, Natasha, 2015. *Troubling Freedom: Antigua and the Aftermath of British Emancipation.* Durham, NC: Duke University Press.

Lindfors, Bernth. 2014. *Early African Entertainments Abroad: From the Hottentot Venus to Africa's First Olympians.* Madison: University of Wisconsin Press.

Lindsey, Treva B., and Jessica Marie Johnson. 2014. "Searching for Climax: Black Erotic Lives in Slavery and Freedom." *Meridians: Feminism, Race, Transnationalism* 12 (2): 169–95.

Lipsitz, George. 1998. *The Possessive Investment in Whiteness: How White People Profit from Identity Politics.* Philadelphia: Temple University Press.

Lloyd, Sheila. 2011. "Sara Baartman and the 'Inclusive Exclusions' of Neoliberalism." *Meridians: Feminism, Race, Transnationalism* 11 (2): 212–37.

Lott, Eric. (1998) 2013. *Love and Theft: Blackface Minstrelsy and the American Working Class.* 20th anniv. ed. New York: Oxford University Press.

Lowe, Lisa. 2009. "Autobiography out of Empire." *Small Axe* 13 (1): 98–111.

Lowe, Lisa. 2015. *The Intimacies of Four Continents.* Durham, NC: Duke University Press.

Luckett, Robert E., Jr. 2018. "For My People: The Margaret Walker Center." *Public Historian* 40 (3): 173–92.

Lynch, Emma. 2005. *The Life of Mary Seacole.* London: Heinemann.

MacKinnon, Catharine A. 1983. "Feminism, Marxism, Method, and the State: Toward Feminist Jurisprudence." *Signs* 8 (4): 635–58.

Magubane, Zine. 2001. "Which Bodies Matter? Feminism, Poststructuralism, Race, and the Curious Theoretical Odyssey of the 'Hottentot Venus.'" *Gender and Society* 15 (6): 816–34.

Marcus, Sharon. 2019. *The Drama of Celebrity.* Princeton, NJ: Princeton University Press.

Marsh, Jan, ed. 2005. *Black Victorians: Black People in British Art, 1800–1900.* London: Lund Humphries.

"Mary Seacole Activities." n.d. My Learning. Accessed October 7, 2017. https://www.mylearning.org/resources/mary-seacole-activities.

"Marys Seacole." 2019. Lincoln Center Theater: Shows. https://www.lct.org/shows/marys-seacole/.

"Matilda" [pseud.]. 1796. "On Reading the Poems of Phillis Wheatley, the African Poetess." *New York Magazine*, October, 549–50.

Mbeki, Thabo. 2002. "Speech at the Funeral of Sarah Bartmann, 9 August 2002." South African History Online. https://www.sahistory.org.za/archive/speech-funeral-sarah -bartmann-9-august-2002.

Mbembe, Achille. 2003. "Necropolitics." *Public Culture* 15 (1): 11–40.

McBride, Dwight. 2001. *Impossible Witnesses: Truth, Abolitionism, and Slave Testimony*. New York: New York University Press.

McCauley, Robbie. n.d. "Sally's Rape." Robbie McCauley Company, accessed December 1, 2019. http://robbiemccauleyncompany.com/portfolio/sallys-rape/.

McCune, Jeffrey Q., Jr. 2014. *Sexual Discretion: Black Masculinity and the Politics of Passing*. Chicago: University of Chicago Press.

McDowell, Deborah E. 1987. "'The Changing Same': Generational Connections and Black Women Novelists." *New Literary History* 18 (2): 281–302.

McGarrity, Maria. 2006. "Mary Seacole's 'Wonderful Adventures': An Eastward Economy of Disease." *VIJ: Victorians Institute Journal* 34:127–44.

McGuire, Danielle L. 2011. *At the Dark End of the Street: Black Women, Rape, and Resistance—A New History of the Civil Rights Movement from Rosa Parks to the Rise of Black Power*. New York: Vintage.

McKay, Nellie Y. 1998. "Naming the Problem That Led to the Question 'Who Shall Teach African American Literature?'; or, Are We Ready to Disband the Wheatley Court?" *PMLA* 113 (3): 359–69.

McKittrick, Katherine. 2006. *Demonic Grounds: Black Women and the Cartographies of Struggle*. Minneapolis: University of Minnesota Press.

McMahon, Deirdre. 2008. "'My Own Dear Sons': Discursive Maternity and Proper British Bodies in *Wonderful Adventures of Mrs. Seacole in Many Lands*." In *Other Mothers: Beyond the Maternal Ideal*, edited by Ellen Bayuk Rosenman and Claudia C. Klaver, 181–201. Columbus: Ohio State University Press.

McMillan, Uri. 2015. *Embodied Avatars: Genealogies of Black Feminist Art and Performance*. New York: New York University Press.

McWhorter, Ladelle. 2013. "Post-Liberation Feminism and Practices of Freedom." *Foucault Studies* 16 (September). http://dx.doi.org/10.22439/fs.v0i16.4117.

Melman, Billie. 1995. *Women's Orients: English Women and the Middle East, 1718–1918*. Ann Arbor: University of Michigan Press.

Mercer, Lorraine. 2005. "'I Shall Make No Excuse: The Narrative Odyssey of Mary Seacole." *Journal of Narrative Theory* 35 (1): 1–24.

Metz, Christian. (1975) 1982. *The Imaginary Signifier: Psychoanalysis and the Cinema*. Bloomington: Indiana University Press.

Miller, Monica L. 2009. *Slaves to Fashion: Black Dandyism and the Styling of Black Diasporic Identity*. Durham, NC: Duke University Press.

Miller-Young, Mireille. 2014. *A Taste for Brown Sugar: Black Women in Pornography*. Durham, NC: Duke University Press.

Mills, Charles W. 1997. *The Racial Contract*. Ithaca, NY: Cornell University Press.

Mitchell, Michele. 1999. "Silences Broken, Silences Kept: Gender and Sexuality in African-American History." *Gender and History* 11 (3): 433–44.

Mitropoulos, Angela. 2012. *Contract and Contagion: From Biopolitics to Oikonomia*. Brooklyn, NY: Minor Compositions.

Moorcroft, Christine, and Magnus Magnusson. 1998. *Mary Seacole, 1805–1881*. London: Channel Four Learning.

Moore, Alexandra Schultheis. 2015. *Vulnerability and Security in Human Rights Literature and Visual Culture*. London: Routledge.

Morgan, Jennifer L. 2004. *Laboring Women: Reproduction and Gender in New World Slavery*. Philadelphia: University of Pennsylvania Press.

Morrison, Toni. (1987) 2004. *Beloved*. New York: Vintage.

Morrison, Toni. 1992. *Playing in the Dark: Witnesses and the Literary Imagination*. Cambridge, MA: Harvard University Press.

Morrison, Toni. (1973) 2004. *Sula*. New York: Vintage.

Moten, Fred. 2003. *In the Break: The Aesthetics of the Black Radical Tradition*. Minneapolis: University of Minnesota Press.

Moten, Fred. 2008. "The Case of Blackness." *Criticism* 50 (2): 177–218.

Moudileno, Lydie. 2009. "Returning Remains: Sarah Baartman, or the 'Hottentot Venus' as Transnational Postcolonial Icon." *Forum for Modern Language Studies* 45 (2): 200–212.

Moyn, Samuel. 2012. *The Last Utopia: Human Rights in History*. Cambridge, MA: Harvard University Press.

Mulla, Sameena. 2014. *The Violence of Care: Rape Victims, Forensic Nurses, and Sexual Assault Intervention*. New York: New York University Press.

Muñoz, José Esteban. 2006. "The Vulnerability Artist: Nao Bustamante and the Sad Beauty of Reparation." *Women and Performance: A Journal of Feminist Theory* 16 (2): 191–200.

Munshi, Sherally. 2014. "The Archivist of Affronts: Immigration, Representation, and Legal Personality in Early Twentieth Century America." PhD diss., Columbia University.

Munshi, Sherally. 2019. "White Slavery and the Crisis of Will in the Age of Contract." *Yale Journal of Law and Feminism* 30 (2). https://digitalcommons.law.yale.edu/yjlf/vol30/iss2/4.

Murray, Rolland. 2009. "African-American Literary Studies and the Legacies of Black Nationalism." *American Literary History* 21 (4): 923–37.

Murray, Rolland. 2015. *Our Living Manhood: Literature, Black Power, and Masculine Ideology*. Philadelphia: University of Pennsylvania Press.

Musser, Amber Jamilla. 2014. *Sensational Flesh: Race, Power, and Masochism*. New York: New York University Press.

Musser, Amber Jamilla. 2016. "Queering Sugar: Kara Walker's Sugar Sphinx and the Intractability of Black Female Sexuality." *Signs: Journal of Women in Culture and Society* 42 (1): 153–74.

Myers, Walter Dean. 1999. *At Her Majesty's Request: An African Princess in Victorian England*. New York: Scholastic.

Naimou, Angela. 2015. *Salvage Work: U.S. and Caribbean Literatures amid the Debris of Legal Personhood*. New York: Fordham University Press.

Nash, Jennifer C. 2014a. "Black Anality." *GLQ: A Journal of Lesbian and Gay Studies* 20 (4): 439–60.

Nash, Jennifer C. 2014b. *The Black Body in Ecstasy: Reading Race, Reading Pornography*. Durham, NC: Duke University Press.

Nash, Jennifer C. 2017. "Intersectionality and Its Discontents." *American Quarterly* 16 (1): 117–29.

Nash, Jennifer C. 2019a. *Black Feminism Reimagined: After Intersectionality*. Durham, NC: Duke University Press.

Nash, Jennifer C. 2019b. "Black Maternal Aesthetics." *Theory and Event* 22 (3): 551–75.

Newell, Martha Hill. 1981. *Phillis: A Life of Phillis Wheatley*. Rowayton, CT: New Plays.

Nguyen, Mimi Thi. 2012. *The Gift of Freedom: War, Debt, and Other Refugee Passages*. Durham, NC: Duke University Press.

Nussbaum, Felicity A. 2003. *The Limits of the Human: Fictions of Anomaly, Race, and Gender in the Long Eighteenth Century*. Cambridge: Cambridge University Press.

Nussbaum, Martha. 2003. "Capabilities as Fundamental Entitlements: Sen and Social Justice." *Feminist Economics* 9 (2–3): 33–59.

Nussbaum, Martha C. 2011. *Creating Capabilities: The Human Development Approach*. Cambridge, MA: Belknap Press of Harvard University Press.

Nwankwo, Ifeoma C. K. 2002. "Caribbean Compositions: New Histories of Writing and Identity." *Callaloo* 25 (3): 990–94.

Nyong'o, Tavia. 2009. *The Amalgamation Waltz: Race, Performance, and the Ruses of Memory*. Minneapolis: University of Minnesota Press.

O'Callaghan, Evelyn. 1994. "(Ex)Tending the Boundaries: Early Travel Writing by Women and the Construction of the 'West Indies.'" *Caribbean Studies* 27 (3–4): 255–77.

O'Connor, Stephen. 2016. *Thomas Jefferson Dreams of Sally Hemings: A Novel*. New York: Penguin.

Oliviero, Kathryn Elizabeth. 2010. "Vulnerable Sensations: Compositions of Imperiled Personhood, Intimacy and Citizenship in 21st Century Social Changes." PhD diss., University of California, Los Angeles.

Oliviero, Katie. 2018. *Vulnerability Politics: The Uses and Abuses of Precarity in Political Debate*. New York: New York University Press.

Ong, Aihwa. 1999. *Flexible Citizenship: The Cultural Logics of Transnationality*. Durham, NC: Duke University Press.

Ovington, Mary White. 1932. *Phillis Wheatley*. New York: Schulte.

Owens, Emily A. 2015. "Fantasies of Consent: Black Women's Sexual Labor in 19th Century New Orleans." PhD diss., Harvard University.

Owens, Emily A. 2017. "Promises: Sexual Labor in the Space between Slavery and Freedom." *Louisiana History* 58 (2): 179–216.

Owens, Emily A. 2019. "Keyword 7 Consent." *Differences* 30 (1): 148–56.

Oxford English Dictionary (*OED*), online ed. 2017. www.oed.com.

Oyěwùmí, Oyèrónkẹ́. 1997. *The Invention of Women: Making an African Sense of Western Gender Discourses*. Minneapolis: University of Minnesota Press.

Oyěwùmí, Oyèrónkẹ́. 2005. "Visualizing the Body: Western Theories and African Subjects." In *African Gender Studies: A Reader*, edited by Oyèrónkẹ́ Oyěwùmí, 3–21. New York: Palgrave Macmillan.

Paik, A. Naomi. 2016. *Rightlessness: Testimony and Redress in U.S. Prison Camps since World War II*. Chapel Hill: University of North Carolina Press.

Painter, Nell Irvin. 1996. *Sojourner Truth: A Life, a Symbol*. New York: Norton.

Paquet, Sandra Pouchet. 1992. "The Enigma of Arrival: *The Wonderful Adventures of Mrs. Seacole in Many Lands*." *African American Review* 26 (4): 651–63.

Paquet, Sandra Pouchet. 2002. *Caribbean Autobiography: Cultural Identity and Self-Representation*. Madison: University of Wisconsin Press.

Paravisini-Gebert, Lizabeth. 2003. "Mrs. Seacole's *Wonderful Adventures in Many Lands* and the Consciousness of Transit." In *Black Victorians/Black Victoriana*, edited by Gretchen Holbrook Gerzina, 17–87. New Brunswick, NJ: Rutgers University Press.

Paredez, Deborah. 2014. "Lena Horne and Judy Garland: Divas, Desire, and Discipline in the Civil Rights Era." *TDR/The Drama Review* 58 (4): 105–19.

Parikh, Crystal. 2017. *Writing Human Rights: The Political Imaginaries of Writers of Color*. Minneapolis: University of Minnesota Press.

Parker, Morgan. 2016. "Hottentot Venus." *Paris Review* 216 (Spring). https://www .theparisreview.org/poetry/6446/hottentot-venus-morgan-parker.

Parker, Morgan. 2017. *There Are More Beautiful Things Than Beyoncé*. Portland, OR: Tin House.

Parks, Suzan-Lori. 1996. "The Rear End Exists." *Grand Street*, no. 55.

Parks, Suzan-Lori. 1997. *Venus*. Performed 1996. New York: Theatre Communications Group.

Pateman, Carole. 1988. *The Sexual Contract*. Palo Alto: Stanford University Press.

Pateman, Carole, and Charles Mills. 2007. *Contract and Domination*. Malden, MA: Polity.

Patterson, Orlando. 1982. *Slavery and Social Death: A Comparative Study*. Cambridge, MA: Harvard University Press.

Patterson, Orlando. 1991. *Freedom in the Making of Western Culture*. New York: Basic Books.

Phan, Hoang Gia. 2013. *Bonds of Citizenship: Law and the Labors of Emancipation*. New York: New York University Press.

Phelan, Peggy. (1993) 2003. *Unmarked: The Politics of Performance*. New York: Routledge.

Pinto, Samantha. 2013. *Difficult Diasporas: The Transnational Feminist Aesthetic of the Black Atlantic*. New York: New York University Press.

Platon, Adelle. 2016. "Beyonce 'in No Way' Tied to Sarah Baartman Film." *Billboard*, January 5. https://www.billboard.com/articles/columns/hip-hop/6828940/beyonce -saartjie-baartman-film.

Pointon, Marcia. 1993. *Hanging the Head: Portraiture and Social Formation in Eighteenth-Century England*. New Haven, CT: Yale University Press.

Poon, Angelia. 2007. "Comic Acts of (Be)Longing: Performing Englishness in *Wonderful Adventures of Mrs. Seacole in Many Lands*." *Victorian Literature and Culture* 35 (2): 501–16.

Powell, Richard J. 2009. *Cutting a Figure: Fashioning Black Portraiture*. Chicago: University of Chicago Press.

Puar, Jasbir K. 2017. *The Right to Maim: Debility, Capacity, Disability*. Durham, NC: Duke University Press.

Quashie, Kevin. 2009. "The Trouble with Publicness: Toward a Theory of Black Quiet." *African American Review* 43 (2–3): 329–43.

Quashie, Kevin. 2012. *The Sovereignty of Quiet: Beyond Resistance in Black Culture*. New Brunswick, NJ: Rutgers University Press.

Qureshi, Sadiah. 2004. "Displaying Sara Baartman, the 'Hottentot Venus.'" *History of Science* 42 (2): 233–57.

Radway, Janice A. 1984. *Reading the Romance: Women, Patriarchy, and Popular Literature*. Chapel Hill: University of North Carolina Press.

Rankine, Claudia. 2015. "The Condition of Black Life Is One of Mourning." *New York Times*, June 22.

Rappaport, Helen. 2007. *No Place for Ladies: The Untold Story of Women in the Crimean War*. London: Aurum.

Reddy, Sujani K. 2015. *Nursing and Empire: Gendered Labor and Migration from India to the United States*. Chapel Hill: University of North Carolina Press.

Rezek, Joseph. 2012. "The Print Atlantic: Phillis Wheatley, Ignatius Sancho, and the Cultural Significance of the Book." In *Early African American Print Culture*, edited by Lara Langer Cohen and Jordan Alexander Stein, 19–39. Philadelphia: University of Pennsylvania Press.

Rezek, Joseph. 2015. "Print, Writing, and the Difference Media Make: Revisiting 'The Signifying Monkey' after Book History." *Early American Literature* 50 (3): 891–900.

Richards, Phillip M. 1992. "Phillis Wheatley and Literary Americanization." *American Quarterly* 44 (2): 163–91.

Rifkin, Mark. 2017. *Beyond Settler Time: Temporal Sovereignty and Indigenous Self-Determination*. Durham, NC: Duke University Press.

Rinaldi, Ann. 1993. *Wolf by the Ears*. New York: Scholastic.

Rinaldi, Ann. 2005. *Hang a Thousand Trees with Ribbons: The Story of Phillis Wheatley*. Orlando, FL: HMH Books for Young Readers.

Roach, Joseph. 2007. *It*. Ann Arbor: University of Michigan Press.

Roberts, Dorothy. 1998. *Killing the Black Body: Race, Reproduction, and the Meaning of Liberty*. New York: Penguin Random House.

Roberts, Neil. 2015. *Freedom as Marronage*. Chicago: University of Chicago Press.

Robinson, Amy. 1994. "Authority and the Public Display of Identity: *Wonderful Adventures of Mrs. Seacole in Many Lands*." *Feminist Studies* 20 (3): 537–57.

Robinson, Jane. 2005. *Mary Seacole: The Charismatic Black Nurse Who Became a Heroine of the Crimea*. London: Constable.

Rosen, Hannah. 2009. *Terror in the Heart of Freedom: Citizenship, Sexual Violence, and the Meaning of Race in the Postemancipation South*. Chapel Hill: University of North Carolina Press.

Royster, Francesca T. 2003. *Becoming Cleopatra: The Shifting Image of an Icon*. New York: Palgrave Macmillan.

Rubin, Gayle. 1975. "The Traffic in Women: Notes on the 'Political Economy' of Sex." In *Toward an Anthropology of Women*, edited by Rayna R. Reiter, 157–94. New York: Monthly Review Press.

Rushdie, Salman. (1988) 2008. *The Satanic Verses: A Novel*. New York: Random House.

Rushdy, Ashraf H. A. 1999. *Neo-Slave Narratives: Studies in the Social Logic of a Literary Form.* New York: Oxford University Press.

Russell, W. H. (1857) 2005. Preface to Mary Seacole, *Wonderful Adventures of Mrs. Seacole in Many Lands*, edited by Sara Salih, 5. New York: Penguin.

Salih, Sara. 2004. "'A Gallant Heart to the Empire': Autoethnography and Imperial Identity in Mary Seacole's *Wonderful Adventures.*" *Philological Quarterly* 83 (2): 171–95.

Salih, Sara. 2005. Introduction to Mary Seacole, *Wonderful Adventures of Mrs. Seacole in Many Lands*, edited by Sara Salih, xv–l. New York: Penguin.

Salih, Sara. 2010. *Representing Mixed Race in Jamaica and England from the Abolition Era to the Present.* New York: Routledge.

Samimian-Darash, Limor, and Paul Rabinow, eds. 2015. *Modes of Uncertainty: Anthropological Cases.* Chicago: University of Chicago Press.

Samuelson, Meg. 2007. *Remembering the Nation, Dismembering Women? Stories of the South African Transition.* Scottsville, South Africa: University of KwaZulu-Natal Press.

Saturday Night Live. 2002. Season 28, episode 7, Sally Hemings skit. Aired December 7. https//www.nbc.com/saturday-night-live/video/thomas-jefferson-meets-sally-hemings/n11650.

Schuller, Kyla. 2018. *The Biopolitics of Feeling: Race, Sex, and Science in the Nineteenth Century.* Durham, NC: Duke University Press.

Scott, Darieck. 2010. *Extravagant Abjection: Blackness, Power, and Sexuality in the African American Literary Imagination.* New York: New York University Press.

Scott, David. 2004. *Conscripts of Modernity: The Tragedy of Colonial Enlightenment.* Durham, NC: Duke University Press.

Scott, David. 2013. "The Paradox of Freedom: An Interview with Orlando Patterson." *Small Axe* 17 (1): 96–242.

Scott, Joan Wallach. 2011. *The Fantasy of Feminist History.* Durham, NC: Duke University Press.

"Seacole." 1905. *Kingston Daily Gleaner*, July 27.

Seacole, Mary. (1857) 2005. *Wonderful Adventures of Mrs. Seacole in Many Lands.* Edited by Sara Salih. New York: Penguin.

Sedgwick, Eve Kosofsky. 2008. *Epistemology of the Closet.* Updated with a new preface. Berkeley: University of California Press.

Sedgwick, Eve Kosofsky. (1985) 2016. *Between Men: English Literature and Male Homosocial Desire.* 30th anniv. ed. New York: Columbia University Press.

Sen, Amartya. 2001. *Development as Freedom.* Oxford: Oxford University Press.

Sen, Amartya. 2004. "Capabilities, Lists, and Public Reason: Continuing the Conversation." *Feminist Economics* 10 (3): 77–80.

Serpell, C. Namwali. 2014. *Seven Modes of Uncertainty.* Cambridge, MA: Harvard University Press.

Sharpe, Christina. 2010. *Monstrous Intimacies: Making Post-Slavery Subjects.* Durham, NC: Duke University Press.

Sharpe, Christina. 2016. *In the Wake: On Blackness and Being.* Durham, NC: Duke University Press.

Sharpe, Jenny. 2003. *Ghosts of Slavery: A Literary Archaeology of Black Women's Lives.* Minneapolis: University of Minnesota Press.

Sharpley-Whiting, T. Denean. 1999. *Black Venus: Sexualized Savages, Primal Fears, and Primitive Narratives in French.* Durham, NC: Duke University Press.

Shaw, Gwendolyn DuBois. 2006. *Portraits of a People: Picturing African Americans in the Nineteenth Century.* Seattle: University of Washington Press.

Shields, John C. 2010. *Phillis Wheatley and the Romantics.* Knoxville: University of Tennessee Press.

Shockley, Evie. 2006. *a half-red sea.* Durham, NC: Carolina Wren.

Shockley, Evie. 2011. *The New Black.* Middletown, CT: Wesleyan University Press.

Shyllon, Folarin. 2006. "The Nigerian and African Experience on Looting and Trafficking in Cultural Objects." In *Art and Cultural Heritage: Law, Policy, and Practice,* edited by Barbara T. Hoffman, 137–44. Cambridge: Cambridge University Press.

Simmons, LaKisha Michelle. 2015. *Crescent City Girls: The Lives of Young Black Women in Segregated New Orleans.* Chapel Hill: University of North Carolina Press.

Simpson, LaJuan. 2001. "Architecting Humanity through Autobiography: Mary Seacole's 'Wonderful Adventures of Mrs. Seacole in Many Lands.'" *Revista/Review Interamericana* 31 (1–4): 1–10.

Singh, Julietta. 2018. *Unthinking Mastery: Dehumanism and Decolonial Entanglements.* Durham, NC: Duke University Press.

Slaughter, Joseph R. 2007. *Human Rights, Inc.: The World Novel, Narrative Form, and International Law.* New York: Fordham University Press.

Slauter, Eric. 2006. "Looking for Scipio Moorhead: An 'African Painter' in Revolutionary America." ResearchGate. doi: 10.1017/CBO9781139021845.005.

Slauter, Eric. 2009. *The State as a Work of Art: The Cultural Origins of the Constitution.* Chicago: University of Chicago Press.

Smith, Anna Deavere. 2003. *House Arrest: A Search for American Character in and around the White House, Past and Present.* New York: Dramatists Play Service.

Smith, Zadie. 2016. *Swing Time.* New York: Penguin.

Snorton, C. Riley. 2014. *Nobody Is Supposed to Know: Black Sexuality on the Down Low.* Minneapolis: University of Minnesota Press.

Sommerville, Diane Miller. 2004. *Rape and Race in the Nineteenth-Century South.* Chapel Hill: University of North Carolina Press.

Spillers, Hortense J. 1987. "Mama's Baby, Papa's Maybe: An American Grammar Book." *Diacritics* 17 (2): 64–81.

Spires, Derrick R. 2019. *The Practice of Citizenship: Black Politics and Print Culture in the Early United States.* Philadelphia: University of Pennsylvania Press.

Spivak, Gayatri Chakravorty. 1999. *A Critique of Postcolonial Reason: Toward a History of the Vanishing Present.* Cambridge, MA: Harvard University Press.

Stallings, L. H. 2015. *Funk the Erotic: Transaesthetics and Black Sexual Cultures.* Urbana: University of Illinois Press.

Stanley, Amy Dru. 1998. *From Bondage to Contract: Wage Labor, Marriage, and the Market in the Age of Slave Emancipation.* Cambridge: Cambridge University Press.

Steinfeld, Robert J. 2001. *Coercion, Contract, and Free Labor in the Nineteenth Century.* Cambridge: Cambridge University Press.

Stephens, Michelle Ann. 2005. *Black Empire: The Masculine Global Imaginary of Caribbean Intellectuals in the United States, 1914–1962.* Durham, NC: Duke University Press.

Stephens, Michelle Ann. 2014. *Skin Acts: Race, Psychoanalysis, and the Black Male Performer.* Durham, NC: Duke University Press.

Sterne, Julia A. 1997. *The Plight of Feeling: Sympathy and Dissent in the Early American Novel.* Chicago: University of Chicago Press.

Stevenson, Brenda E. 1996. *Life in Black and White: Family and Community in the Slave South.* New York: Oxford University Press.

Stevenson, Brenda E. 2013. "What's Love Got to Do with It? Concubinage and Enslaved Black Women and Girls in the Antebellum South." *Journal of African American History* 98 (1): 99–125.

"A Stir for Seacole." 1856. *Punch, or the London Chiarivari.* December 6.

Stockman, Farah. 2018. "'She Was Part of This Family': Jefferson Descendants Reflect on Sally Hemings Exhibit." *New York Times,* June 16.

Stockman, Farah, and Gabriella Demczuk. 2018. "Monticello Is Done Avoiding Jefferson's Relationship with Sally Hemings." *New York Times,* June 16.

Stockton, Kathryn Bond. 2006. *Beautiful Bottom, Beautiful Shame: Where "Black" Meets "Queer."* Durham, NC: Duke University Press.

Stoever, Jennifer Lynn. 2016. *The Sonic Color Line: Race and the Cultural Politics of Listening.* New York: New York University Press.

Stoler, Ann Laura. 1995. *Race and the Education of Desire: Foucault's History of Sexuality and the Colonial Order of Things.* Durham, NC: Duke University Press.

Stoler, Ann Laura. 2001. "Tense and Tender Ties: The Politics of Comparison in North American History and (Post) Colonial Studies." *Journal of American History* 88 (3): 829–65.

Stoler, Ann Laura. 2010. *Carnal Knowledge and Imperial Power: Race and the Intimate in Colonial Rule.* Berkeley: University of California Press.

Streeter, Caroline A. 2012. *Tragic No More: Mixed-Race Women and the Nexus of Sex and Celebrity.* Amherst: University of Massachusetts Press.

Sullivan, Margaret. 2015. "Time Regrets 'Slave Mistress' in Julian Bond's Obituary." *New York Times,* August 20.

Tate, Claudia. 1998. *Psychoanalysis and Black Novels: Desire and the Protocols of Race.* New York: Oxford University Press.

Taylor, Christopher. 2018. *Empire of Neglect: The West Indies in the Wake of British Liberalism.* Durham, NC: Duke University Press.

Taylor, Diana. 2003. *The Archive and the Repertoire: Performing Cultural Memory in the Americas.* Durham, NC: Duke University Press.

Taylor, Keeanga-Yamahtta. 2016. *From #Blacklivesmatter to Black Liberation.* Chicago: Haymarket.

Tchaprazov, Stoyan. 2008. "A Virtuous Nurse and a Pícara: Mary Seacole's Self-Characterization in *Wonderful Adventures of Mrs. Seacole in Many Lands.*" In *Before Windrush: Recovering an Asian and Black Literary Heritage within Britain,* edited by Pallavi Rastogi and Jocelyn Fenton Stitt, 72–87. Newcastle, UK: Cambridge Scholars.

Thomas, Deborah A. 2004. *Modern Blackness: Nationalism, Globalization, and the Politics of Culture in Jamaica.* Durham, NC: Duke University Press.

Thompson, Krissah. 2017. "For Decades They Hid Jefferson's Relationship with Her: Now Monticello Is Making Room for Sally Hemings." *Washington Post*, February 19.

Thompson, Krista A. 2015. *Shine: The Visual Economy of Light in African Diasporic Aesthetic Practice.* Durham, NC: Duke University Press.

Thompson, Shirley Elizabeth. 2009. *Exiles at Home: The Struggle to Become American in Creole New Orleans.* Cambridge, MA: Harvard University Press.

Threadcraft, Shatema. 2016. *Intimate Justice: The Black Female Body and the Body Politic.* New York: Oxford University Press.

Tillet, Salamishah. 2009. "Black Girls in Paris: Sally Hemings, Sarah Baartman, and French Racial Dystopias." *Callaloo* 32 (3): 934–54.

Tillet, Salamishah. 2012. *Sites of Slavery: Citizenship and Racial Democracy in the Post–Civil Rights Imagination.* Durham, NC: Duke University Press.

Tinsley, Omise'eke Natasha. 2010. *Thiefing Sugar: Eroticism between Women in Caribbean Literature.* Durham, NC: Duke University Press.

Trethewey, Natasha. 2012. "Enlightenment." In *Thrall: Poems*, 68–71. New York: Houghton Mifflin Harcourt.

Trollope, Anthony. (1859) 1968. *The West Indies and the Spanish Main.* London: Cass.

"UN Doc. E/1993/22." 1993. https://tbinternet.ohchr.org/_layouts/15/treatybodyexternal /Download.aspx?symbolno=E%2F1993%2F22(SUPP)&Lang=en.

Vogel, Shane. 2009. *The Scene of Harlem Cabaret: Race, Sexuality, Performance.* Chicago: University of Chicago Press.

Waldstreicher, David. 2011. "The Wheatleyan Moment." *Early American Studies* 9 (3): 522–51.

Walker, Alice. 1983. "In Search of Our Mothers' Gardens." In *In Search of Our Mothers' Gardens: Womanist Prose*, 231–43. New York: Harcourt Brace Jovanovich.

Wanzo, Rebecca. 2009. *The Suffering Will Not Be Televised: African American Women and Sentimental Political Storytelling.* Albany: State University of New York Press.

Ward, Jesmyn. 2016. *The Fire This Time: A New Generation Speaks about Race.* New York: Simon and Schuster.

Warren, Calvin L. 2018. *Ontological Terror: Blackness, Nihilism, and Emancipation.* Durham, NC: Duke University Press.

Washington, George. (1775–76) 1931. *The Writings of George Washington from the Original Manuscript Sources, 1745–1799.* Edited by John F. Fitzpatrick. Vol. 4, *October 1775– April 1776.* Washington, DC: US Government Printing Office.

Watt, Billie Lou. 1967. *Phillis: A Musical Drama in Three Acts, Based on the Life of Phillis Wheatley, American Poet.* New York: Friendship.

Weeks, Kathi. 2011. *The Problem with Work: Feminism, Marxism, Antiwork Politics, and Postwork Imaginaries.* Durham, NC: Duke University Press.

Weems, Carrie Mae. 2001. *The Jefferson Suite* (installation). http://carriemaeweems.net /galleries/jefferson-suite.html.

Weheliye, Alexander G. 2014. *Habeas Viscus: Racializing Assemblages, Biopolitics, and Black Feminist Theories of the Human.* Durham, NC: Duke University Press.

Wells, Shallyn. 2017. "Feminism, False Consciousness, and Consent: A Third Way Notes." *Georgetown Journal of Gender and the Law* 18 (1): 251–77.

Wheatley, Phillis. 1988. *The Collected Works of Phillis Wheatley*. New York: Oxford University Press.

Wheatley, Ronald B. 2013. *The Trial of Phillis Wheatley*. Scotts Valley, CA: CreateSpace.

White, Alan. 2014. "You'll Never Guess Who This Woman's Godmother Was." BuzzFeed, April 6. https://www.buzzfeed.com/alanwhite/youll-never-guess-who-this-womans -godmother-was.

White, Deborah Gray. 1999. *Ar'n't I a Woman?: Female Slaves in the Plantation South*. New York: Norton.

Wicomb, Zoë. 1998. "Shame and Identity: The Case of the Coloured in South Africa." In *Writing South Africa: Literature, Apartheid, and Democracy, 1970–1995*, edited by Derek Attridge and Rosemary Jolly, 91–107. Cambridge: Cambridge University Press.

Wicomb, Zoë. 2002. *David's Story*. New York: Feminist Press at CUNY.

Wiegman, Robyn. 2012. *Object Lessons*. Durham, NC: Duke University Press.

Wilcox, Kirstin. 1999. "The Body into Print: Marketing Phillis Wheatley." *American Literature* 71 (1): 1–29.

Williams, Brian. 2009. *Mary Seacole*. Oxford, UK: Heinemann Library.

Williams, Patricia J. 1991. *The Alchemy of Race and Rights*. Cambridge, MA: Harvard University Press.

Willis, Deborah, ed. 2010. *Black Venus 2010: They Called Her "Hottentot."* Philadelphia: Temple University Press.

Winters, Lisa Ze. 2016. *The Mulatta Concubine: Terror, Intimacy, Freedom, and Desire in the Black Transatlantic*. Athens: University of Georgia Press.

Wong, Edlie L. 2009. *Neither Fugitive nor Free: Atlantic Slavery, Freedom Suits, and the Legal Culture of Travel*. New York: New York University Press.

Wong, Edlie L. 2015. *Racial Reconstruction: Black Inclusion, Chinese Exclusion, and the Fictions of Citizenship*. New York: New York University Press.

Wright, Nazera Sadiq. 2016. *Black Girlhood in the Nineteenth Century*. Urbana: University of Illinois Press.

Wynter, Sylvia. 2003. "Unsettling the Coloniality of Being/Power/Truth/Freedom: Towards the Human, After Man, Its Overrepresenation—An Argument." *CR: The New Centennial Review* 3 (3): 257–337.

Wynter, Sylvia. 2015. *No Humans Involved: On the Blackness of BLACKNUSS*. Portland, OR: Publication Studio.

Young, Hershini Bhana. 2017. *Illegible Will: Coercive Spectacles of Labor in South Africa and the Diaspora*. Durham, NC: Duke University Press.

Zerilli, Linda, M. G. 2005. *Feminism and the Abyss of Freedom*. Chicago: University of Chicago Press.

Index

exceptionalism: of Baartman, 116; of Seacole, 156–57, 158, 172; of Wheatley, 33, 36, 61

Exiles at Home (Thompson), 158

extraordinary ordinariness, 10–11, 174, 180, 194

Fairview (Drury), 169

false consciousness, 70, 175

fame, 167; contract between performer and audience, 130; democratization of, 11, 51, 174; denial of to black women, 1, 3; freedom and, 48–49; intersection of race, sexuality, gender, and nation in relics of, 13; Wheatley as epitome of, 31–32. *See also* celebrity; infamy

fantasy: black criticism of Wheatley, 38–39; of citizenship, 192–93; collective, around Wheatley, 40; of consent, 65; corrective histories and, 41–42; of freedom, 26, 29, 35, 53–54, 57, 113–15; of the political, 57–61; as psychoanalytic term, 35; as scene of political formation, 60; uncertainty and historic corrections, 39–49; use and possibilities of, 40; vulnerability and, 35, 65

fatigue. *See* critical fatigue

feminized public sphere, 3–4, 9, 12, 62

Ferguson, Roderick A., 15, 171

fetishization, 24, 40, 43, 49, 62, 82

Fineman, Martha Albertson, 20–21

Fish, Cheryl, 143

flawlessness, 203–5

Fleetwood, Nicole R., 6, 16, 17, 61, 117, 127, 174, 175; black male bodies, reading of, 133; on tension between veneration and denigration, 2, 190; viability, 130

flesh, 22, 179, 180

"flesh memory: an invocation in cento" (brown), 62

Forbes, Frederick (Captain), 180–86, 191

"Formation" (Beyoncé), 2

Foucault, Michel, 6, 9, 12, 36–37, 112, 184

Founding Fathers, 34, 54, 58, 61, 80. *See also* Jefferson, Thomas; Washington, George

Fox, Regis, 16

Fox-Genovese, Elizabeth, 167

France, relations to blackness, 94

Frederick, Rhonda, 158, 160

freedom, 4, 26, 31–63; American ideal under slavery, 58; as becoming, 37–38; black women as foundational political subjects of, 66–67, 75–78, 88, 95–96, 183–86; children's books about, 45–48, *46, 47*; definitions of, 31, 36, 178; emancipation itself as issue in Baartman trial, 106, 112; embodiment and, 26, 29–30, 34, 37–39, 53–54, 180; enslaved sexuality as foundation of, 66–67, 75–78, 88, 95–96; fame and, 48–49; fantasies of, 26, 29, 35, 53–54, 57, 113–15; fiction of, 146; as form of currency, 31, 37, 40, 52, 58; legal, 37–38; "owning" and, 62, 185; as (a) property, 185; as relation, 31, 36–37; slavery required for full form of, 37, 75; "something akin to," 14, 37, 51–52, 84, 112, 141; sovereignty and coercion of black subjects, 182–83, 186; as "success," 124; uncertainty of, 37–38, 40, 94. *See also* Wheatley, Phillis

"free labor," fictions of, 15, 102, 105, 112

free-subject-on-ship spectrum, 180

The Frenzy of Renown (Braudy), 130

Freud, Sigmund, 77–78

friendship, black women's, 54–57

Fuentes, Marisa, 85

futures, black feminist and political, 4, 6, 18, 30, 38, 99–103, 123

Garvey, Marcus, 173, 198

Gates, Henry Louis, Jr., 34, 35

genre: expectations of, 83; humanity, genres of, 79; neo-slave narrative form, 83–85; romance, 76–77, 118–19. *See also* romance

Gerzina, Gretchen Holbrook, 177

Gezo, King (Dahomey/Benin), 181–82, 184–86, 187

gift economy, black women as subjects of, 183–84

Gilroy, Paul, 15, 35, 180, 210n2

globalization, 142, 146

The Good Life (photographic series), *131,* 131–32

Gordon, Avery, 5

Gordon-Reed, Annette, 65, 68–69, 72–73, 76, 94

Goudie, Sean X., 160

governmentality, 183–84

Goyal, Yogita, 43

Graham, Shirley (Du Bois), 48–49

grief work, 211n17

Griffin, Farah Jasmine, 207n5

Gross, Kali N., 170

Grosz, Elizabeth, 35

Gunning, Sandra, 160, 164

Gussow, Mel, 57, 58

habeas corpus, 106, 116, 124

a half-red sea (Shockley), 31, 54, 95

Hancock, John, 48

Hanging the Head (Pointon), 41

Hark, A Vagrant! (Beaton), 150

Harlem Renaissance authors, 43

Harris, Cheryl, 152

Harris, Lyle Ashton, *131,* 131–32, *132*

Hartman, Saidiya V., 3, 15, 68, 72, 75, 79, 182–83, 201; critical fabulation, 2, 5, 23, 126; impossibility of representation, 2, 24, 63, 91; *Scenes of Subjection,* 16, 65; "Venus in Two Acts," 2, 207n11; *Wayward Lives, Beautiful Experiments,* 56, 204

Hegel, G. W. F., 185

Hemings, Harriet, 48, 77

Hemings, James, 84

Hemings, Madison, 73, 79, 91, 105, 137

Hemings, Sally, 3, 26–27, 35, 54, 62, 65–103, 113, 213n9, 214n18; afterlives of, 66, 69–70, 95, 101; agency and, 66–67, 77, 80, 82, 88, 92–93, 95, 97–98, 100; corrective histories of, 90–91, 102; five terrains of representation of, 79; "loophole" of retreat, 100; memorialization of, 85–99, *86, 87, 89*; narratives and alibis